POCKET **ROUGH GUIDE**
BERLIN

CONTENTS

BERLIN

Of all today's European capitals, Berlin carries the biggest buzz. In the two and a half decades since it was reunified, the city has developed into a heady meld of grit and glamour that's vastly different from anywhere else in Germany – or the rest of the world for that matter. Its edgy cultural and fashion scenes, unsurpassed nightlife and radical anti-gentrification agenda regularly make global headlines, as does its reputation as "poor but sexy" – a term coined by former mayor Klaus Wowereit and quickly adopted as the city's unofficial motto.

Statues in front of Berliner Dom

The crackle of youthful energy that characterizes much of the inner city – especially areas such as trendy Mitte (Spandauer Vorstadt and around), student-heavy Friedrichshain and artist and expat haven Neukölln – mingles incongruously with the scars of Berlin's less glamorous past. Holocaust memorials, concentration camps and a wealth of thought-provoking museums, such as Daniel Libeskind's celebrated Jewish Museum, join bullet holes and empty spaces to provide visitors with constant reminders of the horrors of National Socialism and World War II. The fragments of the Berlin Wall, scattered around the city like broken concrete teeth, testify to its painful division – sometimes still reflected in the mindsets of the city's formerly divided neighbourhoods, many of which have retained their pre-reunification identities.

So overwhelming is Berlin's twentieth-century history and its twenty-first century grab for the future, that it's easy to forget that the city has a longer and more illustrious history. Originally two cities – Cölln, an island in the middle of the city, now the site of the Museum Island, and Alt Berlin, formerly a fishing village – Berlin was formed in 1237. Located at the intersection of significant trade routes, it quickly prospered, rising to power as the seat of the Hohenzollern dynasty following the Thirty Years' War. During the

Oberbaum Bridge

eighteenth century, Frederick the Great (1712–86) established Berlin – and neighbouring Potsdam, with its magnificent summer palace Sanssouci – as a grand capital for the Prussian monarchy; it was during this time that many of the buildings on Unter den Linden were constructed. When Germany was united in 1871, Berlin became its capital.

Following the defeat of World War I, during the Weimar Republic (1919–33) the city rivalled Paris as a centre for the cultural avant-garde, the legacy and spirit of which live on in contemporary Berlin. World War II reduced seventy percent of the city to ruins, and it was partitioned into

When to visit

Berlin is a great city to visit at any time of year with plenty to do and see – but like most places, it really comes alive in the warmer months. If you're not a fan of cold weather, be warned that the winter months can be brutally chilly thanks to winds blowing in from the east. In general though, the city enjoys a cool and humid climate with an average summer temperature of around 25°C as well as the occasional heatwave. Spring and autumn are often lovely seasons.

What's new

Berlin has taken up the craft beer 'n' burgers craze with real zest. For artisan brews, check out *Kaschk* (see page 37) – particularly strong on Nordic ales – and *Vagabund Brauerei* (see page 88), which was in the vanguard of Europe's crowd-sourced breweries. When the time comes to soak it all up, we heartily recommend *The Bird* (see page 83), which offers a greasy slice of US-style goodness, or *Marienburgerie* (see page 84), a little venue with a lot of big burgers.

American, British and French zones in the West and a Soviet zone in the East. The three Western-occupied zones eventually merged into West Berlin, while the Soviet zone in the East remained defiantly separate – the city's division was fully realized with the building of the Berlin Wall in August 1961 by the East German government.

The fall of the Wall in 1989 provided a rare opportunity for a late twentieth-century rebirth. Berlin still carries an unfinished air and change remains an exciting constant in the city, though it's not without its growing pains, with gentrification

a red-hot topic: Prenzlauer Berg and Mitte have been yuppified beyond recognition, while in Friedrichshain, Kreuzberg and Neukölln cars are torched, windows smashed in and hip cafés spray-painted with graffiti in an effort to resist.

Political forces and ideals continue to battle it out in Berlin, rendering the city a vibrant and vertiginous place to be: an irresistible combination of entrepreneurial possibility and creative energy rubbing shoulders with a fully developed tourist destination overflowing with museums, sights and events. What's not to like?

Hackescher Markt

Where to...

Shop

Berlin's fashion scene has been going from strength to strength in the past decade or so, with a string of local designers constantly upping the ante. The city is awash with small boutiques, with clusters around Neue Schönhauser Strasse and Münzstrasse in Spandauer Vorstadt (Mitte) and between Kantstrasse and Ku'damm in Charlottenburg, while Kreuzberg and Friedrichshain have a surfeit of street fashion stores. More commercial shopping can be found around Hackescher Markt and along Ku'damm.

OUR FAVOURITES: do you read me?, see page 32. Mall of Berlin, see page 52. Bikini Berlin, see page 126.

Eat

The dining scene in Berlin has come on leaps and bounds since the Wall fell. Cheap eats are abundant all over the city, with snack stalls – *Imbisse* – hawking everything from burgers and *Currywurst* to Asian food. At the other end, you can dine in style at a decent selection of high-end, Michelin-starred spots – particularly in upscale areas such as Unter den Linden, Potsdamer Platz and Charlottenburg. The area in between – mid-priced restaurants – make up the majority of eating options, again all over the city, and vary from authentic and traditional German restaurants to stylish dens of cool. A particular Berlin favourite is the weekend brunch buffet, served in cafés across the city – Prenzlauer Berg is a good bet for these.

OUR FAVOURITES: Cocolo, see page 110. Katz Orange, see page 34. Tempo-Box, see page 96

Drink

The majority of bars are independent, and relaxed licensing laws means they can usually close when they like. Though there are a decent spread of bars everywhere, the biggest concentration is around Mitte, Prenzlauer Berg, Kreuzberg and Neukölln, with many operating as cafés during the day serving snacks and light meals, and then as bars later on, staying open all the way through to the early hours.

OUR FAVOURITES: Schwarze Traube see page 113. Lemke Am Alex see page 62. Vagabund Brauerei see page 88

Party

Berlin's nightlife scene is the envy of, well, most of the world, and its large creative scene means that people have fairly flexible schedules. The city's nightclubs not only stay open later than most (some don't close for days) but also purvey some of the most cutting-edge house and techno around, attracting clubbers from around the globe who come to the city just to party the weekend away at heavyweight places like *Berghain* and *Watergate*. There's a strong concentration of clubs in Friedrichshain and East Kreuzberg, particularly along the River Spree, which divides these two neighbourhoods.

OUR FAVOURITES: Berghain, see page 98. Clärchens Ballhaus, see page 38. B-Flat, see page 38.

Berlin at a glance

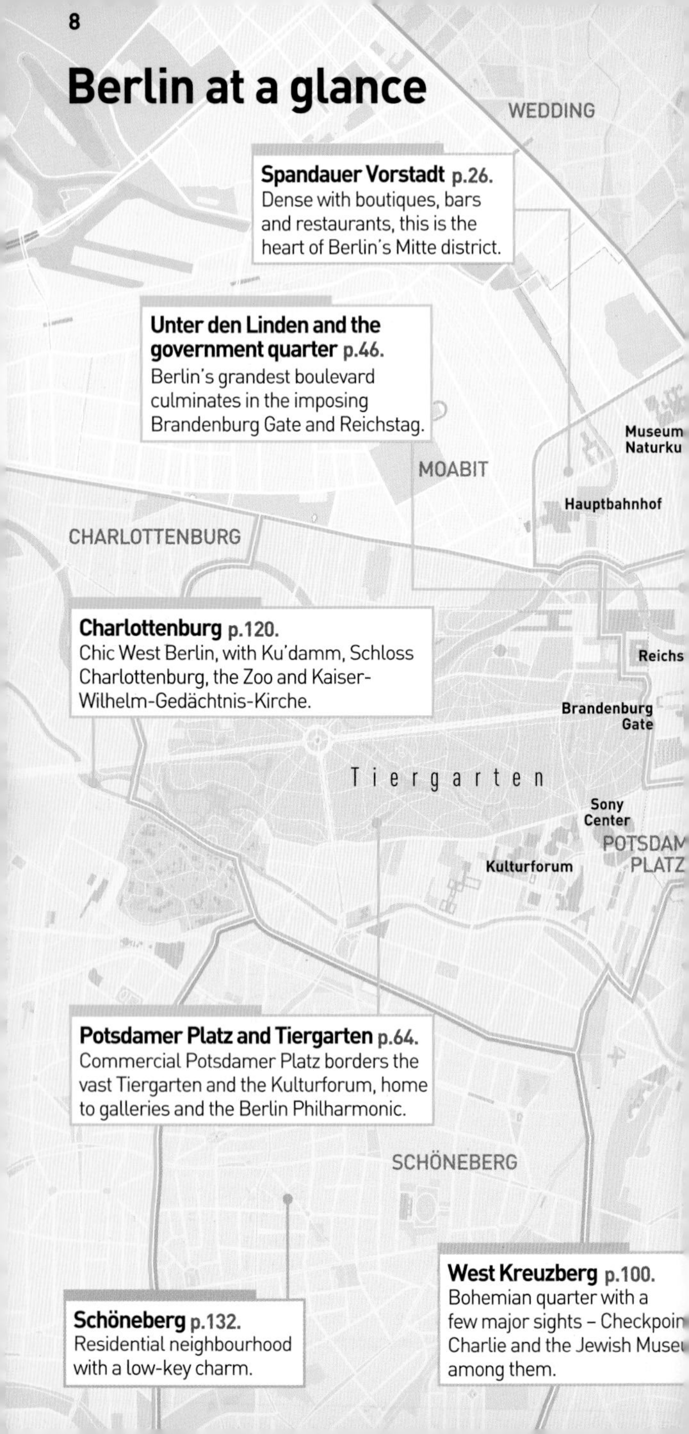

WEDDING

Spandauer Vorstadt p.26.
Dense with boutiques, bars
and restaurants, this is the
heart of Berlin's Mitte district.

**Unter den Linden and the
government quarter** p.46.
Berlin's grandest boulevard
culminates in the imposing
Brandenburg Gate and Reichstag.

Museum
Naturku

MOABIT

Hauptbahnhof

CHARLOTTENBURG

Charlottenburg p.120.
Chic West Berlin, with Ku'damm, Schloss
Charlottenburg, the Zoo and Kaiser-
Wilhelm-Gedächtnis-Kirche.

Reichs

Brandenburg
Gate

T i e r g a r t e n

Sony
Center

POTSDAM
PLATZ

Kulturforum

Potsdamer Platz and Tiergarten p.64.
Commercial Potsdamer Platz borders the
vast Tiergarten and the Kulturforum, home
to galleries and the Berlin Philharmonic.

SCHÖNEBERG

West Kreuzberg p.100.
Bohemian quarter with a
few major sights – Checkpoin
Charlie and the Jewish Museu
among them.

Schöneberg p.132.
Residential neighbourhood
with a low-key charm.

Prenzlauer Berg and Wedding p.76.

Prenzlauer Berg appeals thanks to its leafy squares filled with cafés and boutiques. Neighbouring Wedding has an edgier sort of charm.

PRENZLAUER BERG

Gedenkstätte
Berliner Mauer

Alexanderplatz and the Nikolaiviertel p.56.

The main square of old East Berlin and neighbouring Nikolaiviertel, a reconstruction of a medieval quarter.

SPANDAUER
VORSTADT

Neue
Synagoge ✡   Hackesche
Höfe

Volkspark
Friedrichshain

ALEXANDER-
PLATZ

Pergamon-
museum

Friedrichshain p.90.

East Berlin district that's home to an alternative bars and club scene.

UNTER
DEN LINDEN

Fernsehturm

NIKOLAIVIERTEL

Nikolaikirche

FRIEDRICHSHAIN

MUSEUM
ISLAND

Ostbahnhof

East Side Gallery

Checkpoint
Charlie

The Museum Island p.40.

Five world-class museums, impressively renovated and housing collections of art and antiquities.

WEST
KREUZBERG

Jewish
Museum
Berlin

EAST
KREUZBERG

Kottbusser
Tor

East Kreuzberg p.108.

The more counter-cultural half of Kreuzberg, with a series of superb independent bars.

Neukölln p.116.

Berlin's fastest-changing district is a hipster haven of bars, galleries, cafés and lots of buzz.

NEUKÖLLN

15 Things not to miss

It's not possible to see everything that Berlin has to offer in one trip – and we don't suggest you try. What follows is a selective taste of the city's highlights, from eye-catching architecture to exceptional art.

> **Berliner Fernsehturm**
See page 56
Buy an online fast track ticket to beat the queues and better enjoy the peerless city views from this Berlin landmark.

< **Gemäldegalerie**
See page 65
The undisputed heavyweight of the Kulturforum boasts hundreds of exquisite Old Masters.

∨ **Memorial to the Murdered Jews of Europe**
See page 50
Nineteen thousand square metres of dramatic, disorienting concrete stelae, plus a highly emotive underground museum.

< Hamburger Bahnhof
See page 31
This former train station now houses Berlin's largest collection of cutting-edge international art.

∨ Jewish Museum
See page 103
Daniel Libeskind's Jewish Museum is notable not only for its content but also for its architectural prowess.

< **Reichstag**
See page 51
Having survived fascism, revolution, bombardment and neglect, today the Reichstag is a symbol of the city's reunification.

∨ **Schloss Charlottenburg**
See page 125
The largest palace in Berlin is also a fine example of Prussian-era architecture, built in stunning Rococo and Baroque style.

THINGS NOT TO MISS

∧ Gedenkstätte Berliner Mauer
See page 76
The Wall memorial on Bernauer Strasse has fascinating free indoor and outdoor exhibitions.

< Berliner Dom
See page 40
The interior of Berlin's neo-Renaissance cathedral is as dramatic as its outsized exterior.

∧ Panoramapunkt
See page 65
Take a high-speed ride to the top of the Art Deco Kollhoff Tower for soaring vistas over Potsdamer Platz and beyond.

∨ Deutsches Technikmuseum
See page 101
A jaw-dropping ensemble of German technical innovations, past and present.

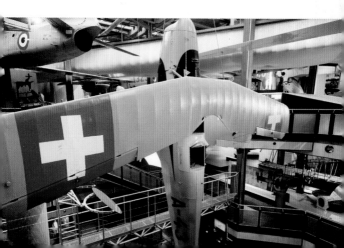

∧ Topography of Terror
See page 101
Located where the SS headquarters used to be, this museum unflinchingly explores the rise of the Nazi party and its atrocities.

⟨ Museum Island
See page 40
A treasure trove of ancient and modern art spread over five world-class museums.

< **Brandenburger Tor**
See page 49
One of Berlin's most iconic landmarks now comes with a multimedia museum that showcases its fascinating history.

∨ **East Side Gallery**
See page 91
This significant remaining stretch of the Berlin Wall doubles as one of the world's longest open-air art galleries.

THINGS NOT TO MISS

Day one

Breakfast. See page 46. The café of the Deutsches Historisches Museum is a refined and classic place to start the day with a hearty breakfast before throwing yourself into the museum.

Deutsches Historisches Museum. See page 46. Check out two thousand years of German history neatly and thoughtfully arranged throughout this beautiful museum, spread across two contrasting buildings.

Neue Wache. See page 46. Visit SchinkVel's famous Neoclassical monument and its moving tributes to victims of wartime, including the emotive Käthe Kollwitz sculpture *Mother with her Dead Son*.

Lunch For a tasty budget option in the area try sushi at *Ishin* (see page 53); for classic Austro-German dishes opt for *Lutter & Wegner* (see page 54).

Brandenburg Gate. See page 49. Berlin's foremost landmark and one of its biggest tourist attractions. A must see for first-time visitors, either with a leisurely stroll via Unter den Linden or with a visit to the neighbouring museum.

Reichstag. See page 51. Climb the Norman Foster-designed dome of this historic building to find great views across the city. Make sure you book a guided tour ahead.

Memorial to the Murdered Jews of Europe. See page 50. Visit the controversial memorial with its rows of stelae above ground and sobering visitor centre below.

Dinner. See page 53. End the day with some quality European-nouveau meat or fish dishes and fine service at *Crackers*.

Deutsches Historisches Museum

Brandenburg Gate location

Reichstag

Day two

Breakfast. See page 131. West Berlin's *Schwarzes Café* is a vaguely bohemian 24-hour café with a relaxed, spacious interior upstairs (more of a "Black Café" downstairs) and decent breakfasts.

Berlin Zoo and Aquarium. See page 120. One of the biggest zoos in Europe – hippos are among the celebrated residents – with an equally comprehensive aquarium right around the corner.

Kaiser-Wilhelm-Gedächtnis-Kirche. See page 121. Don't let the shattered spire put you off, this memorial church has a wonderful interior to investigate.

Käthe Kollwitz Museum. See page 124. The biggest collection of work from Berlin's pre-eminent sculptor displayed in a lovely villa on Fasanenstrasse.

Lunch. See page 130. Linger over coffee or a budget lunch at *Café Savigny*.

Story of Berlin. See page 124. This museum does precisely what it says on the tin, covering eight centuries of Berlin's history in an insightful and impressive manner.

Shopping on Ku'damm. See page 126. Since you're on the mighty Kurfürstendamm it'd be a shame not to indulge in some retail therapy. Don't forget to check the side streets too for a host of excellent, independent boutiques.

Dinner. See page 128. Try some thoroughly old-fashioned Silesian and Pomeranian food at *Marjellchen*, a marvellous timewarp.

Berlin Zoo

Kaiser-Wilhelm-Gedächtnis-Kirche

Käthe Kollwitz Museum

GDR Berlin

Take an "Ostalgie" tour through former East Berlin, its monumental sights, kitsch icons and memorials to the city's divided past.

DDR Museum. See page 57. Get hands on with GDR culture at this interactive museum, which evokes both the lighter and darker sides of life in communist East Germany. Nearby stand statues of Marx and Engels, tucked into a corner of the Marx-Engels-Forum park.

Berliner Fernsehturm. See page 56. Gape at the bleak GDR architecture of Alexanderplatz before taking a trip up the Fernsehturm for tremendous views over the city.

Lunch. See page 57. For the complete television tower experience, book ahead for a meal in the revolving restaurant, *Sphere*.

Karl-Marx-Allee. See page 91. Admire the Soviet architecture along this impressive historical boulevard, formerly known as Stalinallee, including the original Kino International, as featured in the film *Good Bye Lenin!*

Coffee. See page 97. Grab coffee and cake (or ice cream) at *Café Sybille*, which also hosts a small but informative museum about Karl-Marx-Allee.

East Side Gallery. See page 91. Finish up at the largest remaining section of the Berlin Wall, also one of the world's largest open-air galleries.

Sleep. See page 147. For a complete Ostalgie experience, book a night at the GDR-themed *Ostel* in Friedrichshain, which is also well placed for the neighbourhood's nightlife.

DDR Museum

Café Sybille

Ostel

Budget Berlin

Berlin's not necessarily an expensive city, and there are plenty of fun ways to explore on the cheap.

Breakfast. See page 87. Tuck into the weekend veggie breakfast at *Morgenrot* in Prenzlauer Berg, where the amount you pay depends on your income.

Take the bus. See page 152. Public buses #100 and #200 will give you a guided tour of some of the city's main sights at a fraction of the cost.

Free art. See pages 65 and 47. For free contemporary art, check out Daimler Contemporary (always free) and DB Kunsthalle (free Mon).

Museum of Things

Lunch. See page 73. *Joseph Roth Diele*, a charming restaurant near Potsdamer Platz, is dedicated to the Jewish author and has excellent lunch deals.

Topography of Terror. See page 101. Built on the grounds of the former SS Headquarters, this memorial of Gestapo horrors will leave you reeling.

Gedenkstätte Berliner Mauer. See page 76. The Wall memorial on Bernauer Strasse has fascinating indoor and outdoor exhibitions for free.

Joseph Roth Diele

Cheap and quirky museums. See page 108. You can access the delightful Museum der Dinge (Museum of Things) for just €6 while the Ramones Museum (€4.50) is the only one of its kind in the world.

Drinks. See page 38. Drink and make merry at one of the *Weinerei* bars, low-key, hipster hangouts where you pay what you feel is fair for the wine.

Drinking at Weinerei Forum

Berlin nightlife

Berlin's nightlife is justifiably renowned around the globe, with several distinct nightlife districts making it easy to spend an evening – or even an entire weekend – exploring the city's multitude of bars and clubs.

Clärchens Ballhaus. See page 38. Start the night with a pizza and Pilsner at this charming century-old ballhouse, which hosts a variety of nights from Tango to classical concerts.

B-Flat. See page 38. A great jazz spot in the city, B-Flat is one of the most dynamic with regular international guests and weekly jam sessions. A great place to get into the swing of things.

Schokoladen. See page 39. For more live music, head to intimate Schokoladen which hosts indie-pop and upcoming acts in a bare brick (former squat, former chocolate factory) interior.

Club der Visionäre. See page 113. A top pre-club spot, this CdV has the advantage of being mostly set outdoors on a floating deck. The dancefloor is small but the vibes can be big on the right night.

Salon zur Wilden Renate. See page 99. One of the most reliably fun nightspots in the city, the parties have an arty aesthetic and favour a house and disco soundtrack over the usual techno.

Rosi's. See page 99. Upbeat and oddball, a visit to Rosi's feels like crashing a house party – you can even chill out in the kitchen, or over a game of ping pong, in between sessions on the dancefloors, where indie, punk and electro pound.

Berghain. See page 98. It's notoriously tough to get into, but if you can penetrate Berlin's world-famous techno temple you'll realise why it's considered one of the best in the world. The Saturday night party runs until Monday morning.

Clärchens Ballhaus

Club der Visionäre

Salon zur Wilden Renate

Open spaces

Although it's known more for its urban thrills, the German capital is a surprisingly green city. Its many parks are not only easy to get to, but often come with plenty of options for activities, along with lots of history.

Mauerpark. See page 76. Salvaged by local residents after the fall of the Wall, this scruffy but popular park was once the Wall's "death strip" between East and West Berlin. Visit on a Sunday to find life-affirming public karaoke and a popular flea market.

Viktoriapark. See page 104. This much-loved Kreuzberg park is famous for having the tallest peak in the city. It also offers a pretty waterfall in summer and lots of hills for winter sledging.

Tiergarten. See page 71. The city's most famous park used to be a hunting ground for the Kaiser and his cohorts. Nowadays it provides ample running and walking tracks, lakes and a couple of great beer gardens.

Tempelhofer Park. See page 104. One of the largest and most unique parks in Europe, this former Nazi airport is now a vast community space where residents and visitors can rollerblade and kite-surf along the former runway.

Volkspark Friedrichshain. See page 90. GDR-era memorials abound at this sprawling city park, which also offers a picturesque nineteenth-century fountain, a great recreational area with climbing walls and sandy volleyball courts, and a couple of beer gardens.

Pfaueninsel. See page 140. Take to the water to escape the city for a fantasy island getaway – now a car-free nature reserve, stalked by a flock of peacocks, Pfaueninsel also features a mini-Schloss and gardens landscaped by the original designer of the Tiergarten.

Mauerpark

Viktoriapark

Tempelhof Park

PLACES

The Reichstag

DEUTSCHEN VOLKE

Spandauer Vorstadt

Arcing elegantly above the Spree between Friedrichstrasse and Alexanderplatz, the Spandauer Vorstadt was an eighteenth-century suburb that today serves as Berlin's primary "downtown" area, and is the heart of the Mitte district. Before World War II it was a significant hub for Jewish and French Huguenot exiles; after the Wall fell it became an artists' enclave, playing a vital role in the transferral of the city's art scene from West to East. Two decades of commercialization have resulted in a vibrant but touristic part of the city that's dense with boutiques, bars and restaurants, mainly around Hackescher Markt and the adjacent Oranienburger Strasse, as well as galleries along Auguststrasse and Torstrasse. Key insights into local Jewish life remain at the Neue Synagoge, the Jewish cemetery on Grosse Hamburger Strasse, and a trio of museums in the Haus Schwarzenberg.

Hackesche Höfe

MAP P.28, POCKET MAP E12
Rosenthaler Str. 40/41 & Sophienstr. 6
⑤ Hackescher Markt ☎ 030 28 09 80 10,
ⓦ www.hackesche-hoefe.com. Open various hours (residential parts close 10pm).
The extensive series of interconnected courtyards known as the Hackesche Höfe, located just across from S-Bahn station Hackescher Markt, are one of the best-known sights in this area. Having formerly hosted a Jewish girls' club, ballroom, factories, apartments – even a poets' society – the courtyards were remixed post-Wall into a more commercial enterprise, albeit with a vaguely arty twist. Today you'll find a cinema, several theatres, a jumble of smart restaurants and shops – and a throng of tourists, attracted by the impressive Art Nouveau restoration.

Haus Schwarzenberg

MAP P.28, POCKET MAP E12
Rosenthaler Str. 39 ⑤ Hackescher Markt
ⓦ www.haus-schwarzenberg.org.
Haus Schwarzenberg is the grungy alternative to gentrified Hackesche Höfe, located just a couple of doors away. It has only been minimally refurbished and at least part of its allure is its wonderful crumbling facades. Inside is an aptly unpretentious selection of cafés, bars and shops plus a cinema and galleries (street-art lovers will want to visit Neurotitan Gallery), as well as the **Monsterkabinett**, a collection of moving mechanical monsters (ⓦ www.monsterkabinett. de; check website for opening times; €8). Of particular interest is a trio of small museums that explore Jewish life in the area during the Third Reich. The **Gedenkstätte Stille Helden** (☎ 030 26 39 59 20, ⓦ gedenkstaette-stille-helden.de; Mon–Wed, Fri 9am–6pm, Sat–Sun 10am–6pm, Thur until 8pm; free) commemorates local residents who risked their lives to rescue persecuted Jews, documenting both heroic successes and tragic failures via photographs, documents and oral testimonies. Among the heroes is Otto Weidt, a German entrepreneur who helped save a number of his

blind Jewish employees at his workshop. Now called the **Museum Blindenwerkstatt Otto Weidt** (☎030 28 59 94 07, ⓦmuseum-blindenwerkstatt.de; daily 10am–8pm; free), it preserves photographs and personal mementoes of Weidt and his workers and the claustrophobic, hidden room, located behind a backless wardrobe, where he hid Jewish families when the Gestapo came knocking. Finally, the **Anne-Frank-Zentrum** (☎030 28 88 65 600, ⓦwww.annefrank.de; Tues–Sun 10am–6pm; €5) is a modern, surprisingly engaging exhibition on her life.

Sammlung Hoffmann

MAP P.28, POCKET MAP D11

Sophie-Gips-Höfe, Sophienstr. 21 ⓢ Hackescher Markt ☎030 28 49 91 20, ⓦ www.sammlung-hoffmann.de. By appointment only: Sat 11am–4pm; closed Aug. €10.

Started by avid art collectors Erika and Rolf Hoffmann, this sizeable private museum displays their personal collection of contemporary art, which spans painting, sculpture, photography and video over two floors filled with natural light. Organized subjectively – there are no names, descriptions or over-arching curatorial themes – the exhibition features internationally renowned names such as Jean-Michel Basquiat, Andy Warhol and Bruce Nauman. The collection is rearranged every year. Entry is by guided tour (English tours available) – a pleasantly interactive and informative way of experiencing such major works.

Neue Synagoge

MAP P.28, POCKET MAP D12

Oranienburger Str. 28–30 ⓢ Oranienburger Str. ☎030 88 02 83 00, ⓦ centrumjudaicum.de. April–Sept: Mon–Fri 10am–6pm, Sun 10am–7pm; Oct–March Mon–Thurs 10am–6pm, Fri 10am–3pm, Sun 10am–7pm. Permanent exhibition €7; temporary exhibitions €4.50; entry to the dome €3.

Topped with a golden, glittering dome that almost rivals the Reichstag's for prowess and recognition, the Moorish Neue Synagoge (New Synagogue) is a building with a long and largely brutal history. Consecrated on Rosh Hashanah in 1866, it quickly became the most important

Neue Synagoge

SPANDAUER VORSTADT

Spandauer Vorstadt

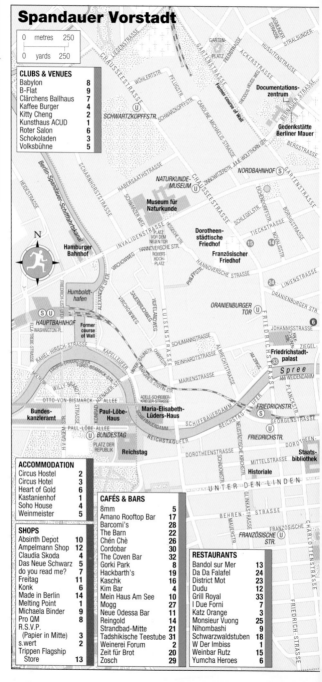

| 0 | metres | 250 |
| 0 | yards | 250 |

CLUBS & VENUES

Babylon	8
B-Flat	9
Clärchens Ballhaus	7
Kaffee Burger	4
Kitty Cheng	2
Kunsthaus ACUD	1
Roter Salon	6
Schokoladen	3
Volksbühne	5

ACCOMMODATION

Circus Hostel	2
Circus Hotel	3
Heart of Gold	6
Kastanienhof	1
Soho House	4
Weinmeister	5

SHOPS

Absinth Depot	10
Ampelmann Shop	12
Claudia Skoda	4
Das Neue Schwarz	5
do you read me?	7
Freitag	11
Konk	6
Made in Berlin	14
Melting Point	1
Michaela Binder	9
Pro QM	8
R.S.V.P. (Papier in Mitte)	3
s.wert	2
Trippen Flagship Store	13

CAFÉS & BARS

8mm	5
Amano Rooftop Bar	17
Barcomi's	28
The Barn	22
Chén Chè	26
Cordobar	30
The Coven Bar	32
Gorki Park	8
Hackbarth's	19
Kaschk	16
Kim Bar	4
Mein Haus Am See	10
Mogg	27
Neue Odessa Bar	11
Reingold	14
Strandbad-Mitte	21
Tadshikische Teestube	31
Weinerei Forum	2
Zeit für Brot	20
Zosch	29

RESTAURANTS

Bandol sur Mer	13
Da Da Falafel	24
District Mot	23
Dudu	12
Grill Royal	33
I Due Forni	7
Katz Orange	3
Monsieur Vuong	25
Nihombashi	9
Schwarzwaldstuben	18
W Der Imbiss	1
Weinbar Rutz	15
Yumcha Heroes	6

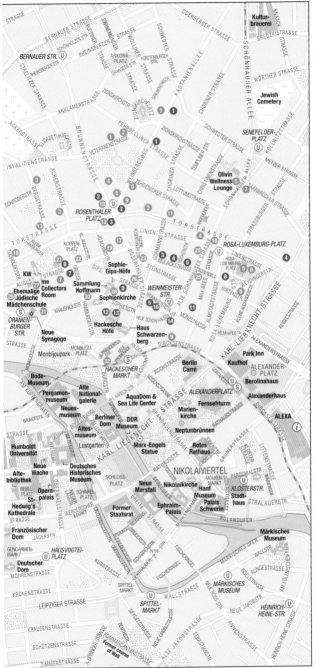

Me Collectors Room

Me Collectors Room – a platform for international private art collections – was conceived and built by chemist and endocrinologist Thomas Olbricht to showcase his private art collection – which happens to be among the most comprehensive in Europe, including works by John Currin, Franz Gertsch, Marlene Dumas and Gerhard Richter – via a series of alternating exhibitions. The "me" stands for "moving energies": the collection spans painting, sculpture, photography, installation and new media works from the early sixteenth century to the present day. A permanent part of the museum is the **Wunderkammer**, which rekindles an older tradition, popular during the Renaissance and Baroque periods, of bringing together eccentric curiosities and "wonders" from around the world. The spacious café downstairs serves lunches, snacks and coffee (Wed–Mon noon–6pm).

synagogue in Berlin; in its prime it could house over three thousand worshippers. Its fortunes changed under the Nazis and the synagogue was heavily vandalized during *Kristallnacht* (1938), bombed by Allied planes (1945) and demolished by the GDR in the 1950s. Rebuilt and restored in the 1990s, it stands proudly today both as a memorial to Jewish suffering in Germany and a depository of local Jewish culture. Sadly it wasn't possible to restore all of the synagogue and its interior, so the front section (or **Centrum Judaicum**) displays the oldest surviving elements – original carvings, entrance vestibules and anterooms – and hosts exhibitions, which mostly focus on the history of the building and Jewish Berlin. You can get an idea of the building's former dimensions by visiting a gravel-covered area outside, which marks the original layout of the synagogue.

Me Collectors Room

MAP P.28, POCKET MAP D11
Auguststr. 68 ⑤ Oranienburger Str. ☏ 030 86 00 85 10, ⓦ www.me-berlin.com. Wed–Mon noon–6pm. €8.

KW Institute for Contemporary Art

MAP P.28, POCKET MAP D11
Auguststr. 69 ⑤ Oranienburger Str.
☏ 030 24 34 590, ⓦ www.kw-berlin.de.
Mon–Wed & Fri–Sun 11am–7pm, Thurs 11am–9pm. €8.

The KW Institute for Contemporary Art was one of the prime movers in the post-*Wende* (reunification) transformation of Auguststrasse into what has been dubbed Berlin's "art mile". Once a nineteenth-century margarine factory, KW was turned into a dedicated art space by Klaus Biesenbach and a group of fellow art-lovers in the early 1990s. The elegant facade leads into a lovely, tree-filled courtyard surrounded by artist studios, the glass-walled *Café Bravo* (designed by American artist Dan Graham) and a series of modern, white spaces that include an exhibition hall by Berlin architect Hans Düttmann.

The institute mainly exhibits cutting-edge international works from both up-and-coming and major names such as Doug Aitken, Dinos and Jake Chapman and Paul Pfeiffer. KW also runs Berlin's immensely popular Biennale for Contemporary Art.

Ehemalige Jüdische Mädchenschule

MAP P.28, POCKET MAP D11

Auguststr. 11–13 ⓢ Oranienburger Str. ⓣ 030 33 00 60 70, ⓦ maedchenschule. org. Daily 8am–midnight; specific opening hours vary according to venue.

Built in the late 1920s as one of the last major Jewish structures before the Nazis took over, this charming, former Jewish girls' school opened as a space for art and cuisine in 2012 following a sensitive restoration. The former classrooms and corridors are now used for cultural venues such as the Rooftop Playground and Michael Fuchs galleries, and Museum Frieder Burda's Salon Berlin, an offshoot of the modern art museum in Baden-Baden. As for cuisine, the one-Michelin-star *Pauly-Saal* offers an ambitious menu made from the best of the region, the more relaxed (and affordable) *Mogg* Jewish deli brings NYC flavour, and the cultivated *Pauly Bar* provides some evening buzz.

Friedrichstadt-Palast

MAP P.28, POCKET MAP C12

Friedrichstr. 107 ⓢ Friedrichstr. ⓣ 030 23 26 23 27, ⓦ www.palast.berlin.

Founded in the 1860s, this theatre has a long and distinguished history, having been a market hall, circus, theatre and, during the Nazi era, the Theater des Volkes when it staged bourgeois operettas. Its current incarnation – an imposing GDR-style block – was opened in 1984. The stage is a whopping 2800 square metres and the main hall holds up to two thousand people for its programme of revue shows.

Museum für Naturkunde

MAP P.28, POCKET MAP A10

Invalidenstr. 43 ⓤ Naturekundemuseum ⓣ 030 20 93 85 91, ⓦ naturkundemuseum-berlin.de. Tues–Fri 9.30am–6pm, Sat & Sun 10am–6pm. €8.

Inaugurated in 1889 by Emperor Wilhelm II, Berlin's natural history museum is the largest of its kind in Germany, counting some thirty million objects within its collections. Highlights include the largest mounted dinosaur in the world – a *Brachiosaurus brancai* composed of fossilized bones – plus a 2015 T. rex skeleton found in Montana and an impressive room of stuffed animals that showcase biodiversity.

Hamburger Bahnhof

MAP P.28, POCKET MAP A11

Invalidenstr. 50 ⓢ/ⓤ Hauptbahnhof ⓣ 030 266 42 42 42, ⓦ www.smb.museum. Tues, Wed & Fri 10am–6pm, Thurs 10am–8pm, Sat & Sun 11am–6pm. €14. Free guided tours (in English) Sat & Sun noon.

Occupying a capacious and architecturally interesting space (formerly one of the city's first terminal stations), Berlin's contemporary art museum (Museum für Gegenwart) is one of the city's major modern art venues. Its permanent collection, which features holdings from the Nationalgalerie, focuses on the major movements of the late twentieth century up to the present day, with an emphasis on installation art and a number of large-scale sculptures by Joseph Beuys, to whom the entire west wing is dedicated. The museum's Marx Collection has works by Anselm Kiefer and Andy Warhol, while Friedrich Christian Flick's collection, donated in 2004, added works by artists like Isa Genzken, Bruce Nauman, Pipilotti Rist and Wolfgang Tillmans. The museum also hosts temporary exhibitions by international artists at the forefront of their respective fields. The adjacent restaurant, an elegant affair run by German celebrity chef Sarah Wiener, is a good lunch spot.

Shops

Absinth Depot

MAP P.28, POCKET MAP E11

Weinmeisterstr. 4 ⓤ Weinmeisterstr. ☏ 030 28 16 789. Mon–Fri 2pm–midnight, Sat 1pm–midnight.

The place not only to find all kinds of "Green Fairy" liquor but also a wide variety of props for the true absinth experience. You can even have a little taste.

Ampelmann Shop

MAP P.28, POCKET MAP D11

Rosenthaler Str. 40–41 ⓤ Weinmeisterstr. ☏ 030 44 72 65 15, ⓦ ampelmann.de. Mon–Sat 9.30am–10pm, Sun 1pm–6pm.

Everything here is based on the Ampelmännchen – the distinctive (and stylish) traffic light men once present on all East German traffic lights, who were saved from extinction after the Wall fell by various high-profile campaigns.

Claudia Skoda

MAP P.28, POCKET MAP E11

Mulackstr. 8 ⓤ Weinmeisterstr. ☏ 030 40 04 18 84. Mon–Sat 12.30–6.30pm.

Skoda's renowned knitwear is unapologetically chic (and correspondingly expensive). The clothes are geared mostly for women but there's a small men's section too.

Das Neue Schwarz

MAP P.28, POCKET MAP E11

Mulackstr. 38 ⓤ Weinmeisterstr. ☏ 030 27 87 44 67, ⓦ www.dasneueschwarz. de. Mon–Sat 10.30am–6.30pm.

"The New Black" stocks innovative garments for men and women, often from previous seasons to keep the prices down. Expect handbags, shoes, suits and jackets from top designer brands.

do you read me?

MAP P.28, POCKET MAP D11

Auguststr. 28 ⓤ Rosenthaler Platz ☏ 030 69 54 96 95, Mon–Sat 10am–7.30pm.

A magazine lover's paradise, this multilingual store offers a vast assortment of magazines and reading material from around the world, covering fashion and photography, art and architecture, culture and literature.

Freitag

MAP P.28, POCKET MAP E11

Max-Beer-Str. 3 ⓤ/ⓢ Alexanderplatz ☏ 030 24 63 69 61, ⓦ www.freitag.ch. Mon–Fri 11am–8pm, Sat 11am–7pm.

The Mitte flagship store features concrete, couches and catwalk lighting – all of which provides the perfect backdrop for Markus Freitag's creations: 1600 colourful, durable bags in every shape imaginable.

Konk

MAP P.28, POCKET MAP D11

Kleine Hamburger Str. 15 ⓢ Oranienburger Str. ☏ 030 28 09 78 39. Mon–Fri noon–7pm, Sat noon–6pm.

Featuring collections from many of Berlin's esteemed labels (Anntian, Boessert/Schorn, Marina Hoermannseder), this women's boutique features cutting-edge fashions, jewellery and other glamorous accessories that flit between fashion and art.

Made in Berlin

MAP P.28, POCKET MAP E12

Neue Schönhauser Str. 19 ⓤ Weinmeisterstr. ☏ 030 21 23 06 01, ⓦ picknweight.de. Mon–Sat noon–8pm.

One of four shops that sell cutting-edge, mostly vintage clothes for girls and boys. Tuesday noon till 3pm is happy hour (20 percent off all vintage).

Melting Point

MAP P.28, POCKET MAP E10

Kastanienallee 55 ⓤ Rosenthaler Platz ☏ 030 44 04 71 31. Mon–Sat noon–8pm.

Opened in the mid-1990s, Melting Point records has stayed true to Berlin's techno and house culture, though it also sells funk, Afro, Latin and more. Masses of vinyl.

Michaela Binder

MAP P.28, POCKET MAP E11

Gipsstr. 13 Ⓤ Weinmeisterstr. ☎ 030 28 38 48 69. Tues–Fri noon–7pm, Sat noon–4pm.
Michaela Binder's smart shop stocks her stylish rings, bracelets, ear studs and necklaces in clean, basic shapes, from silver and gold. There's also a line of (cheaper) steel and stone vases.

Pro QM

MAP P.28, POCKET MAP F11
Almstadtstr. 48 Ⓤ Rosa-Luxemburg-Platz ☎ 030 24 72 85 20, Ⓦ pro-qm.de. Mon–Sat 11am–8pm.
Run by an artist and an architecture professor, this smart and surprisingly spacious shop specializes in books and magazines dedicated to these subjects, as well as design and craft, and spans lifestyle as well as academic publications.

R.S.V.P. (Papier in Mitte)

MAP P.28, POCKET MAP E11
Mulackstr. 14 Ⓤ Weinmeisterstr. ☎ 030 31 95 64 10. Mon–Sat 11am–7pm.
From rare international notebooks to the store's own unique cards and journals, R.S.V.P. sells elegant stationery and related products from international artists. A shop at no. 26 sells wrapping paper, boxes and envelopes.

s.wert

MAP P.28, POCKET MAP D10
Brunnenstr. 191 Ⓤ Rosenthaler Platz ☎ 030 40 05 66 55. Mon–Fri 11am–7pm, Sat 11am–6pm.
Interested in special Berliner "architecture pillows", or unique designs of wrapping paper? s.wert sells all this and more, including stylish drinking cups, dresses and curtains.

Trippen Flagship Store

MAP P.28, POCKET MAP D11
Hackesche Höfe, Hofs 4 & 6, Rosenthaler Str. 40/41 Ⓢ Hackescher Markt (also Alte Schönhauser str. 45 in Spandauer Vorstadt) ☎ 030 28 39 13 37. Mon–Sat 11am–7.30pm, Trippen sells men's and women's shoes for every occasion. There are several branches around, but this flagship store has the best range. Footwear also made to order.

Restaurants

Bandol sur Mer

MAP P.28, POCKET MAP D11
Torstr. 167 Ⓤ Rosenthaler Platz ☎ 030 67 30 20 51. Mon–Thurs & Sun 6–11pm
A former kebab kiosk refurbished into a tiny, Michelin-starred French restaurant. The menu, chalked up on the all-black walls, consists of regional French cuisine like snails, entrecote and foie gras. As well as à la carte options (mains around €32), there are also seven-course menus available for €113. The sister restaurant next door, 3 minutes sur mer (Ⓦ 3minutessurmer.de), serves more typical French cuisine.

Da Da Falafel

MAP P.28, POCKET MAP C11
Linienstr. 132 Ⓤ Oranienburger Tor ☎ 030 27 59 69 27, Ⓦ www.dadafalafel.de. Mon–Wed & Sun 10am–1am, Thurs–Sat 10am–2am.
Berlin isn't exactly short of falafels but *Da Da* stands out thanks to their fresh salads and an excellent

Made in Berlin

Bandol sur Mer

array of sauces. The Dada Teller (€8) will set you up for a day's sightseeing, though expect long queues at lunchtimes.

District Mot

MAP P.28, POCKET MAP E11
Rosenthaler Str. 62 Ⓤ Rosenthaler Platz
ⓣ 030 20 08 92 84, Ⓦ www. districtmot. com. Daily noon–midnight.

A Vietnamese street food restaurant, serving dishes you would find on the streets of Saigon, such as Cá Kho Tho (braised Mekong fish in caramel sauce) or Chân Gá Nuong (grilled chicken feet) for more adventurous eaters. Décor is typical Vietnamese street food style: simple with stools and cutlery (read chopsticks) all ready to go in a bowl on the table.

Dudu

MAP P.28, POCKET MAP D11
Torstr. 134 Ⓤ Rosenthaler Platz ⓣ 030 51 73 68 54, Ⓦ www.dudu-berlin.de, Mon–Sat noon–midnight, Sun 1pm–midnight.

This trendy Asian spot, hidden away behind a walled garden on Torstrasse, draws a cosmopolitan Mitte crowd. The menu includes very good Japanese dishes alongside flavoursome Vietnamese soups, and

you can sit inside the chic, minimal interior or at picnic tables in the cosy garden area.

Grill Royal

MAP P.28, POCKET MAP C12
Friedrichstr. 105b Ⓤ Oranienburger Tor
ⓣ 030 28 87 92 88, Ⓦ www.grillroyal.com.
Daily from 6pm.

The steaks are definitely high end at this celeb-friendly restaurant. Some of the best Argentine, German and French cuts in town are served, as well as excellent seafood and wines. In summer try and reserve a seat out on the Spree-facing terrace. Steaks from €29 to – wait for it – €125.

I Due Forni

MAP P.28, POCKET MAP F10
Schönhauser Allee 12 Ⓤ Senefelderplatz
ⓣ 030 44 01 73 33. Daily noon–midnight.

This famous Italian joint serves up cheap and tasty brick-oven pizzas (€5.50–8.50) and pasta dishes, in an idiosyncratic atmosphere, aided by the punk staff (all Italian) and – in summer – a large beer garden. Service is appropriately blasé.

Katz Orange

MAP P.28, POCKET MAP D10

Bergstr. 22 ⓤ/ⓢ Nordbahnhof ⓣ 030 98 32 08 430, ⓦ www.katzorange.com. Daily from 6pm.

Tucked away in a restored, nineteenth-century brewery in Mitte, the (slightly) glamorous "orange cat" offers a pleasant blend of casual and fine dining with an international menu that runs from salads to quality fish and meat dishes. There's also a cocktail bar and a lovely courtyard terrace for warmer weather.

Monsieur Vuong

MAP P.28, POCKET MAP E11
Alte Schönhauser Str. 46 ⓤ Rosa-Luxemburg-Platz ⓣ 030 99 29 69 24, ⓦ www.monsieurvuong.de. Mon–Thurs noon–11pm, Fri–Sun noon–midnight.

The light, simple and cheap Vietnamese food served at *Monsieur Vuong* has made it one of the most popular dining spots in Mitte. The menu changes every few days but there's always good fresh soups, noodle salads and fruit cocktails. You may have to wait for a table, especially at peak times. Specials from €7.80.

Nihombashi

MAP P.28, POCKET MAP E10
Weinbergsweg 4 ⓤ Rosenthaler Platz ⓣ 0176 222 234 15, ⓦ nihombashi.de. Daily noon–midnight.

Brightly decorated Japanese spot that serves good-quality sushi (with red rice as well as white), soups and sashimi, plus tasty *kushiyaki* skewers with meat, vegetables and fish. The basketball hoops in the toilets are a cute touch.

Schwarzwaldstuben

MAP P.28, POCKET MAP C11
Tucholskystr. 48 ⓢ Oranienburger Str. ⓣ 030 28 09 80 84. Mon–Fri noon–midnight, Sat–Sun 9am–11pm

This Mitte mainstay doubles as a casual restaurant serving hearty Swabian food – think Sauerkraut, *Maultaschen* (filled pasta) and *Flammkuchen* (a type of thin-crust pizza, from €7.50) – and a friendly bar in the evenings with decent German beers on draught.

W Der Imbiss

MAP P.28, POCKET MAP H2
Kastanienallee 49 ⓤ Senefelderplatz ⓣ 030 43 35 22 06, ⓦ w-derimbiss.de. Mon–Thurs & Sun noon–10pm, Fri & Sat noon–11pm.

Easily identified by its cheekily inverted *McDonald's* sign (and orange tables), *Imbiss W* serves up fusion food that includes such unusual items as naan pizza and other bright ideas. The results can be a bit hit and miss, but they're generally good and the reasonable prices (items begin at €2) and outdoor seating make this a good budget option.

Weinbar Rutz

MAP P.28, POCKET MAP B11
Chausseestr. 8 ⓤ Naturkundemuseum ⓣ 030 24 62 87 60, ⓦ rutz-restaurant.de. Tues–Sat: wine bar 4–11pm; restaurant 6.30–10.30pm.

Double-Michelin-starred cuisine on the second floor and over eight hundred wines on offer make this a de rigueur stop for foodies. It's expensive – six-course menu €158 or eight courses for €198 – but the bar sells slightly cheaper (but still great) home-style dishes.

Yumcha Heroes

MAP P.28, POCKET MAP E16
Weinbergsweg 8 ⓤ Rosenthaler Platz ⓣ 030 76 21 30 35, ⓦ yumchaheroes.de. Daily noon–midnight.

With the same owners as nearby Portuguese café *Galao*, *Yumcha Heroes* is *the* place in Mitte for dumplings – steamed, baked or in a tasty broth. The food is handmade and MSG-free, cooked in an open kitchen and served in a small, but stylish interior.

Cafés and bars

8mm

MAP P.28, POCKET MAP F10
Schönhauser Allee 177b ⓤ Senefelderplatz ⓦ 8mmbar.com. Mon–Thurs from 7pm, Fri 8pm, Sat 9pm.

It's just a small, blacked-out room with a small bar, a DJ spinning anything from rock to northern soul and 8mm films projected onto one wall – but it's a superb place for low-key, late-night hedonism.

Amano Rooftop Bar

MAP P.28, POCKET MAP E11
Auguststr. 43 ⓤ Rosenthaler Platz ⓣ 030 80 94150, Ⓦ www.amanogroup.de. May–Sept: Every day from 4pm till late.
The rooftop bar at the *Amano* hotel has become a firm summer favourite, not only for the see-and-be-seen ambience and views across Mitte's rooftops but also for its excellent array of summery wines and cocktails.

Barcomi's

MAP P.28, POCKET MAP D11
Sophienstr. 21, Sophie-Gips-Höfe
ⓤ Weinmeisterstr. ⓣ 030 28 59 83 63, Ⓦ www.barcomis.de. Mon–Sat 9am–9pm, Sun 10am–9pm.
This second outlet from American baker Cynthia Barcomi is tucked away in a lovely courtyard and offers excellent bagels, brunches, coffee and cakes – the cheesecake is justly famous. Reservations essential at weekends.

Amano Rooftop Bar

The Barn

MAP P.28, POCKET MAP D11
Auguststr. 58 ⓤ Rosenthaler Platz
Ⓦ thebarn.de. Mon–Fri 8am–6pm, Sat 9am–6pm,Sun 10am–6pm.
Wooden shelves stacked with delicious products for sale, some of the best coffee in town, home-made cakes, and sandwiches using bread from local artisan bakeries all make *The Barn* well worth a visit. They also have a spacious roastery-café in Prenzlauer Berg (Schönhauser Allee 8) and a couple of other locations in the city.

Chén Chè

MAP P.28, POCKET MAP E11
Rosenthaler Str. 13 ⓤ Rosenthaler Platz
ⓣ 030 28 88 42 82, Ⓦ chenche-berlin.de. Daily noon–midnight.
This charming Vietnamese tea room, with its high ceilings and elegant, handmade lanterns, has a small but considered menu featuring a selection of starters and mains as well as great teas and coffees. Try one of the weekend breakfasts for something a bit different.

Cordobar

MAP P.28, POCKET MAP D11
Grosse Hamburger Str. 32 Ⓢ Oranienburger Str. ⓣ 030 27 58 12 15, Ⓦ cordobar.net. Tues–Sat 6.30pm–midnight.
Berlin has finally overcome its dearth of serious wine bars, and *Cordobar* is a refreshing mix of high-end viticulture and accessible atmosphere. There are over nine hundred selections on the menu, including many rarities, plus a small, creative food menu.

The Coven Bar

MAP P.28, POCKET MAP H2
Kleine Präsidenten Str. 3 Ⓢ Hackescher Markt. ⓣ 015 11 49 825 24, Ⓦ www.thecovenberlin.com. Sun–Thur 8pm–2am, Fri & Sat 9pm–3am.
This excellent cocktail bar is well known in the LGBT community as for its 'manly cool' but that shouldn't stop you from visiting

this well designed, uber-modern bar. The service is friendly and the atmosphere relaxed: there isn't a better way to end your evening in this area.

Gorki Park

MAP P.28, POCKET MAP E10
Weinbergsweg 25 Ⓤ Rosenthaler Platz
ⓣ 030 448 72 86, Ⓦ www.gorki-park.de.
Mon–Fri 8am–1am, Sat & Sun 9am–1am.
A network of lounge-style rooms decked out with interesting furniture and retro wallpaper. Despite the Russian theme, mostly evident in the name and the blini and borscht available, there's a very Berlin-esque "Wohnzimmer" (living room) feel to the place.

Hackbarth's

MAP P.28, POCKET MAP D11
Auguststr. 49a Ⓤ Rosenthaler Platz ⓣ 030 28 27 704. Mon–Sat from 9am.
With its simple wooden interior and crowd of regulars, *Hackbarth's* is a casually tasteful option. Snacks and freshly baked cakes are offered during the day.

Kaschk

MAP P.28, POCKET MAP F11
Linienstr. 40 Ⓤ Rosa-Luxemburg-Platz
Ⓦ kaschk.de. Mon–Thurs 8am–2am, Fri 8am–3am, Sat 10am–3am, Sun 10am–2am.
This hip place serves top-notch third-wave coffee, a great selection of local and international (especially Nordic) craft beers and – downstairs – Germany's first ever shuffleboards.

Kim Bar

MAP P.28, POCKET MAP D10
Brunnenstr. 10 Ⓤ Rosenthaler Platz
Ⓦ kim-bar.com. Mon–Sat 8pm–late.
Art space, bar and locals' hangout, *Kim* is a firm favourite among Mitte's trend-conscious residents. There's no sign on the door, just a glass facade (the entrance is through the adjacent courtyard). The dark, grey-walled space hosts an array of art, film and DJ nights.

Mein Haus Am See

MAP P.28, POCKET MAP D16
Brunnenstr. 197–198 Ⓤ Rosenthaler Platz
ⓣ 030 27 59 08 73, Ⓦ mein-haus-am-see.
club. Open 24hr.
A spacious café/bar, stumbling distance from Rosenthaler Platz, *Mein Haus am See* is filled with comfy flea-market furnishings and is as good a spot for reading a book as it is for a drink late at night, when DJs play anything from disco to Latin.

Mogg

MAP P.28, POCKET MAP D11
Auguststr. 11–13 Ⓤ Oranienburger Str.
ⓣ 030 330 06 07 70, Ⓦ moggmogg.
com. Mon–Fri 11am–10pm, Sat & Sun 10am–10pm.
Breezy and chic deli, located inside the former Jewish Girls' School (see page 31) that serves up delicious, Jewish-inspired food, including one of the best pastrami sandwiches in the city (€9.50/€13.50) and a range of delicious salads, lentil and hummus dishes (from €7).

Neue Odessa Bar

MAP P.28, POCKET MAP E10
Torstr. 89 Ⓤ Rosenthaler Platz/Rosa-Luxemburg-Platz ⓣ 0171 839 89 91,
Ⓦ www.neueodessabar.de. Daily from 7pm.
Neue Odessa Bar is now something of a place-to-be thanks to a well-thought-out combination of attractive, swanky interior, reasonably made cocktails and table service. Perpetually busy.

Reingold

MAP P.28, POCKET MAP C11
Novalisstr. 11 Ⓤ Oranienburger Tor ⓣ 030 28 38 76 76, Ⓦ .cms.reingold.de. Tues–Sat from 8pm.
Featuring one of the most impressive bars in town – certainly one of the longest – this classy 1920s-themed watering hole offers impeccably attired waiters who make meticulous cocktails.

Strandbad-Mitte

MAP P.28, POCKET MAP D11

Kleine Hamburger Str. 16 ⓢ Oranienburger Str. ⓣ 030 24 62 89 63, ⓦ strandbad-mitte. de. Daily 9am–midnight.

This laidback café, with breezy, green-tiled, seaside-themed decor, is slightly off the tourist routes and has a correspondingly local vibe. The food and coffee and cakes are good and the staff friendly.

Tadshikische Teestube

MAP P.28, POCKET MAP D11
Oranienburger Str. 27 ⓢ Oranienburger Str. ⓣ 030 20 41 112, ⓦ www.tadshikische-teestube.de. Tues–Fri 4–11pm, Mon until 10pm, Sat & Sun noon–10pm.

This delightful "Tajik Tea Room" has an Oriental cushions-and-carpets interior, a vast tea menu (tea ceremony around €8) and a kids' storyteller on Mondays spinning fairytales in German.

Weinerei Forum

MAP P.28, POCKET MAP E10
Shop: Veteranenstr. 14; bar: Fehrbellnir Str. 57 ⓤ Rosenthaler Platz ⓣ 030 44 06 983, ⓦ weinerei.com. Shop: Mon–Fri 1–8pm, Sat 11am–8pm; bars 10am–midnight.

This "underground" members-club-style wine shop and bar operates on an honesty-box system after 8pm: you pay what you feel is fair for your drinks. As such it's popular with a mix of leftie sympathizers, students and freeloaders. The wine is decidedly average, but the atmosphere is friendly. The owners run other ventures nearby.

Zeit für Brot

MAP P.28, POCKET MAP E11
Alte Schönhauser Str. 4 ⓤ Rosa-Luxemburg-Platz ⓣ 030 28 04 67 80, ⓦ zeitfuerbrot.com. Mon–Fri 7am–8pm, Sat 8am–8pm, Sun 8am–6pm.

This café offers a mellow, pastel-coloured interior, large windows and an eye-catching assortment of artisanal breads (you can see the bakers working away through a Perspex window). The quiches, sandwiches and sweets are organic and delicious. There is another branch in Charlottenburg.

Zosch

MAP P.28, POCKET MAP C11
Tucholskystr. 30 ⓤ Oranienburger Str. ⓣ 030 280 76 64, ⓦ zosch-berlin.de. Daily 4pm till late.

Alternative place that started as a squat when the Wall came down and has retained an early 90s feel. A good place for gigs and club nights in the cellar, where a fun-loving local Creole jazz band often plays amid the smoky ambience and constant chatter.

Clubs and venues

Babylon

MAP P.28, POCKET MAP F11
Rosa-Luxemburg-Str. 30 ⓤ Rosa-Luxemburg-Platz ⓣ 030 24 25 969, ⓦ www.babylonberlin.eu.

This striking Berlin *Kino* opened in 1929 and remains one of the defining architectural landmarks of Rosa-Luxemburg-Platz. Today the cinema shows a mix of indie, trash, silents with live organ music and cult movies, as well as hosting concerts and over forty film festivals annually.

B-Flat

MAP P.28, POCKET MAP E11
Dircksenstr. 40 ⓤ Rosenthaler Platz ⓣ 030 28 33 123, ⓦ b-flat-berlin.de. Daily from 8pm; concerts start at 9pm.

This cosy jazz club offers a mix of local musicians and the occasional international act. There's a free jam session on Wednesdays (from 9pm).

Clärchens Ballhaus

MAP P.28, POCKET MAP D11
Auguststr. 24 ⓤ Rosenthaler Platz dor Weinmeisterstr. ⓣ 030 28 29 295, ⓦ www.ballhaus.de. Daily 11am–late.

This authentic pre-war ballroom still hosts dance classes, but at weekends the downstairs is taken over by one of the most diverse crowds (young, old, straight, gay) in Berlin, drawn by the unique atmosphere of a live covers band

and an unpretentious good time. Tasty pizzas too.

Kaffee Burger

MAP P.28, POCKET MAP E11
Torstr. 60 ⓤ Rosa-Luxemburg-Platz ☏ 030 28 04 64 95, ⓦ www.kaffeeburger.de. Daily from 9pm.

Kaffee Burger has been throwing parties and events beloved of students and culture vultures for years. In recent years, its programme has become less cultural and more focused on DJ and live music events that span hip-hop and disco to world music.

Kitty Cheng

MAP P.28, POCKET MAP E10
Torstr. 99 ⓤ Rosa-Luxemburg-Platz ☏ 030 92 36 89 75, ⓦ kittycheng.de. Thurs–Sat 9pm–6am.

With its vague Renaissance theme – red-and-white-striped walls, regal furnishings – and lengthy drinks list, this slightly under-the-radar spot manages to attract the attention of Mitte's buzzy (and spoiled-for-choice) party crowd. The best parties are at the weekend and the music is refreshingly diverse.

Kunsthaus ACUD

MAP P.28, POCKET MAP D10
Veteranenstr. 21 ⓤ Rosenthaler Platz ☏ 030 98 35 26 13, ⓦ acud.de. Entry and opening times vary.

One of the few cultural spaces left from the immediate post-Wall era, ACUD contains a theatre, cinema, club, bar and studio, and puts on regular concerts.

Roter Salon

MAP P.28, POCKET MAP F11
Rosa-Luxemburg-Platz 1 ⓤ Rosa-Luxemburg-Platz ☏ 030 24 06 55, ⓦ volksbuehne.berlin. Wed–Sat 11pm–4am.

Set within the Volksbühne theatre, this long-running venue's lurid red decor and chintzy furniture give it the feel of a cultured 1950s brothel. Readings, concerts and talks are

Babylon

held here. Entry varies according to event.

Schokoladen

MAP P.28, POCKET MAP D10
Ackerstr. 169 ⓤ Rosenthaler Platz ☏ 030 28 26 527, ⓦ www.schokoladen-mitte.de. Daily from 8.30pm.

A small live venue (in a former chocolate factory) that is a bit like visiting a private lounge – albeit one with cheap drinks, a friendly atmosphere and a consistently good line-up of indie-pop bands and upcoming singer/songwriters.

Volksbühne

MAP P.28, POCKET MAP F11
Rosa-Luxemburg-Platz (Linienstrasse 227) ⓤ Rosa-Luxemburg-Platz ☏ 030 24 06 57 77, ⓦ www.volksbuehne-berlin.de.

Built just before World War I, the Volksbühne ("People's Theatre") has its origin in the free people's theatre movement. Damaged during World War II, it was rebuilt in the 1950s and is now established as one of Germany's most experimental theatres. The venue also hosts club nights and concerts.

The Museum Island

The world-renowned Museum Island (Museumsinsel) comprises five of Berlin's most famous museums and is an absolute must for any visitor to Berlin, if only to stroll around and take in the lovely buildings and waterside atmosphere. Friedrich Wilhelm III commissioned the Royal Museum (now the Altes Museum) in 1830, but the plan for an island of museums – intended as the embodiment of Enlightenment ideas about culture – came to fruition under Friedrich Wilhelm IV of Prussia. The site was further developed under successive Prussian kings. The range of artwork and architecture is startling, spanning two thousand years and featuring such treasures as the Roman gate of Miletus and the bust of Nefertiti as well as a dizzying range of paintings and sculptures. Though badly damaged during World War II, with the collections divided during the Cold War, sensitive renovations have seen the buildings revived.

Berliner Dom (Cathedral)

MAP P.42, POCKET MAP D13
Am Lustgarten 1 ℹ 030 20 26 91 36,
ⓦ berlinerdom.de. Mon–Sat 9am–8pm,
Sun noon–8pm, Oct–March closes 7pm. €7,
audioguide €3. Guided tours of the dome are available (ℹ 030 20 26 91 19). Designed by Julius Raschdorff in Baroque style with Italian Renaissance influences, Berlin's

Berliner Dom

Lustgarten

Protestant cathedral was intended as a counterpart to St Peter's Basilica in Rome. The present structure dates from 1905, but stands on the site of several earlier buildings, including the St Erasmus Chapel and a Neoclassical design by Schinkel dating from 1822. Restoration of the current interior began in 1984 and in 1993 the church reopened. It's a handsome and interesting building to explore, with notable eye candy including Sauer's organ, stained-glass windows designed by Anton von Werner and a marvellous dome intricately decorated with mosaics. You can get an excellent close-up view of the dome – and the entire interior – by climbing the 270 steps to the gallery. The most historically significant feature of the cathedral is its crypt, which holds more than eighty sarcophagi of Prussian royals, including those of Friedrich I and his queen, Sophie Charlotte.

Lustgarten

MAP P.42, POCKET MAP D13

Berlin's "Pleasure Garden" is a fundamental part of the Museum Island landscape. It's difficult to believe that this charming rectangular park, a great spot for picnics or taking a pause

Museum Island practicalities

The **phone number** and **website** for all Museum Island enquiries are: ☎ 030 26 64 24 242 (Mon–Fri 9am–4pm), ⓦ www.smb.museum. The nearest **station** for all museums is ⓢ Hackescher Markt.

Three-day tickets for all state museums (including those in the Kulturforum, see page 64) and a wealth of private museums can be bought for €29 (discounted €14.50), though these do not include special exhibitions. Note that entrance is always free for anyone under 18.

The **Berlin Welcome Card Museum Island** includes admission to many museums including the Museum Island, travel for up to 72 hours and up to 50 percent discount on many top attractions in Berlin for €46. See ⓦ www.visitberlin.de.

A new visitor centre, the **James Simon-Galerie**, opened in 2019, between the Neues Museum and Kupfergraben.

people here). Bombed in the War and renamed Marx-Engels-Platz by the GDR, its current incarnation harks back to Peter Joseph Lenné's early nineteenth-century design with a central 13m-high fountain, as re-envisioned by German landscape architect Hans Loidl.

Altes Museum

MAP P.42, POCKET MAP D13
Am Lustgarten. Tues–Sun 10am–6pm (Thurs till 8pm). €10. Guided tours by arrangement.

The Altes Museum, built between 1823 and 1830 after a design by Karl Friedrich Schinkel, is Berlin's oldest museum. It's also one of the city's most important Classicist statements and a marvellous piece of architecture, all fluted Ionic columns, a beautiful rotunda filled with sculptures of Greek gods and a grand staircase that more than nods to Athens and Rome. As

Neues Museum

between museum visits, has been used variously as a military parade ground (for Wilhelm I and Napoleon), mass protests (a huge anti-Nazi demo here in 1933 prompted the banning of demonstrations) and rallies (Hitler addressed up to a million

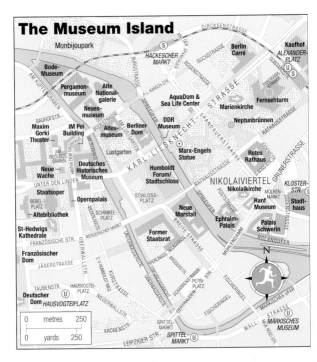

Pergamonmuseum

well as Greek statues downstairs, the upper floor contains a colossal range of Roman and Etruscan art – urns, shields, sarcophagi, friezes – all chronologically and thematically arranged.

Neues Museum

MAP P.42, POCKET MAP D13
Bodestr. 1–3. Ⓦ www.neues-museum.de. Daily 10am–6pm (Thurs till 8pm). €12.

One of the Museum Island's undoubted highlights, the misleadingly named Neues Museum was opened in 1859 to cater for the overspill of the by-then overcrowded Altes Museum. Largely destroyed during World War II, it was only reopened in 2009, fully restored by British architect David Chipperfield, whose distinguished makeover has melded the old with the new, maintaining traces of war damage. Over three floors you'll find no less than twenty exhibition halls, each impressively designed and connected via a stunning winding staircase. As well as the archeological collections of the Egyptian museum and papyrus collection, there's plenty of pre- and early history, as well as works from classical antiquity. The big draw is the bust of Egyptian Queen Nefertiti – famously described as "the world's most beautiful woman" – but you could happily spend an entire day absorbing the endless exhibits. Note that due to the popularity of the exhibitions you need to reserve a time slot, either by purchasing one from the nearby sales cabin or on the museum's website in advance.

Pergamonmuseum

MAP P.42, POCKET MAP D12
Bodestr. 1–3. Daily 10am–6pm (Thurs till 8pm). €19. Guided tours by arrangement.

The Pergamonmuseum was built by Alfred Mussel in 1930 to house the artefacts from the nineteenth-century excavations of German archeologists in

Pergamon and Asia Minor, perhaps most famously the controversial "Priam's treasure" – a cache of gold and other artefacts discovered by classical archeologist Heinrich Schliemann, but whose authenticity and relationship to Homeric king Priam has long been in doubt. Essentially three museums in one, the museum offers a collection of Classical antiquities (part of which is also on display in the Altes Museum); the museum of the Ancient Near East; and the museum of Islamic Art. As with the Neues Museum, you can spend a day here easily, though some of the main highlights – specifically the reconstructed (and mind-bogglingly large) Pergamon Altar from the second century BC and the Gallery of Hellenistic Art – have been affected by current renovations that are expected to last until 2023. Depending on what's on display at the time, check out the facade of the throne hall of King Nebuchadnezzar, the Market Gate of Miletus (an important example of Roman architecture) or the bright blue, glazed-brick Ishtar Gate of Babylon from the sixth century BC instead.

Alte Nationalgalerie

MAP P.42, POCKET MAP D12
Bodestr. 1–3. Tues–Sun 10am–6pm (Thurs until 8pm). €10.

The Neoclassical Alte Nationalgalerie (Old National Gallery), designed to resemble a Greek temple, houses one of the country's most significant collections of nineteenth-century painting. Built between 1866 and 1876, the museum reopened in 2001 to showcase its wealth of Classical, Romantic, Impressionist and early Modernist masterpieces. Highlights include the Goethe-era landscapes, works by Jakob Philipp Hackert and Anton Graff and Romantic paintings by the likes of Caspar David Friedrich and Karl Friedrich Schinkel (a

Alte Nationalgalerie

Schlossplatz

The reconstruction of Berlin's **Stadtschloss** (City Palace) is just one of the many controversial components of Berlin's cityscape – not least because of its projected €590 million cost. The original palace, which featured architectural elements designed, built and inspired by Schlüter, Stüler, Schinkel and Goethe was the seat of the Prussian rulers (Hohenzollerns) from the fifteenth century onwards. The Stadtschloss was at the centre of the Revolution of 1848 and its last resident, Kaiser Wilhelm II, quit the palace and throne in 1918 following Germany's surrender in World War I.

The palace was damaged during World War II and pulled down in 1950 by the GDR, who replaced it with their own **Palast der Republik**, a bronze-tinted, blocky behemoth that became surprisingly popular with many East Germans. Nonetheless, after reunification this building was also pulled down, leaving a vast empty space and a lot of heated discussion about whether to rebuild the original palace or something more suited to the modern city. In 2007, the Bundestag (parliament) reached a compromise of sorts by deciding to rebuild the exterior facade with a modern interior – the new building is to be called the **Humboldt Forum** and will house parts of Humboldt University, two museums relocated from Dahlem (see page 139) and various shops and restaurants. At the time of writing, the opening was scheduled to coincide with Humboldt's 250th birthday in September 2019.

gifted landscape painter as well as Berlin's foremost architect). The Impressionist section, with its international "big guns" Manet, Monet, Renoir and Rodin, is worth the visit alone.

Bode-Museum

MAP P.42, POCKET MAP D12
Am Kupfergraben 1. Tues–Sun 10am–6pm (Thurs till 8pm). €12.

The stately Bode-Museum, with its recognizable dome, was originally called the Kaiser Friedrich Museum, and was renamed in 1956 after its inaugural curator Wilhelm van Bode. Opened after extensive refurbishments in 2006, the building is notable for its refined architectural details – the opulent staircases, monumental pilasters and demi-columns – as well as a wealth of art and artefacts from the Byzantine and Medieval periods. These are mainly from Germany but also come from major European art centres such as the Netherlands, Italy, France and Spain, and are culled from three major state museum collections: the sculpture collection, with highlights including the terracotta statues from Luca della Robbia, the Madonna from Donatello and the sculptures of Desiderio da Settignano; the Museum of Byzantine Art – the only one of its kind in Germany; and the Numismatic Collection, a vast and impressive collection of coins (and other forms of currency) that range from the seventh century BC to the twenty-first century.

On summer Sundays, the Bode-Museum hosts popular outdoor classical concerts. Entry is free (donations welcome) and the setting, on the elegant Monbijou Bridge, spectacular.

Unter den Linden and the government quarter

Berlin's grand boulevard, named for the Linden (lime) trees that line it, runs east–west from the site of the former royal palace to the Brandenburg Gate. The road originated as a bridle path for Duke Friedrich Wilhelm in the seventeenth century; by the nineteenth century it was a popular gathering place for many Berliners and Unter den Linden was furnished with new buildings, including the Neoclassical Neue Wache. Despite appearances, most of the buildings are reconstructions. Nonetheless it maintains its upscale aura, reflected in the fine-dining restaurants and expensive shops that predominate. Beyond the Brandenburg Gate lies the modern, yet no less authoritative Regierungsviertel ("government quarter"), a cluster of buildings starting with the Reichstag that stretch along the Spree. A stroll along the river past the striking Paul Löbe Haus and the Bundeskanzleramt, towards the Hauptbahnhof, is a pleasant and architecturally interesting way to pass a couple of hours.

Deutsches Historisches Museum

MAP P.48, POCKET MAP D13
Unter den Linden 2 ⓤ/ⓈFriedrichstr.
ⓣ 030 20 30 40, ⓦ dhm.de. Daily 10am–6pm. €8.

The fascinating German Historical Museum (Deutsches Historisches Museum) is spread across two buildings: the unique Baroque Zeughaus (armoury) and a modern exhibition hall designed by Chinese-American architect I.M. Pei. The **Zeughaus** was first used as a museum for German history during the years of the GDR (1952–90), essentially to espouse the Marxist-Leninist concept of history. In 2006 a permanent exhibition "German history in images and artefacts" was inaugurated in the three-hundred-year-old building (the oldest on Unter den Linden), which showcases two thousand years of German history via eight thousand objects from the museum's extensive collections. Supplementing this are special temporary exhibitions displayed on the four floors of the spacious **Pei building**, with its glass-and-steel lobby and winding staircase. There's also a very tasteful and little-known **cinema**, entered from the Spree side of the museum, with a historically protected interior, and a refined **café** serving great breakfasts, lunches and cakes.

Neue Wache

MAP P.48, POCKET MAP D13
Unter den Linden 4 ⓤ/ⓈFriedrichstr.
ⓣ 030 25 00 25. Daily 10am–6pm.

The Neue Wache (New Guard House) was Karl Friedrich Schinkel's first major commission in Berlin – he rose to the occasion by building a leading example of German Neoclassicism. Originally constructed as a guardhouse for the troops of the crown prince of Prussia, the building became a memorial to the Wars of Liberation (Napoleonic Wars) until 1918. From 1931 onwards it was a memorial for World War I, and the inner courtyard was covered over, apart from a small opening in the roof letting through a slither of symbolic light. Post World War II, the GDR leadership turned it into the monument for the victims of fascism and militarism. An eternal flame was placed in a cube above the ashes of an unknown concentration camp prisoner and an unknown fallen soldier. After German reunification, the GDR memorial piece was removed and replaced by an enlarged version of Käthe Kollwitz's sculpture *Mother with her Dead Son* (*Pietá*). This sculpture is directly under the oculus, its exposure to the elements a metaphor for the suffering of civilians during World War II.

Bebelplatz

MAP P.48, POCKET MAP C13
Ⓤ Französische Str.

This historical square on the south side of Unter den Linden was constructed between 1741 and 1743 and was originally known as Opernplatz. Though framed by the opulent **Staatsoper** (see page 55), a library and the swanky *Hotel de Rome* (see page 145), it remains best known for the 1933 Nazi book burning that took place here, as instigated by propaganda minister Joseph Goebbels. The Nazis burned some twenty thousand books, including works by Thomas Mann, Erich Maria Remarque, Heinrich Heine and Karl Marx. At the centre of the square is a **memorial** of the burning by Micha Ullman, which consists of a glass-covered view into an underground chamber of empty bookshelves. Nearby, an engraving of a line from Heinrich Heine translates as: "Where they burn books, they ultimately burn people".

DB Palais Populaire

MAP P.48, POCKET MAP C13
Unter den Linden 5 Ⓢ Französisches Str. ☎ 030 20 20 930, Ⓦ www.db-palaispopulaire.de. Daily 10am–8pm (Thurs till 9pm). €9, free on Mon.

Located in the 18th century Prinzessin Palais (the rooms were redesigned by Kuehn Malvezzi)

Neue Wache

– three times the size of the former DB Kunsthalle – the Palais Populaire opened in mid 2018. It showcases all manner of things from local, global and future cultures and strives to be an "open house" – combining an innovative forum for visitors with art, culture and sports. The Palais Populaire's opening exhibition, "The World on Paper", showcased 300 works of contemporary art, the most comprehensive works from the DB collection. Besides art, the museum hosts lectures and other events like "ClubPopulaire" and "PalaisLecture". Visit the website to see what's on.

Gendarmenmarkt

MAP P.48, POCKET MAP C14
Ⓤ Hausvogteiplatz/Französische Str./ Stadtmitte.

The Gendarmenmarkt, one of Berlin's most beautiful squares, was created at the end of the seventeenth century as a market place (then called the Linden Markt) but its current name comes from the Regiment Gens d'Armes that had their stables here from 1736 to 1773. Despite its inherent grandness, it's a surprisingly quiet place defined by three landmark buildings: the Französischer Dom, Deutscher Dom and the **Konzerthaus** (Concert Hall, see page 55), which frame a central statue of Friedrich Schiller. The **Französischer Dom** and **Deutscher Dom** are two seemingly identical churches facing each other across the square, poised in a standoff for visitor attention. The Französischer Dom (French Cathedral) is older, built between 1701 and 1705 by the Huguenot community, and contains a Huguenot museum, a restaurant on the top floor and a viewing platform. The pentagonal Deutscher Dom (German Cathedral), at the southern end

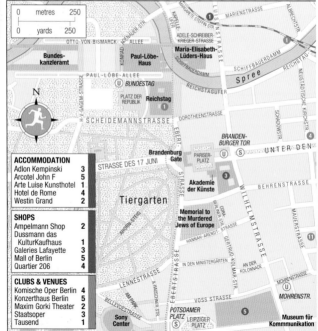

ACCOMMODATION
Adlon Kempinski	3
Arcotel John F	5
Arte Luise Kunsthotel	1
Hotel de Rome	4
Westin Grand	2

SHOPS
Ampelmann Shop	2
Dussmann das KulturKaufhaus	1
Galeries Lafayette	3
Mall of Berlin	5
Quartier 206	4

CLUBS & VENUES
Komische Oper Berlin	4
Konzerthaus Berlin	5
Maxim Gorki Theater	2
Staatsoper	3
Tausend	1

of the square, was designed by Martin Grünberg, built in 1708 by Giovanni Simonetti and modified in 1785 after a design by Carl von Gontard, who added the domed tower. A popular Christmas market is held on the square during the holidays.

Akademie der Künste

MAP P.48, POCKET MAP B14
Pariser Platz 4 (and Hanseatenweg 10, Tiergarten) Ⓤ/Ⓢ Brandenburger Tor
☎ 030 20 05 71 000, Ⓦ www.adk.de.
General visits daily 10am–8pm; exhibitions Tues–Sun 11am–7pm. Admission varies.

Founded as the Prussian Academy of Arts in 1696 by Friedrich III, this public corporation continues its original mission to support and foster the arts. Its prestigious members have included Goethe, Mendelssohn-Bartholdy and Brecht; Max Liebermann headed the institution in the 1920s after the academy introduced a literature section. Under Hitler it was used as a headquarters for architect Albert Speer to redesign Berlin into "Germania", before being bombed almost to the ground (only the exhibition halls remained intact). During the GDR era it was turned into studios for Academy members like the sculptor Fritz Cremer and several master scholars such as Wieland Förster and Werner Stötzer. The glass-facade building, designed by Günter Behnisch, lies directly in front of what's left of the original academy, and its current members include German Nobel laureate Günter Grass, architects Daniel Libeskind and Sir Norman Foster and composer Sir Harrison Birtwistle. The venue holds a number of lectures, exhibits and workshops.

Brandenburg Gate

MAP P.48, POCKET MAP A13
Pariser Platz Ⓤ/Ⓢ Brandenburger Tor.

CAFÉS & BARS	
Café Nö!	11
Einstein	4
Newton Bar	12
Windhorst	2

RESTAURANTS	
Bocca di Bacco	7
Borchardt	9
Charlotte & Fritz	8
Cookies Cream	5
Crackers	6
Ishin	3
Käfer Dachgarten	1
Lutter & Wegner	10

Unter den Linden and the government quarter

Brandenburg Gate

A former city gate (the only remaining of the period), the Brandenburg Gate (Brandenburger Tor) is one of the most recognizable icons of Berlin, if not Europe. Commissioned by Friedrich Wilhelm II of Prussia as a sign of peace, and built by Carl Gotthard Langhans in 1788 from a design based upon the Propylaea (the gateway to the Acropolis in Athens), the gate has at various times been a symbol of victory, peace, division and unity. After the 1806 Prussian defeat at the Battle of Jena-Auerstedt, Napoleon took the Quadriga (added in 1793 by Johann Gottfried Schadow) to Paris. After Napoleon's defeat in 1814 and the Prussian occupation of Paris by General Ernst von Pfuel, the Quadriga was restored to Berlin. The Gate survived World War II and was one of the damaged structures still standing in the ruins of Pariser Platz in 1945. In December 2000, the Brandenburg Gate was closed for a €4 million private refurbishment by the Stiftung Denkmalschutz Berlin (Berlin Monument Conservation Foundation), reopening less than two years later. Today, it still draws punters by the busload. The best way to enjoy it is to stroll towards it via Unter den Linden, taking in the trees and run of shops, glamorous theatres and excellent museums along the way. It's a very touristy spot, so for a bit of peace and quiet pop into the Room of Silence on the north side, built specifically for visitors to rest and reflect. Since 2016, a museum right next to the Brandenburg Gate on Pariser Platz has offered a 300-year history of the city as witnessed via its iconic gate (030 236 078 436, brandenburggate-museum.com; admission €5; daily 10am–6pm).

Memorial to the Murdered Jews of Europe

MAP P.48, POCKET MAP A14

Cora-Berliner-Str. 1 U/S Brandenburger Tor holocaust-mahnmal.de. Guided tours: 030 26 39 43 36; memorial open 24hr; information centre Tues–Sun: April–Sept 10am–8pm (last entrance 7.15pm), Oct–March 10am–7pm (last entrance 6.15pm).

Peter Eisenman's hugely controversial 2711 sombre concrete slabs (stelae) are arranged in a neat grid spread across 19,000 square metres of prime Berlin real estate near the Brandenburg Gate, the memorial's grand scale intended as a reminder of the magnitude of the Holocaust. The slabs are purposefully varying in height to give visitors walking among them a sense of disorientation and confusion, though from above the slabs appear to make a wave-like form. Soon after construction began in 2003, a Swiss newspaper reported that a subsidiary of the company hired to produce the anti-graffiti substance to cover the stelae, Degussa, had created the poison gas used to exterminate so many in the Nazi death camps of the Holocaust. Rather than spend an additional €2 million to undo the work and hire another company, work continued.

As impressive as the memorial is, it's really the 800-square-metre underground **information centre** (located in the southeastern corner) that leaves you reeling. The centre holds factual exhibits to balance the abstract memorial above, including personal information about many of the victims and a video archive ("Voices of Survival") where you can listen to Holocaust survivor testimonies in many languages, or even search for specific places, people or events in the database.

The Reichstag

MAP P.48, POCKET MAP A13

Platz der Republik 1 ⓤ Bundestag ⓣ 030 22 73 21 52, ⓦ bundestag.de. Roof terrace and dome accessible on prearranged guided tours only (daily 8am–midnight, last entry 10pm; free) or with a restaurant reservation (daily 9am–4.30pm & 6.30pm–midnight; ⓣ 030 22 62 99 33).

The Reichstag, the seat of the German Parliament, has played a crucial role in several of the city's most significant historic events. After the founding of the German Empire in 1872, German architect Paul Wallot was commissioned to create this imposing neo-Renaissance parliament building. It was constructed between 1884 and 1894, mainly funded with wartime reparation money from France – following Prussia's defeat of France in 1871. The famous inscription "Dem Deutschen Volke" (To the German People) was added in 1916 by Wilhelm II. In 1933 a fire destroyed much of the Reichstag. Though it remains uncertain how the fire started, the Communists were blamed, giving a boost to Hitler and the Nazis, who would soon come to power. The building was further damaged at the end of the War, when the Soviets entered Berlin. The picture of a Red Army soldier raising the Soviet flag on the Reichstag is one of the most famous twentieth-century images and symbolized Germany's defeat. The Reichstag was rebuilt between 1958 and 1972, but the central dome and most of the ornamentation were removed. During Berlin's division the West German parliament assembled here once a year as a way to indicate that Bonn was only a temporary capital – and indeed, after reunification, the Bundestag relocated here. The building was renovated again from 1995 to 1999, when the glass dome designed by Sir Norman Foster was added. At first the subject of much controversy, the dome has become one of the city's most recognized landmarks. Since April 1999, the Reichstag is once again the seat of the Bundestag – and also one of the city's largest attractions. Not all the building is open to the public: the most popular (and accessible) part is the glass dome, which features a roof terrace, restaurant and fantastic views over the city. It's currently only open to visitors with a restaurant reservation, who have registered to attend a sitting or lecture, or who sign up in advance for a guided tour. The audioguides (free) last twenty minutes and give all the facts about the building and the surroundings as you ascend and descend the 230m spiral staircase to the top.

St Hedwig's Cathedral

MAP P.48, POCKET MAP D14

Hinter der Katholischen Kirche 3 ⓤ Französische Str. ⓣ 030 20 34 810, ⓦ hedwigs-kathedrale.de. Visiting times (outside services) Mon–Sat 10am–5pm, Sun 1–5pm. Guided tours available on request.

The seat of the archbishop of Berlin, St Hedwig's Cathedral was the first Catholic church to be built in Germany after the Protestant Reformation. Consecrated in 1773, it was completely destroyed by Allied bombs in 1943, but reconstruction began in 1952 and was finally completed in 1963. The exterior is striking, but it's also worth popping inside to see the interior of the dome, composed of 84 reinforced concrete segments, and the impressive hanging organ (built in 1978 to replace one destroyed in the War), made by Klais of Bonn. At the time of writing, the Cathedral was closed for renovation; check the website for the latest updates.

Shops

Ampelmann Shop

MAP P.48, POCKET MAP C13
Unter den Linden 35 Ⓤ Franzözische Str./Ⓢ Friedrichstr. ☏ 030 20 62 52 69, Ⓦ ampelmann.de. Mon–Sat 9.30am–10pm, Sun 1pm–6pm.

The very first traffic lights to feature Karl Peglau's red and green Ampelmännchen stood on Unter den Linden. Fitting then, that this flagship store is here to pay tribute in the shape of thirty sets of traffic lights from all over the world, and a wealth of related gifts and souvenirs. There's also a small café selling coffee and snacks.

Dussmann das KulturKaufhaus

MAP P.48, POCKET MAP C13
Friedrichstr. 90 Ⓤ/Ⓢ Friedrichstr. ☏ 030 20 25 11 11, Ⓦ kulturkaufhaus.de. Mon–Fri 9am–midnight, Sat 9am–11.30pm.

This giant store has five levels of books, CDs, vinyl, DVDs and a large section of books in English and ten other foreign languages across two floors.

Galeries Lafayette

MAP P.48, POCKET MAP C14
Friedrichstr. 76–78 Ⓢ Stadtmitte ☏ 030 20 94 80, Ⓦ galerieslafayette.de. Mon–Sat 10am–8pm.

This elegant branch of the Parisian store opened in 1996. Housed in a glass temple designed by Jean Nouvel, it stocks every super-exclusive brand you can think of, from Agent Provocateur to Yves Saint Laurent. There's also a vast variety of gourmet foods.

Mall of Berlin

MAP P.48, POCKET MAP B15
Leipziger Platz 12 Ⓢ Potsdamer Platz ☏ 030 20 62 17 70, Ⓦ mallofberlin.de. Mon–Sat 10am–9pm.

Housed on the site of the city's former Wertheim Department Store (an architectural and retail highlight during the Weimar era), this is Germany's biggest shopping centre. Housing 270 stores, apartments and a hotel, it's a modern, elegant space with a mix of high-street names (Zara, H&M), independent fashion boutiques and luxury outlets (Hugo Boss, Karl Lagerfeld). There's a third-floor food court.

Galeries Lafayette

Quartier 206

MAP P.48, POCKET MAP C14
Friedrichstr. 71 ⓤ Stadtmitte ☎ 030 20
94 65 00, ⓦ www.q206berlin.de. Mon–Sat
10.30am–7.30pm.

Unapologetically posh department store with flagships for the likes of Etro, Gant, Wolford and Galerie Mensing, all set in a lavish, Art Deco-inspired interior.

Restaurants

Bocca di Bacco

MAP P.48, POCKET MAP C14
Friedrichstr. 167–168 ⓤ Französische
Str. ☎ 030 20 67 28 28, ⓦ boccadibacco.
de. Mon–Sat noon–midnight, Sun 6pm–
midnight.

Bocca di Bacco blends a down-to-earth atmosphere with high-quality cuisine, inspired by Tuscany and other parts of Italy. The menu includes pasta, game, fish and plenty of wonderful desserts. The three-course lunch is a pretty good deal.

Borchardt

MAP P.48, POCKET MAP C14
Französische Str. 47 ⓤ Französische Str.
☎ 030 81 88 62 62, ⓦ www.borchardt-
restaurant.de. Daily 11.30am–midnight.

A reincarnation of a nineteenth-century meeting place for high society, *Borchardt* mark two is a tasteful facsimile with marble columns, plush seating and an Art Nouveau mosaic that was discovered during renovations. The place draws politicians, celebrities and tourists, and cuisine is high-quality French-German, though if you're not a regular, service is likely to be offhand at best.

Charlotte & Fritz

MAP P.48, POCKET MAP C14
Regent Berlin, Charlottenstr. 49
ⓤ Französische Str. ☎ 030 20 33 63 63,
ⓦ charlotteundfritz.com. Daily 6.30–
10.30am, noon–2pm & 6.00–10.30pm.

Charlotte & Fritz (formerly *Fischers Fritz*) is headed by Jörg Lawerenz, who has created a menu based on regional cuisine specialities, while focusing on fine meats. At lunchtime, it also offers weekly changing business lunches.
There's a price for Lawerenz's expertise of course, namely €80 for four courses.

Cookies Cream

MAP P.48, POCKET MAP C13
Behrenstr. 55 ⓤ Französische Str. ☎ 030
27 49 29 40, ⓦ www.cookiescream.de.
Tues–Sat 6–11pm.

Deliberately difficult to find (it's behind the *Westin Grand* on Friedrichstr.; see website for creative directions) this stylish restaurant is worth seeking out. Chef Stephan Hentschel has made this one of the best vegetarian restaurants in the city. At €49 for a three-course menu and €25 for a main, it's pricey but far from prohibitive, and the seasonal, inventive food is worth it.

Crackers

MAP P.48, POCKET MAP C13
Friedrichstr. 158 ⓤ Französische Str. ☎ 030
68 07 30 488, ⓦ crackersberlin.com. Daily
6.30pm–midnight.

Downstairs from *Cookies Cream* (see above), the equally chic *Crackers* offers a European-nouveau menu of meat and fish (and some vegetarian options), a great cocktail bar and hip service. DJ dinner sets on Fri & Sat. Mains €18–36.

Ishin

MAP P.48, POCKET MAP C13
Mittelstr. 24 ⓤ/ⓢ Brandenburger Tor/
Friedrichstr. ☎ 030 20 67 48 29, ⓦ ishin.
de. Mon–Fri 11.30am–9.30pm, Sat
noon–9.30pm.

There are four *Ishin* restaurants in Berlin. The interior of this central one is slightly functional but the decent, fresh sushi, good prices (full menus from €6.50) and quick service make it very popular, especially for lunch. There's a happy hour all day Wednesday and

Saturday (plus Mon, Tues, Thurs & Fri till 4pm), plenty of veggie dishes and free green tea.

Käfer Dachgarten

MAP P.48, POCKET MAP A13

Platz der Republik 1 ⓤ Bundestag ⓣ 030 22 62 990, ⓦ feinkost-kaefer.de/berlin. Daily 9am–5pm & 7pm–midnight (last orders 9.15pm).

Famous for its location on the roof of the Reichstag and its 180-degree view of eastern Berlin, this restaurant specializes in gourmet renditions of regional German dishes (mains €17.50–30). A reservation here also means you get to avoid the registration process through the Bundestag.

Lutter & Wegner

MAP P.48, POCKET MAP C14

Charlottenstr. 56 ⓤ Französische Str. ⓣ 030 20 29 5415, ⓦ www.l-w-berlin.de. Daily 11am–midnight.

This refined, airy Austro-German restaurant is the finest of the *Lutter & Wagner* mini empire – it was here the wine merchant started (in 1811). Prices are high (set menus around €35, mains from €15.50) but that's what happens when The *New York Times* crowns your Wiener Schnitzel the best outside Vienna (though the Sauerbraten is the real highlight). There's a cheaper bistro with a shorter menu too.

Cafés and bars

Café Nö!

MAP P.48, POCKET MAP B14

Glinkastr. 23 ⓤ Französische Str. ⓣ 030 20 10 871, ⓦ cafe-noe.de. Mon–Fri noon–1am.

This wine bar-restaurant serves good food for good prices. The menu includes *Flammkuchen* (from €8.50) and the like, plus lunch deals (Mon–Fri noon–3pm) for €10–13.

Einstein

MAP P.48, POCKET MAP B13

Unter den Linden 42 ⓤ/Ⓢ Brandenburger Tor ⓣ 030 20 43 632, ⓦ einstein-udl.com. Daily 7am–11pm (Sat & Sun from 8am)

The younger sibling to the famous *Café Einstein* (see page 134), this branch doesn't have the same panache, but it's popular with Berlin's cultural elite and serves excellent Austro-Hungarian specialities. Also good for a coffee and cake.

Newton Bar

MAP P.48, POCKET MAP C14

Charlottenstr. 57 ⓤ Stadtmitte ⓣ 030 20 29 54 21, ⓦ www.newton-bar.de. Sun–Wed 10am–3am, Thurs–Sat 10am–4am.

Dedicated to photographer Helmut Newton, this classy cocktail bar, all leather chairs and oak furnishings, is popular with a mature, well-heeled crowd. The large windows look out onto Gendarmenmarkt, though since a huge Newton photograph called *Big Nudes* covers one wall, you won't be short on eye candy either way.

Windhorst

MAP P.48, POCKET MAP C13

Dorotheenstr. 65 ⓤ/Ⓢ Friedrichstr. ⓣ 030 20 45 00 70. Mon–Fri 6pm–late, Sat 9pm–late.

Though it's not in a residential area, this tucked-away cocktail haven feels like a neighbourhood spot. It's a smart, fairly simple place, but the cocktails are above average and go well with the jazz (on vinyl) that they love to play.

Clubs and venues

Komische Oper Berlin

MAP P.48, POCKET MAP C13

Behrenstr. 55–57 ⓤ Französische Str. ⓣ 030 47 99 74 00, ⓦ www.komische-oper-berlin.de.

Presenting everything from opera and German operetta to musicals and baroque, the Comic Opera – the smallest of Berlin's three opera houses – was built between 1891 and 1892. Since

Einstein

2004 it has been operated by the Berliner Opernstiftung.

Konzerthaus Berlin

MAP P.48, POCKET MAP C14
Gendarmenmarkt Ⓤ Französische Str. ⓘ 030 20 30 92 101 (tickets), Ⓦ konzerthaus.de.
The concert house was built on the ruins of the national theatre by Schinkel in 1821. Since 1984 it has been the home of the Konzerthausorchester Berlin and is numbered amongst the best classical concert venues in the world. Daily tours are available (for example Sat 1pm; 75min, €3).

Maxim Gorki Theater

MAP P.48, POCKET MAP D13
Am Festungsgraben 2 Ⓤ/Ⓢ Friedrichstr. ⓘ 030 20 221 115, Ⓦ www.gorki.de.
Named after the Russian socialist-realist author, this large theatre hosts classic dramas by him plus contemporary works by the likes of Fassbinder. All shows except premieres have English surtitles.

Staatsoper

MAP P.48, POCKET MAP D13
Unter den Linden 7 Ⓤ Unter den Linden
ⓘ 030 20 35 45 55, Ⓦ staatsoper-berlin.de.
This is one of the world's leading opera houses, its history going back to the eighteenth century and including illustrious conductors like Richard Strauss.

Tausend

MAP P.48, POCKET MAP B12
Schiffbauerdamm 11, Albrechtstr. Ⓤ/Ⓢ Friedrichstr. ⓘ 030 27 58 20 70, Ⓦ tausendberlin.com. Tues–Sat from 7pm. €10.
Decorated with an enormous eye that emits a golden glow over the tunnel-shaped space, this upmarket bar-club, quite anonymous from the outside, attracts a dapper crowd, so it's advisable to turn up looking the part. Inside you'll find a mix of upbeat disco, jazz and R&B. At the back of the club you'll find a hidden, high-end Ibero-Asian fusion restaurant, *Cantina*, by chef Octavio Osés Bravo, who creates his dishes to surprise you with a touch of the Middle or even Far East – think freekeh risotto, gazpacho verde and halawa cinnamon balls for desert. Reservations essential.

Alexanderplatz and the Nikolaiviertel

Alexanderplatz – or Alex, as it's colloquially known – is one of Berlin's ugliest, bleakest and best-known squares. Named in honour of a visit from Russian Tsar Alexander I in 1805, by the start of the twentieth century it had become a commercial centre busy enough to rival Potsdamer Platz. Under the GDR it was a nondescript pedestrianized area and in 1989 was the site of the Peaceful Revolution, the largest demonstration in the history of East Germany. Today its grey, concrete GDR tower blocks, themselves towered over by the needle-like spire of the Fernsehturm (TV Tower), join more recent buildings like the Alexa shopping mall and the Saturn electronics store to create a thoroughly charmless transport hub. More scenic, though touristy, is the adjacent Nikolaiviertel, with its pretty old-town feel and various museums, a reconstruction of the historical heart of the city that dates back to the thirteenth century.

Berliner Fernsehturm

MAP P.58, POCKET MAP F12
Panoramastr. 1a Ⓤ/Ⓢ Alexanderplatz
☎ 030 24 75 75 875, Ⓦ www.tv-turm.de.

Daily: March–Oct 9am–midnight; Nov–Feb 10am–midnight. €16.50.
The city's most visible structure, the 368m concrete spike known

Berliner Fernsehturm

as the Fernsehturm (television tower), is the building most likely to crop up in all your photographs when you get home – whether you realized you'd been photographing it or not. Built in 1969 as a broadcasting system for East Berlin, and intended as a showpiece structure for the GDR, visible in West Berlin, it has a visitor platform at 203m – a lift zooms you up in forty seconds – and a small photographic exhibition in the lobby where you can see how the tower was built (it took four years). Above the visitor platform, there's also a rotating restaurant, *Sphere*, that serves coffee, snacks and meals while revolving once around the tower's axis every sixty minutes. The tower receives around a million visitors a year and the queues can be long whatever the weather. You don't need a reservation for the tower, but it can be handy for the restaurant (in high season). Another option is to get a Fast Track Ticket (from €21.50 for adults, children aged 4–14 from €12), available on the website in advance, which enables you to dodge the queues and has an option for a table reservation.

If the sun's out when you're out and about, take a look up at the Fernsehturm and see if you can spot the cross that's reflected across the main steel sphere: the religious symbolism caused a great deal of embarrassment for the atheist GDR government.

DDR Museum

DDR Museum

MAP P.58, POCKET MAP E13
Karl-Liebknecht-Str. 1 ⓤ /
Ⓢ Alexanderplatz ⓣ 030 84 71 23 732
(tickets), ⓦ www.ddr-museum.de. Mon-Fri
& Sun 10am–8pm, Sat 10am–10pm. From
€8.50 (discounts sometimes offered via
website).

Located opposite the Berliner Dom (see page 40), this collection of memorabilia from the Deutsche Demokratische Republik (DDR/ GDR) makes for a fun, interactive and informative visit. There are screens to touch, buttons to press, drawers to open – even a Trabant to sit in and a bugged apartment to listen in on.

Divided into three differently themed areas ("Public Life", "State and Ideology", "Life in a Tower Block"), visitors get to inspect a reconstruction of a GDR living room, experience what it's like to have your phone bugged, and ponder the East German penchant for public nudity – little wonder it's one of the most visited museums in Berlin.

Though many of the displays feed on the current penchant for *Ostalgie*, there is also an emphasis on the darker side of GDR life – Party, State, prison – making this a much more rounded experience than it used to be.

Rotes Rathaus

MAP P.58, POCKET MAP E13
Rathausstr. 15 ⓤ Klosterstr. ⓤ /
Ⓢ Alexanderplatz ⓣ 030 90 260. Mon-Fri
9am–6pm. Free (ID required).

This distinctive building gets its name (which means "red town hall") from the red clinker brick of its facade. The building, inspired by Italian High Renaissance architecture, was erected in the 1860s. During communist times, it was East Berlin's town hall, when the red in the name really came into its own; today it's the office of the city mayor, and is the political centre of power in Greater Berlin. Its neo-Renaissance clock tower and frieze depicting Berlin's history until 1879 in 36 terracotta plaques, each 6m long, are its most impressive architectural features. At the top of the grand stairwell is a coat-of-arms hall and some exhibits. The building also has a cafeteria with low-price lunches.

Marienkirche

MAP P.58, POCKET MAP E12
Karl-Liebknecht-Str. 8 ⓤ /
Ⓢ **Alexanderplatz** Ⓦ **marienkirche-berlin. de. Daily: April–Dec 10am–6pm; Jan–Mar 10am–4pm (no visits during services and concerts). Free.**

Standing somewhat incongruously at the edge of Alexanderplatz and the Marx-Engels-Forum, the Marienkirche (church of St Mary) – one of Berlin's oldest churches – is the last remnant of its time in the area. Built some time in the thirteenth century, its oldest part is the granite base, upon which a hall church (Hallenkirche) stands. The tower was added during the fifteenth century, and the steeple in 1790 by Carl Gotthard Langhan, architect of the Brandenburg Gate. The church escaped heavy damage during World War II and was later fully restored. Visitors today can see *The Dance of Death* (*Totentanz*), a large fresco (2m high, 22m long), dating from about 1485, that was discovered in 1860 under layers of paint and depicts various classes of society dancing with Death. Other notable artworks include a bronze baptismal font from 1437, *The Crucifixion* painted by

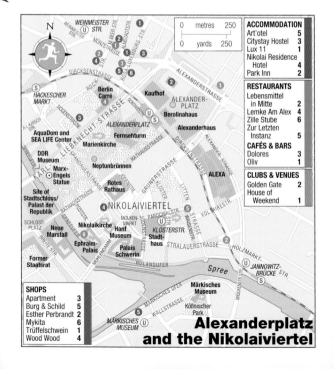

ACCOMMODATION
Art'otel — 5
Citystay Hostel — 3
Lux 11 — 4
Nikolai Residence Hotel — 2
Park Inn — 1

RESTAURANTS
Lebensmittel in Mitte — 2
Lemke Am Alex — 4
Zille Stube — 6
Zur Letzten Instanz — 5

CAFÉS & BARS
Dolores — 3
Oliv — 1

CLUBS & VENUES
Golden Gate — 2
House of Weekend — 1

SHOPS
Apartment — 3
Burg & Schild — 5
Esther Perbrandt — 2
Mykita — 6
Trüffelschwein — 1
Wood Wood — 4

Alexanderplatz and the Nikolaiviertel

Ephraim-Palais

Michael Ribestein in 1562 and an alabaster pulpit created by Andreas Schlüter in 1703, decorated with reliefs of John the Baptist and personifications of Faith, Hope and Love.

AquaDom and SEA LIFE Center

MAP P.58, POCKET MAP E13
Spandauer Str. 3 ⓢ Hackescher Markt
ⓣ 0180 666 690 101, ⓦ visitsealife.com.
Daily 10am–7pm. From €19 (discounted tickets if you book online).

The Sea Life Center's chief claim to fame is the AquaDom – the world's largest cylindrical fish aquarium, a 25m-tall acrylic glass aquarium, with built-in transparent elevator, located right in the lobby of the adjacent *Radisson SAS* hotel. Filled with around 900,000 litres of seawater, the aquarium contains around 1500 fish, covering 56 species. The AquaDom can be visited separately, but visitors who want a broader overview of the underwater world can visit the Sea Life Center first, a succession of themed tunnels that illustrate marine life from various habitats including the Spree and the Pacific Ocean. It's insightful enough and a well-laid-out exhibition, though it lacks the comprehensive scope and diversity – not to mention the manatees and sharks – of the Zoo Aquarium.

Ephraim-Palais

MAP P.58, POCKET MAP E13
Poststr. 16, corner Mühlendamm
ⓤ Klosterstr. or ⓤ/ⓢ Alexanderplatz
ⓣ 030 24 00 21 62, ⓦ stadtmuseum.
de. Tues & Thurs–Sun 10am–6pm, Wed noon–8pm. €7.

This attractive Rococo-style residential palace, located in the southern corner of Berlin's Nikolaiviertel, is a replica of a 1762 original built by Veitel Heine Ephraim, a court jeweller. His original building was torn down in 1935–36 when the Mühlendamm was widened, but a painstaking reconstruction has produced an exquisite place, with its elegantly curving, decorated facade (complete with cherubs), Tuscan columns, wrought-iron balconies and an oval staircase and ornate ceiling crafted by Schlüter. As well as special exhibitions on themes relating to the history and culture

Hanf Museum

of Berlin, the "Salon Ephraim" and the Museum Laboratory offer family-friendly events and workshops.

Märkisches Museum

MAP P.58, POCKET MAP F14
Am Köllnischen Park 5 ⓤ /
ⓢ Jannowitzbrücke ☏ 030 24 00 21 62, ⓦ www.stadtmuseum.de. Tues–Sun 10am–6pm. €7 (free admission every first Wed of the month).

The red-brick Märkisches Museum, built at the turn of the twentieth century, is the headquarters of Berlin's City Museum Foundation. The permanent exhibition "Here is Berlin" invites you to stroll through the city's streets and discover how Berlin has changed over the centuries. The museum also hosts a wide array of art-historic collections in its atmospheric rooms, with medieval sculptures, artefacts and paintings telling the story of Berlin from the first settlers until now (German text only). Thoughtfully divided into sections of the city – Unter den Linden, Friedrichstrasse and so on – favourites include a working mechanical musical instrument that's shown off every Sunday (3pm), seven original graffitied segments of the Berlin Wall and a Kaiserpanorama: a stereoscope dating from around 1900 that produces a fascinating 3D show of images from nineteenth-century Berlin..

Hanf Museum

MAP P.58, POCKET MAP E13
Mühlendamm 5 ⓤ / ⓢ Alexanderplatz or ⓤ Klosterstr. ☏ 030 24 24 827, ⓦ hanfmuseum.de. Tues–Fri 10am–8pm, Sat & Sun noon–8pm. €4.50.

The Hanf Museum is 300 square metres of space devoted exclusively to the agricultural, manufacturing, industrial and legal aspects of hemp – a plant most commonly associated with marijuana. This museum, while slightly dingy, isn't just for the stoners: the aim is to give a broader overview of this fascinating botanical treasure and its myriad applications, from textile and paper to medicine and cosmetics. Texts are in German only.

Shops

Apartment

MAP P.58, POCKET MAP F12

Memhardstr. 8 ⓤ/Ⓢ Alexanderplatz ☎ 030 28 04 22 51, Ⓦ www.apartmentberlin.de. Mon–Sat 2–7pm.

You'll have to be careful not to walk right past what looks like an all-white art space: the goods lie downstairs (follow the spiral staircase), where you'll find jeans, jackets, shoes and accessories with a distinctly Berlin twist.

Burg & Schild

MAP P.58, POCKET MAP E12

Rosa-Luxemburg-Str. 3 ⓤ Rosa-Luxemburg-Platz ☎ 030 24 63 05 01, Ⓦ www.burgundschild.com. Mon–Sat 11am–7pm.

Visit a long-vanished America by way of brands like Iron Heart, Indigofera, Filson and Buzz Rickson's, all on display alongside vintage motorbikes that generate an authentic odour of oil and tar.

Esther Perbandt

MAP P.58, POCKET MAP E12

Almstadtstr. 3 ⓤ Weinmeisterstr. ☎ 030 88 53 67 91, Ⓦ www.estherperbandt.com. Tues–Fri 10am–7pm, Sat noon–6pm.

A relative veteran of the Berlin fashion scene, Esther Perbandt sells (pricey) rock and avant-garde styles with an audaciously gender-bending slant. As well as clothing, expect bags, belts and jewellery.

Mykita

MAP P.58, POCKET MAP F12

Rosa-Luxemburg-Str. 6 ⓤ/Ⓢ Alexanderplatz ☎ 030 67 30 87 15, Ⓦ www.mykita.com. Mon–Fri 11am–8pm, Sat noon–6pm.

Sunglasses and spectacles with a stylish twist, sold in a hip, minimal space with large street-facing windows. Berlin-based Mykita opened in 2003, and has since achieved international prominence.

Trüffelschwein

MAP P.58, POCKET MAP F11

Rosa-Luxemburg-Str. 21 ⓤ Rosa-Luxemburg-Platz ☎ 030 70 22 12 25, Ⓦ www.trueffelschweinberlin.com. Mon–Fri noon–8pm, Sat noon–7pm.

This pleasant, airy store sells everything menswear from sexy shoes and trendy jumpers to belts and dapper swimwear. Labels include Hannes Roether, La Panoplie, Howlin', Superga and La Paz.

Wood Wood

MAP P.58, POCKET MAP E12

Rochstr. 3–4 ⓤ/Ⓢ Alexanderplatz ☎ 030 28 04 78 77, Ⓦ www.woodwood.com. Mon–Fri noon–8pm, Sat noon–7pm.

One of the best stops in the area for all things streetwear, this long-serving Berlin branch of Copenhagen-based Wood Wood stocks an incredible sneaker collection plus contemporary fashion items.

Restaurants

Lebensmittel in Mitte

MAP P.58, POCKET MAP E12

Rochstr. 2 ⓤ Weinmeisterstr. ☎ 030 27 59 61 30. Mon–Fri noon–midnight, Sat 11am–midnight.

Burg & Schild

If you're a fan of "slow" home cooking this unassuming spot on Rochstrasse is a good choice. Specializing in German cuisine (mainly from the south), the menu features hearty soups, sausages, sauerkraut and *Spätzle* (a type of soft egg noodle), as well as a decent selection of German/Austrian wines and Bavarian beer, all served against a homely, elegant backdrop.

Lemke Am Alex

MAP P.58, POCKET MAP F12
Karl-Liebknechtstr 13 /Ⓢ Alexanderplatz.
Ⓣ 030 30 87 89 89, Ⓦ en.lemke.berlin.
Daily noon–midnight.
Always wanted to dine in the middle of a modern Brauhaus (brewery)? Then this is the place to go. This craft beer-meets-German regional food bistro serves dishes like Eisbein (knuckle of pork), bratwurst or Berlin style meatballs – pretty much anything that goes well with craft beer. They also offer guided tours and beer tastings.

Dolores

Zille Stube

MAP P.58, POCKET MAP E13
Spreeufer 3 Ⓤ Klosterstr. Ⓣ 030 24 25 247, Ⓦ zillestube-nikolaiviertel.de. Daily 11am–10pm; Heinrich Zille show every 1st and 3rd Tues 3–5pm.
A great place to break up a stroll around the Nikolaiviertel, the menu here features Berlin specialities like *Currywurst* and *Eisbein* (knuckle of pork), all served in cosy, time-warp surroundings. Named after the area's most famous caricaturist, Heinrich Zille, there's a two-hour show every 1st and 3rd Tuesday at 3pm that transports guests back to the artist's turn-of-the-century Berlin.

Zur Letzten Instanz

MAP P.58, POCKET MAP F13
Waisenstr. 14–16 Ⓤ Klosterstr. Ⓣ 030 24 25 528, Ⓦ www.zurletzteninstanz.de. Mon 6pm–1am, Tues–Sat noon–1am.
Yes it's the oldest restaurant in Berlin (the building goes right back to 1561), yes the interior is textbook Alt Berlin, and yes it's a tourist haunt, but the food here – traditional dishes like pork knuckle, dumplings and Berlin meatballs – is delicious and care is taken to source ingredients from local producers. Portions are hearty and there's Pilsner on draught to wash it all down.

Cafés and bars

Dolores

MAP P.58, POCKET MAP E12
Rosa-Luxemburg-Str. 7 Ⓤ /
Ⓢ Alexanderplatz Ⓣ 030 28 09 95 97,
Ⓦ www.dolores-online.de. Mon–Sat 11.30am–10pm, Sun 1–10pm.
Run by Germans who spent a considerable time in California, Berlin's first burrito shop is a basic but colourful spot that offers pre-prepared "classics", "make-your-own", customizable burritos and also quesadillas, salads and soups. A good spot for a cheap, filling bite (burritos from €5) or

Oliv

takeaway. There is a second branch in Schöneberg (Bayreuther Str. 36 Ⓤ Wittenbergplatz).

Oliv

MAP P.58, POCKET MAP E12
Münzstr. 8 Ⓤ Weinmeisterstr./Rosa-
Luxemburg-Platz Ⓣ 030 89 20 65 40,
Ⓦ www.oliv-cafe.de. Mon–Fri 8.30am–
7pm, Sat 9.30am–7pm, Sun 10am–6pm.
With a modern interior, great coffee and decent, unpreten-tious food (sandwiches, quiches, soups, cakes), *Oliv* is a pleasant spot for breakfast or lunch, and very conveniently located if you're seeking respite from boutique bashing. Cash only.

Clubs and venues

Golden Gate

MAP P.58, POCKET MAP J5
Dircksenstr. 77–78 Ⓤ/Ⓢ Jannowitzbrücke
Ⓣ 030 57 70 42 78, Ⓦ goldengate-berlin.
de. Wed from 10pm, Thurs–Sat from 11pm.
Lurking beneath the tracks near Jannowitzbrücke train station (close to the river Spree), this club consists of two wilfully shabby rooms kitted out in secondhand furniture and is dedicated to two- or three-day-long free-for-alls. The crowds here tend to be a dressed-down, unpretentious lot who arrive well after midnight to try their luck with the difficult bouncers. Music policy is mostly house and techno but there are sometimes surprises.

House of Weekend

MAP P.58, POCKET MAP F12
Alexanderstr. 7 (15th floor and open
rooftop) Ⓤ/Ⓢ Alexanderplatz Ⓣ 0152 24
29 31 40, Ⓦ www.weekendclub.berlin.
Summer daily from 7pm; winter Fri–Sun
from 11pm. €10–12.
Accessed via a lift that shoots punters up to the top of a Communist-era tower block, this chic, spacious club has attained veteran status in the city thanks to its consistently good house and techno parties. International guests and high-profile residents play most weekends. The wonderful roof terrace – open from 7pm daily in summer – is a must.

Potsdamer Platz and Tiergarten

A major public transport hub and popular entertainment district, Potsdamer Platz was one of the liveliest squares in Europe during the 1920s. Reduced to rubble during the War, afterwards it became – literally – a no-man's land, sandwiched between the different sectors. What little remained was levelled when the Berlin Wall went up in 1961. After the Wall fell, it became the largest construction site in Europe as an ambitious rebuilding programme started. Commercial, even futuristic in tone, the centrepiece today is the Sony Center, surrounded by a new U-Bahn station and a few slabs from the old Berlin Wall. Just to the west is the Kulturforum, a fine collection of cultural institutions, built in the 1960s as West Berlin's response to East Berlin's Museumsinsel, including the Gemäldegalerie, and its important collections of Old Masters. Adjacent to the Platz is the Tiergarten, Berlin's oldest and most beautiful park.

Sony Center

MAP P.66, POCKET MAP A15
Potsdamer Str. 4 Ⓤ/Ⓢ Potsdamer Platz
Ⓦ www.sonycenter.de. Free.

The striking, eco-friendly, glass-and-steel Sony Center, by Helmut Jahn, opened in 2000 and cost a cool €750 million to build. The centre houses shops for everything from cosmetics and jewellery to, of course, Sony electronics, plus restaurants, a conference centre, art and film museums, cinemas, including an **IMAX**, and a **Legoland** (daily 10am–7pm; Ⓦlegolanddiscoverycentre.de; €14–25). The "Forum", the semi-enclosed roofed space, is used for occasional cultural and entertainment events. There's plenty to do, although the experience is generally soulless and the shopping expensive (though there is free wi-fi).

Film and Television Museum

MAP P.66, POCKET MAP A15

Potsdamer Str. 2 Ⓤ/Ⓢ Potsdamer Platz
Ⓣ 030 30 09 030, Ⓦ deutsche-kinemathek.de. Wed–Mon 10am–6pm, Thurs till 8pm. €8; free Thurs 4–8pm.

One of the must-sees in the Sony Center is the impressively slick **Deutsche Kinemathek** museum, which collects German cinema under one roof. This "journey through film history" explores the pioneering years, silent-film divas, films from the Weimar era, cinema under the Nazis and goes right up to contemporary cinema, with rooms that cover postwar German filmmakers (1946–80) and the present (from 1981). As well as a special exhibit on Germany's biggest star, Marlene Dietrich, there's memorabilia and model film sets from key directors including Fritz Lang and an exhibit that compares East and West German television broadcasts. The museum also organizes the retrospective section of the Berlinale film festival, and hosts special film series, exhibitions and events.

Kollhoff Tower

MAP P.66, POCKET MAP A15
Potsdamer Platz 1 Ⓤ/Ⓢ Potsdamer Platz
Ⓣ 030 25 93 70 80, Ⓦ panoramapunkt.
de. Platform winter: daily 10am–6pm;
summer: daily 10am–8pm; last lift 30min
before closing. €7.50.

Located on the northern edge of
Potsdamer Platz, the 25-storey
(103m), dark, peat-fired brick
Kollhoff Tower is named after
architect Hans Kollhoff, a
member of the international team
of architects (headed by Renzo
Piano) that designed many of the
buildings for the new Platz. The
ground floor houses a number of
restaurants and shops, the upper
floors are used for office space
and – the real highlight – the
Panoramapunkt on the top floors,
offers an open-air viewing platform,
reached via Europe's fastest elevator.
From the top you can see the
Reichstag, Brandenburg Gate, TV
Tower, Sony Center, Tiergarten and
Kulturforum. Admission includes
entry to the viewing platform, an
exhibition on the history of the
area and there's also a café.

Sony Center

Daimler Contemporary

MAP P.66, POCKET MAP A15
Alte Potsdamer Str. 5, in Haus Huth Ⓤ/
Ⓢ Potsdamer Platz Ⓣ 030 25 94 14 20,
Ⓦ www.collection.daimler.com. Daily
11am–6pm. Free.

The Daimler art collection was set
up in 1977 as a space for twentieth-
century art, initially mainly focused
on German artists. The museum
expanded in the 1990s with works
by other European and American
artists, including Andy Warhol and
Jeff Koons, and moved into the
elaborately renovated Haus Huth
in 1999. The collection includes
approximately 1800 works by
international artists, showcased
in rotating exhibitions across this
attractive 600-square-metre space,
which used to be a restaurant and
storage area. Much of the collection
is modernist in nature – geometric,
challenging and abstract – so not
one for traditionalists.

Gemäldegalerie

MAP P.66, POCKET MAP E6
Matthäikirchplatz 4/6 Ⓤ/Ⓢ Potsdamer
Platz Ⓣ 030 26 62 951, Ⓦ www.smb.

museum. Tues–Fri 10am–6pm (Thurs until 8pm), Sat & Sun from 11 am. €14.

With a history that goes back to 1830, the Gemäldegalerie holds one of the world's most renowned collections of classical European painting. Created from the treasures of the Prussian royalty – including that of Frederick the Great – the collection used to be part of Museum Island (see page 40). The museum – and some of the works – were damaged by Allied bombing during World War II, and the artworks were then split between East and West during the Cold War. After the Wall fell the collection came together again here. Spread across 72 rooms, divided up by country, with sections on Italian, Flemish and Dutch works, the treasures include many high points of European art by including works by Bruegel, a particularly good selection by Cranach (pictured), Dürer, Raphael, Rubens, Vermeer and many others. The Rembrandt room and Caravaggio's exquisite Cupid, *Love Conquers All*, are both well worth seeking out.

Kunstgewerbemuseum

MAP P.66, POCKET MAP E6

Matthäikirchplatz ⓤ/ⓢ Potsdamer Platz ☏ 030 26 64 24 242, ⓦ www.smb. museum. Tues–Fri 10am–6pm, Sat & Sun 11am–6pm. €8.

Following a major renovation, Berlin's Museum of Decorative Arts – one of the oldest in Germany – reopened in 2014 and provides a systematic overview of the key achievements in European design. Over 7000 square metres of white-walled space, the museum covers all major styles and periods, including jaw-dropping silks, tapestries, Renaissance bronzes, contemporary furniture, Rococo glassware, faïence work, porcelain, gold and silver. It includes a Fashion Gallery – which houses around 130 costumes and accessories

Potsdamer Platz and Tiergarten

CAFÉS & BARS	
Café am Neuen See	5
Café Buchwald	2
Kumpelnest 3000	11
Salomon Bagels	8
Schleusenkrug	4
Sushi Express	6
Victoria Bar	13
Weilands Wellfood	9

RESTAURANTS	
Angkor Wat	3
Facil	7
Hugos	10
Joseph Roth Diele	12
Paris-Moskau	1

representing 150 years of fashion history – plus the departments of Design (think Bauhaus classics mixed with contemporary designers like Philippe Starck and Konstantin Grcic), Jugendstil and Art Deco. A second collection can be found at **Schloss Köpenick** (Schlossinsel 1 Ⓢ Köpenick; April–Sept Tues–Sun 11am–6pm; Oct–March Thurs–Sun 11am–5pm; €6), a Baroque palace located in a picturesque setting on an island in the river Dahme. Exhibited here are over five hundred items from the sixteenth to eighteenth centuries, as well as Renaissance, Baroque and Rococo furniture and interior decorations.

Kupferstichkabinett

MAP P.66, POCKET MAP E6
Matthäikirchplatz Ⓤ/Ⓢ Potsdamer Platz ☎ 030 26 64 24 242, ⓦ www.smb. museum. Mon–Fri 10am–6pm, Sat & Sun 11am–6pm; study room Tues–Fri 9am–4pm. €6.

Kunstgewerbemuseum

The Kupferstichkabinett, or "print room", is the largest collection of graphic art in Germany, and one of the four most important

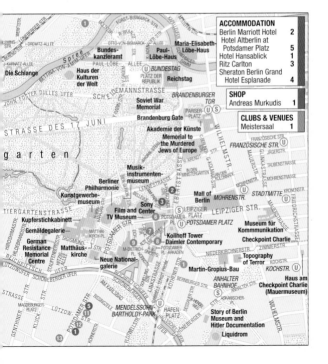

ACCOMMODATION
Berlin Marriott Hotel	2
Hotel Altberlin at Potsdamer Platz	5
Hotel Hansablick	1
Ritz Carlton	3
Sheraton Berlin Grand Hotel Esplanade	4

SHOP
Andreas Murkudis	1

CLUBS & VENUES
Meistersaal	1

Berliner Philharmonie

museums of its kind in the world. The museum houses over 500,000 prints and 110,000 drawings, watercolours, pastels and oil sketches from European artists from the Middle Ages to the present, all on paper. Major artists such as Sandro Botticelli, Albrecht Dürer, Rembrandt, Adolph von Menzel, Pablo Picasso and Andy Warhol are represented. Due to the size and sensitivity of the collection (being largely on paper), there's no permanent display – visitors must check for special exhibitions, or request to see specific artworks via the study room.

Berliner Philharmonie

MAP P.66, POCKET MAP E6
Herbert-von-Karajan-Str. 1 Ⓤ/Ⓢ Potsdamer Platz Ⓣ 030 25 48 80 999 (tickets), Ⓦ www.berliner-philharmoniker.de.
Built by architect Hans Scharoun between 1960 and 1963, the Berliner Philharmonie is one of the most important concert halls in Berlin and home to the world-renowned Berlin Philharmonic. The asymmetrical, tent-like building has an equally distinctive pentagon-shaped concert hall (plus a smaller hall, Kammermusiksaal, which seats 1180) that enables great views from all sides. Guided tours of both the Philharmonic Hall and the Chamber Music Hall are offered daily from 1.30pm (Ⓣ 030 25 48 81 34; €5/€3).

Musikinstrumenten-Museum

MAP P.66, POCKET MAP E6
Tiergartenstr. 1 (visitors' entrance Ben-Gurion-Str.) Ⓤ/Ⓢ Potsdamer Platz Ⓣ 030 25 48 11 78, Ⓦ simpk.de. Tues, Wed & Fri 9am–5pm, Thurs 9am–8pm, Sat & Sun 10am–5pm. €6 including audioguide; guided tours Sat (11am) & Thurs (6pm) €3 extra.
The Musikinstrumenten-Museum embraces Germany's glorious musical history, with over three thousand instruments from the sixteenth to the twenty-first centuries, making it one of the country's largest collections. Many are on permanent display here, including a rare Stradivarius violin, Frederick the Great's flutes, a glass harmonica invented by Benjamin Franklin and – the flamboyant centrepiece – a massive Mighty Wurlitzer theatre organ once

owned by the Siemens family, which is demonstrated every Saturday at noon. The museum also veers into electronic music with electric guitars, mixing stations and other experimental instruments, including the Mixtur-Trautonium on which composer Oskar Sala created sound effects for Hitchcock's film *The Birds*.

Neue Nationalgalerie

MAP P.66, POCKET MAP E6
Potsdamer Str. 50 Ⓤ/Ⓢ Potsdamer Platz
Ⓣ 030 26 64 23 040, Ⓦ smb.museum/nng. Tues, Wed, & Fri 10am–6pm, Thurs 10am–8pm, Sat & Sun 11am–6pm. €10.
The "temple of light and glass" (as it's modestly known) and its sculpture gardens were famously designed by Bauhaus affiliate Ludwig Mies van der Rohe. Opened in 1968, the museum houses an extensive collection of twentieth-century European paintings, and sculptures from the nineteenth century to the 1960s, including household names like Bacon, Picasso, Klee, Dix and plenty of German art (E.L. Kirchner, Beckmann). The museum displays portions of its permanent

collection on a rotating basis, so each visit is different, and a number of special exhibitions also occur throughout the year, during which the permanent collection may not be on view. There's also a café on the ground floor (10.30am–5.45pm). Note, however, that the museum closed at the end of 2015 for refurbishments, with no reopening date specified; see the website for updates.

Museum für Kommunikation

MAP P.66, POCKET MAP C15
Leipziger Str. 16 Ⓤ Stadtmitte Ⓣ 030 20 29 40, Ⓦ www.mfk-berlin.de. Tues 9am–8pm, Wed–Fri 9am–5pm, Sat & Sun 10am–6pm. €6.
Founded in 1872 as the first postal museum of the world, the Museum for Communication experienced a rebirth in 2000, as evidenced by the blue neon writing on the neo-Baroque facade and robots in the lobby. A permanent exhibition showcases the origins, development and future perspectives of the "information society", while highlights of the permanent exhibition are wax seals, postcards and stamps (such

Museum für Kommunikation

POTSDAMER PLATZ AND TIERGARTEN

The German Resistance Memorial Center

as the famous Blue Mauritius), telephones (including some of the first), radios, film, telegraphs and computers. The museum's interactive and lively approach makes it an ideal destination for kids, but adults will appreciate the temporary exhibitions featuring cutting-edge artists.

The German Resistance Memorial Center

MAP P.66, POCKET MAP D6
Stauffenbergstr. 13–14 (entrance through the commemorative courtyard); tram M29 to "Gedenkstätte Deutscher Widerstand"
📞 030 26 99 50 00, 🌐 www.gdw-berlin.de.
Mon–Wed & Fri 9am–6pm, Thurs 9am–8pm, Sat & Sun 10am–6pm. Free.

Located in a historic section of the former headquarters of the Nazi army high command, the site of the assassination attempt on Adolf Hitler on July 20, 1944, the **Gedenkstätte Deutscher Widerstand** (German Resistance Memorial Center) documents the action taken against the Nazis between 1933 and 1945. The permanent exhibition has over five thousand photographs and documents spread across eighteen topics that go beyond Nazi dissent to address the wider context of resistance, including the role of Christian beliefs in protest, opposition by young people specifically and general defiance of wartime environments in daily life. The memorial courtyard, meanwhile, is dedicated to the conspiring German army officers who were killed after the assassination attempt. The exhibition is in German and English.

Bauhaus Museum

MAP P.66, POCKET MAP D6
Klingelhöferstr. 14 Ⓤ Nollendorfplatz
📞 030 25 40 020, 🌐 www.bauhaus. de. Daily except Tues 10am–5pm. €8, concessions €5 (includes audio tour). The museum is closed for renovation; until it's reopening, the Bauhaus Archive will be housed in the Museum für Gestaltung (Knesebeckstr 1–2, Tue–Sun 10am–5pm, Wed till 8pm, €8).

Germany's Bauhaus ("building house") design school may have only lasted from 1919 to 1933 but it went on to became one of the twentieth century's most influential movements – more famous outside the country than Goethe or Schiller. Founded by Walter Gropius, the movement explored the links between fine art and craftsmanship and – a bit later – art and mass production. The Bauhaus Archive and Museum, housed in a distinctive building designed by Gropius himself, is the best place to explore the breadth and depth of Bauhaus's expansive activities. Here are tubular steel furniture from Marcel Breuer, armchairs and desks from Mies van der Rohe, paintings from Itten, Schlemmer, Feininger, Albers and Klee… even dapper wallpaper and beautiful chess sets. The museum shop stocks an impressive range of high-quality reproductions, and there's an adjoining café.

Haus der Kulturen der Welt

MAP P.66, POCKET MAP E5
John-Foster-Dulles-Allee 10 Ⓤ /
Ⓢ Bundestag Ⓣ 030 39 78 71 75, Ⓦ hkw.
de. Daily 10am–7pm. Exhibitions: daily
except Tues 11am–7pm; free entry Mon,
varies at other times.

Known as the "pregnant oyster"
because of its distinctively
curvaceous facade, the House of
World Cultures hosts exhibitions
with a focus on artistic and cultural
movements in contemporary global
societies. Formerly known as the
Kongresshalle conference hall, the
building, designed in 1957 by US
architect Hugh Stubbins Jr, was a
gift from the United States (John
F. Kennedy spoke here during
his 1963 visit to West Berlin). In
1980 the roof collapsed, injuring
many people (and killing one)
and was rebuilt in its original style
in 1987. The building's maze of
rooms include two exhibition
halls, auditorium for concerts
and theatre and a congress hall,
and it is an ideal location for the
colourful variety of events held
here throughout the year. The
eclectic and globally minded spread
of events range from educational
programmes to exhibitions, music,
performing arts, literature festivals
and more.

The Tiergarten

MAP P.66, POCKET MAP D5
Full of paths, forested areas, lakes
and meadows, the luscious and
vast Tiergarten park – bisected by
Strasse des 17. Juni – began its life
as the preferred hunting ground
for the electors of Brandenburg.
Designed in its current form in
1830 by landscape architect Peter
Joseph Lenne, it is now one of the
most relaxing spots in Berlin, and is
dotted with a couple of interesting
attractions, with the Siegessäule its
focal point.

Siegessäule

MAP P.66, POCKET MAP D5
Grosser Stern 1 Ⓤ Hansaplatz. April–Oct
Mon–Fri 9.30am–6.30pm, Sat & Sun
9.30am–7pm; Nov–March Mon–Fri
10am–5pm, Sat & Sun 10am–5.30pm. €3.
You can't miss the huge victory
column at the centre of the
"Grosser Stern" (great star)
roundabout in the Tiergarten. The
cocksure monument is otherwise

Haus der Kulturen der Welt

Siegessäule

known as the-tricky-to-pronounce Siegessäule, built from 1864 to 1873 after a design by Johann Heinrich Stack to commemorate the Prussian victory in the Prusso-Danish war of 1864. It's 69m (25ft) tall, weighs 35 tonnes and features a Goddess of Victory on top, added later after further Prussian victories in wars against Austria and France. At the base you can see bas-reliefs of battles and at the top there's an observatory, which gives great views of the Reichstag, the Brandenburg Gate and the Fernsehturm, but you have to climb the 285 steps to access it. There's also a small café, souvenir shop and small exhibition connecting the column with the events in German history that it represents.

Schloss Bellevue

MAP P.66, POCKET MAP D5
Spreeweg 1 Ⓤ **Hansaplatz. Closed to the public.**
Situated on an area of 20 hectares (about 50 acres) beside the river Spree, Schloss Bellevue was built for Prince August Ferdinand

of Prussia, the younger brother of Frederick II of Prussia. The sparkling white home was designed by architect Philipp Daniel Boumann and has the distinction of being the first Neoclassical building constructed in Germany. It was uninhabited in the nineteenth century and used by various institutions such as a museum of ethnography in the 1930s. In 1938, the building was converted into a guesthouse of the government and the entrance to the palace was redesigned. Severely damaged in World War II, it was renovated during 1954–59 and set up as the official residence of the federal president in Berlin. The main sights include a ballroom designed by Carl Gotthard Langhans, the huge lawn behind the palace and the modern building to the south – known as the "presidential egg" due to its oval shape. The palace is currently closed to visitors.

Buchstabenmuseum

MAP P.66, POCKET MAP C4
Stadtbahnbogen 424 Ⓢ **Bellevue/**
Ⓤ **Hansaplatz** Ⓣ **0177 42 01 587,** Ⓦ **www.buchstabenmuseum.de. Thur–Sun 1–5pm. €12.**
Buchstaben means "letter" (as in "alphabetic character"), and this unique museum – formerly located near Alexanderplatz before moving to this larger space near the Hansaviertel in 2016 – is dedicated solely to the preservation and protection of artisan-esque examples of lettering in the age of digitalization. Though the museum is still building its permanent collection, the assortment of old and new industrial signs is well worth navigating the slightly eccentric opening hours for. Though the museum collects lettering of any language, the ultimate goal is to honour "local colour", which museum founder Barbara Dechant feels is waning.

Shop

Andreas Murkudis

MAP P.66, POCKET MAP E7
Potsdamer Str. 81 Ⓤ Kurfürstenstr. ☏ 030
68 07 98 306, Ⓦ andreasmurkudis.com.
Mon–Sat 10am–7pm.

Set in the former *Tagesspiegel*
newspaper building, this vast,
white, bright space designed by
lead architects Gonzales Haase is
almost all used to highlight the
high end (and sometimes pointedly
eccentric) products selected by
Andreas Murkudis, the brother of
fashion designer Kostas Murkudis.
The latter's designs are here, as
are Valextra briefcases and quality
brands like Pringle and Céline.

Restaurants

Angkor Wat

MAP P.66, POCKET MAP D4
Paulstr. 22 Ⓤ/Ⓢ Hauptbahnhof ☏ 030 39
33 922, Ⓦ www.angkorwatrestaurant.de.
Tues–Fri 6–11pm, Sat & Sun noon–11pm.

This cavernous restaurant serves
a mean Cambodian fondue. The
friendly service makes up for the
exotic decor, and if you don't like
frying your own meat, the menu
extends to other Cambodian
classics with plenty of spices and
creamy coconut.

Facil

MAP P.66, POCKET MAP A15
The Mandala Hotel, Potsdamer Str. 3 Ⓤ/
Ⓢ Potsdamer Platz ☏ 030 59 005 ext 1234,
Ⓦ www.facil.de. Mon–Fri noon–2pm &
7–10pm, closed Sat & Sun.

Michael Kempf's restaurant in
The Mandala Hotel not only offers
amazing food but also splendid
views from its fifth-floor dining
room, surrounded by a lush
bamboo garden. Popular with
business types, politicos and serious
foodies, Kempf's Michelin-starred,
fish-heavy menu has become justly
famous. Evening mains range
from €29 to €64; try a lunch for

something slightly cheaper (€23
for one course, €57 for three;
reservations required).

Hugos

MAP P.66, POCKET MAP C6
Hotel InterContinental, Budapester Str. 2
Ⓤ Zoologischer Garten ☏ 030 26 02 12 63,
Ⓦ www.hugos-restaurant.de. Tues–Sat
6.30–10.30pm, closed first two weeks of Jan,
last weeks of April and mid-July to mid-Aug.

In a gorgeously appointed
room at the top of the *Hotel
InterContinental*, master
chef Eberhard Lange creates
Michelin-starred "New German–
Mediterranean" food that you
can sample – for a price – while
enjoying the restaurant's panoramic
views (menus €98–150).

Joseph Roth Diele

MAP P.66, POCKET MAP E7
Potsdamer Str. 75 Ⓤ Kurfürstenstr. ☏ 030
26 36 98 84, Ⓦ www.joseph-roth-diele.de.
Mon–Thurs 10am–11pm, Fri till midnight.

A splash of charm and colour on
nondescript Potsdamer Strasse,
this quirky restaurant pays homage
to interwar Jewish writer Joseph
Roth. The daily specials are very
reasonable (€4.95–9.95), though

Joseph Roth Diele

the food is far from high end. Popular with a wide range of people at lunchtimes.

Paris-Moskau

MAP P.66, POCKET MAP E4
Alt-Moabit 141 ⓤ/Ⓢ Hauptbahnhof ☏ 030 39 42 081, ⓦ paris-moskau.de. Mon–Fri noon–3pm & from 6pm, Sat from 6pm.
This curious mix of old Berlin and contemporary elegance is set in a nineteenth-century rail signalman's house (it's named after the Paris–Moscow line) and serves hearty meats like ox, fish and dishes like risotto with Alba truffles (€39–89). It's all backed up by a fine wine list and a great summer garden with views of the government quarter.

Cafés and bars

Café am Neuen See

MAP P.66, POCKET MAP C6
Lichtensteinallee 2 ⓤ Zoologischer Garten ☏ 30 25 44 930, ⓦ cafeamneuensee.de. Daily 9am–midnight.
A fine stop-off on any tour of the Tiergarten, this old-school beer garden with modern restaurant (reservations required for larger groups) offers great coffee and draught beers, and a menu including pizza and pasta dishes (€10). It's beautifully set on the Neuen See lake, and there are even rowing boats for rent.

Café Buchwald

MAP P.66, POCKET MAP C4
Bartningallee 29 ⓤ Hansaplatz ☏ 030 39 15 931, ⓦ konditorei-buchwald.de. Daily 9am–7pm.
A short stroll down a pleasant path from Schloss Bellevue, *Café Buchwald* has been standing here for over 160 years. Not just standing but selling some of the best cakes in town – former suppliers to the court, they still make such delicious confections as home-made *Baumkuchen*. There are a few seats in the charming little front garden.

Kumpelnest 3000

MAP P.66, POCKET MAP E7
Lützowstr. 23 ⓤ Kurfürstenstr. ☏ 030 26 16 918, ⓦ www.kumpelnest3000.com. Daily from 7pm.
Hard to believe that this charming den of iniquity is only a few minutes' stroll from Potsdamer Platz. With its deliberately tacky decor, loyal mixed/gay crowd and anything-goes atmosphere, especially at weekends, it's a good place if you're in the area and looking for the lure of the mirrored discoball rather than the commercial glare of the Platz.

Salomon Bagels

MAP P.66, POCKET MAP A15
Alte Potsdamer Str. 7, inside Potsdamer Platz Arkaden ⓤ/Ⓢ Potsdamer Platz ☏ 030 25 29 76 26, ⓦ www.salomon-bagels.de. Mon–Sat 10am–9pm, Sun noon–9pm.
Bagels, bagels, bagels. And sandwiches. And excellent cakes, like their New York-style cheesecake. Located in a mall, this shop does takeaways, but there are sofas too – a good spot for a cheap snack (€6–13).

Schleusenkrug

MAP P.66, POCKET MAP B6
Müller-Breslau-Str. corner Unterschleuse ⓤ/Ⓢ Zoologischer Garten ☏ 030 31 39 909, ⓦ www.schleusenkrug.de. Daily: summer 11am–midnight; winter 11am–7pm.
A classic Berlin beer garden, *Schleusenkrug* is a fine place to tuck into a glass of beer and an organic *Wurst*, enjoy a coffee while watching the boats cruise down the canal, or lap up the live music they sometimes have in the summer.

Sushi Express

MAP P.66, POCKET MAP A15
Potsdamer Platz 2 ⓤ/Ⓢ Potsdamer Platz ☏ 030 26 55 80 55, ⓦ sushi-expressberlin.de. Mon–Fri 11.30am–10pm, Sat noon–10pm, Sun 2–8pm.
It's a bit of a hassle to find, but *Sushi Express* – located in the

Sony Center courtyard in a passage to the S-Bahn – offers a decent range of conveyor-belt sushi, especially when half-price offers are on (daily 11.30am–9pm). Hot dishes and lunchboxes also available, though it's usually packed at lunchtimes. Main courses €5.

Victoria Bar

MAP P.66, POCKET MAP E7
Potsdamer Str. 102 ⓤ Kurfürstenstr. ⓣ 030 25 75 99 77, ⓦ victoriabar.de. Thurs & Sun 6.30pm–3am, Fri & Sat 6.30pm–4am.
This much-loved cocktail bar is great for a low-key and decently mixed drink in the week or a livelier atmosphere at weekends. The long bar, subdued lighting and discreet but upbeat music create a decent buzz.

Weilands Wellfood

MAP P.66, POCKET MAP A15
Marlene-Dietrich-Platz 1 ⓤ/ⓢ Potsdamer Platz ⓣ 030 25 89 97 17, ⓦ weilands-wellfood.de. Mon–Fri 8am–8pm.

Right by a pond near bustling Potsdamer Platz, this health-conscious, fast-food-style store sells food low in calories and high in vitamins: couscous, salads, curries and sandwiches stacked with fresh ingredients. Popular with local workers at lunchtimes.

Clubs and venues

Meistersaal

MAP P.66, POCKET MAP F6
Köthener Str. 38 ⓤ/ⓢ Potsdamer Platz ⓣ 030 32 59 99 710, ⓦ meistersaal-berlin.de.
This hundred-year-old music venue and recording studio has drawn major artists from Kurt Tucholsky and David Bowie to U2 and Herbert Grönemeyer. Built in 1913 in what was once Berlin's music quarter, the building fell into disrepair after World War II. Since then, though, the Meistersaal has become Berlin's version of London's Abbey Road, world-renowned for its excellent acoustics.

POTSDAMER PLATZ AND TIERGARTEN

Schleusenkrug

Prenzlauer Berg and Wedding

Built in the nineteenth century as a working-class district, Prenzlauer Berg was neglected by the GDR after World War II, becoming a crumbling ghetto for intellectuals, punks and bohemians. Following merciless post-Wall gentrification, wealthy creative types and middle-class families have gravitated here, drawn by the area's handsome, cobbled streets, leafy squares like Helmholtzplatz and Kollwitzplatz, and its distinctive Alt Berlin atmosphere, with lots of independent bars and cafés, Kastanienallee's boutiques and the buzzy Sunday flea market at Mauerpark. While Prenzlauer Berg's nightlife has been reduced to a few late-night bars, just over the famous Bösebrücke – where the Bornholmer Strasse border crossing was first officially breached in November 1989 – lies the former Western district of Wedding. Known for its large immigrant population and edgy charm, this up-and-coming borough is peppered with the kind of underground spaces that were once common in Prenzlauer Berg during the 1990s.

Gedenkstätte Berliner Mauer

MAP P.78, POCKET MAP G2
Bernauer Str. 111–119 ⓤ Bernauer Str./
ⓢ Nordbahnhof ☎ 030 46 79 86 666,
ⓦ www.berliner-mauer-gedenkstaette.
de. Open-air exhibition and memorial
grounds daily 8am–10pm; visitor and
documentation centres Tues–Sun
10am–6pm. Free.

Based slightly away from the tourist centre, so avoiding the crowds that throng Checkpoint Charlie, the Berlin Wall Memorial takes a more academic look at Germany's division. A section of the former border strip is the focus for the **memorial**, while an outdoor exhibition on the former death-strip shows the history of Bernauer Strasse and the Wall itself. Stretching 1.4km up to the Mauerpark, it includes traces of border obstacles that retain the appearance of the Wall as it would have been at the time.

The **museum** opposite, expanded in 2014, now hosts a permanent exhibition ("1961–1989: the Berlin Wall"), which documents the lives of those attempting to escape the dictatorship (the most successful escape tunnels were dug near here) and the resistance efforts – sometimes fatal – organized by those living nearby. There's also a separate exhibition on the division of the U-Bahn and S-Bahn lines displayed in the adjacent **Nordbahnhof** station (open during station opening hours). Prayer services for the victims of the Berlin Wall are held in the **chapel** on weekdays at noon.

Mauerpark Flohmarkt

MAP P.78, POCKET MAP H2
Bernauer Str. 63–65 ⓤ Bernauer Str. ☎ 030
29 77 24 86, ⓦ flohmarktimmauerpark.de.
Sun 9am–6pm. Free.

The Mauerpark flea market is a city institution, a popular Sunday stop for hungover students, bargain hunters, families and shade-wearing clubbers who come to scan the international food stalls, clothes shops and nostalgic bric-a-brac that seems to extend forever. You can find everything here from bike parts, 1950s cutlery sets and faded jigsaws to new and vintage clothes, GDR memorabilia, record players and lots of vinyl and CDs. As with most flea markets, there's a decent amount of what might uncharitably be called "junk" but also some genuine antiques. Adjacent to the market you'll find the actual **Mauerpark**, a strip of landscaped green that was once the site of a stretch of Berlin Wall and the associated death-strip, loomed over by the Friedrich-Ludwig-Jahn-Sportpark and the Max-Schmeling-Halle. In warm weather, check out the weekly karaoke session in the "bearpit", which attracts massive crowds from 2.30/3pm.

Kollwitzplatz

MAP P.78, POCKET MAP J2
Kollwitzplatz ⓤ Eberswalder Str./
Senefelderplatz.

Kollwitzplatz is one of Prenzlauer Berg's best-known and most attractive squares. It was named after artist Käthe Kollwitz (1867–1945), who lived in the area at the turn of the twentieth century (a simple plaque commemorates her former home on Kollwitzstr.) and whose squat, serious-looking **sculpture** is one of the main features of the square. From the appearance of the lavishly restored facades it is hard to tell that Kollwitzplatz was once one of Berlin's poorest areas, but Kollwitz's work (see page 124) reveals the area to have once been home to the city's more impoverished and downtrodden citizens. This was one of the first areas to be gentrified when the Wall fell in 1989 and today symbolizes Prenzlauer Berg's yuppie status as well as its bias towards families (some call this part of the city Pramzlauerberg). It's a lovely place to come for a stroll – three **playgrounds** and a leafy **park** lie within the square and endless restaurants, cafés and smart boutiques are scattered around its perimeter. Saturdays are especially popular thanks to the extensive **farmers' market**, offering everything from organic meat and fish, fruit and veg, sweets and coffee and clothes. A smaller (and less crowded) organic market also takes place on Thursdays. In summer especially the fun carries on till late at night.

Jewish cemetery

MAP P.78, POCKET MAP J2
Schönhauser Allee 23–25
ⓤ Senefelderplatz ⓣ 030 44 19 824. Mon–Thurs 8am–4pm, Fri 7.30am–1pm. Free.
A short hop from the Senefelderplatz U-Bahn, Prenzlauer Berg's small but charming Jewish cemetery (Jüdischer Friedhof) was built to cater for the overspill from the one on Mitte's Grosse Hamburger Strasse. It was mostly used between 1827 and 1880, at a time when the Jewish population in this area was thriving, and holds approximately 22,000 graves and almost a thousand hereditary family plots, including the graves of painter Max Liebermann, the

Mauerpark Flohmarkt

Prenzlauer Berg

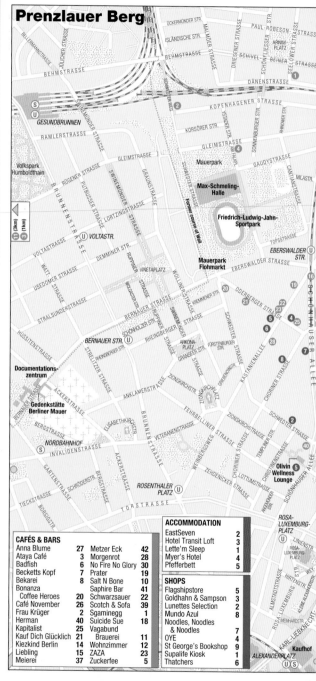

CAFÉS & BARS

Anna Blume	27	Metzer Eck	42
Ataya Café	3	Morgenrot	28
Badfish	6	No Fire No Glory	30
Becketts Kopf	7	Prater	19
Bekarei	8	Salt N Bone	10
Bonanza		Saphire Bar	41
Coffee Heroes	20	Schwarzsauer	22
Café November	26	Scotch & Sofa	39
Frau Krüger	2	Sgaminegg	1
Herman	40	Suicide Sue	18
Kapitalist	25	Vagabund	
Kauf Dich Glücklich	21	Brauerei	11
Kiezkind Berlin	14	Wohnzimmer	12
Liebling	15	ZAZA	23
Meierei	37	Zuckerfee	5

ACCOMMODATION

EastSeven	2
Hotel Transit Loft	3
Lette'm Sleep	1
Myer's Hotel	4
Pfefferbett	5

SHOPS

Flagshipstore	5
Goldhahn & Sampson	3
Lunettes Selection	2
Mundo Azul	8
Noodles, Noodles	
& Noodles	7
OYE	4
St George's Bookshop	9
Supalife Kiosk	1
Thatchers	6

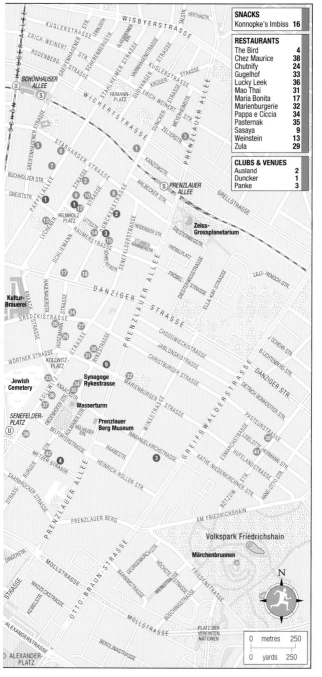

SNACKS

Konnopke's Imbiss	16

RESTAURANTS

The Bird	4
Chez Maurice	38
Chutnify	24
Gugelhof	33
Lucky Leek	36
Mao Thai	31
Maria Bonita	17
Marienburgerie	32
Pappa e Ciccia	34
Pasternak	35
Sasaya	9
Weinstein	13
Zula	29

CLUBS & VENUES

Ausland	2
Duncker	1
Panke	3

Kollwitzplatz

publisher Leopold Ullstein, the composer Giacomo Meyerbeer and German-Jewish banker Joseph Mendelssohn (son of the influential philosopher Moses Mendelssohn). Sadly many gravestones, the original cemetery entrance and mourning chapel were destroyed during World War II and subsequent anti-Semitic vandalism – and many graves are still in a dilapidated state, some riddled with bullet holes. The cemetery was rebuilt in the 1960s, and the adjacent lapidarium – on the site of the former mourning hall – was opened in 2004 as a place to preserve and protect sixty of the most valuable stones, as well as to display panels on Jewish culture and Jewish mourning rituals. Note that men are obliged to cover their heads to visit the cemetery: hats can be borrowed from the lapidarium but visitors are urged to bring their own.

Synagoge Rykestrasse

MAP P.78, POCKET MAP J2
Rykestr. 53 Ⓤ Senefelderstr. ☎ 030 88 02 80, ⓦ www.jg-berlin.org. Open for services only: Fri 6pm (winter), 7pm (summer) & Sat 9.30am.
Built by Johann Hoeniger at the turn of the twentieth century, this gorgeous Neoclassical synagogue (inaugurated in 1904) is one of Germany's largest – and one of Berlin's loveliest. The building

survived *Kristallnacht* in 1938 as it was located between "Aryan" apartment buildings, although precious Torah scrolls were damaged and rabbis and congregation members were deported to Sachsenhausen (see page 136). The synagogue was also used as stables during the war, but was finally restored to its former glory by architects Ruth Golan and Kay Zareh in 2007, who used black-and-white photographs and a €6-million budget to lavishly re-create the remarkable original. Outside of service times, the synagogue can only be visited via prior arrangement.

The Wasserturm

MAP P.78, POCKET MAP J2
Corner of Knaackstr. & Rykestr.
Ⓤ Eberswalder Str./Senefelderplatz.
Designed by Henry Gill, constructed by the English Waterworks Company and finished in 1877, the 30m-high cylindrical brick water tower, known as "Dicker Hermann", has become one of Prenzlauer Berg's unofficial symbols. Among the oldest of its kind in the city, it was one of the first places to provide running water in the country, and remained in use until the 1950s. Its engine house was used as an unofficial prison by the SA in 1933–45 – 28

bodies were later found in the underground pipe network, and a commemorative plaque stands outside the tower on Knaackstrasse. During GDR times the tower was used to store canned fish, which could apparently be smelled across the whole neighbourhood. The building was then abandoned and became a "playground" for local kids. Today the refurbished tower is home to much-coveted cake-wedge-shaped apartments (formerly belonging to the tower's operators), while the underground reservoir space hosts sporadic cultural events.

Olivin Wellness Lounge

MAP P.78, POCKET MAP J3
Schönhauser Allee 177 Ⓤ Senefelderplatz
☎ 030 44 04 25 00, Ⓦ www.olivin-berlin. com. Daily: autumn/winter noon–midnight; summer 5pm–midnight. Entrance costs €14 for four hours.

With its exposed brick walls, saunas and an excellent bamboo garden, this Finnish sauna is a great way to unwind whatever the season. Special offers are available in winter and massages start at €18 for twenty minutes. No access for men on Thursdays. Cash only.

Kulturbrauerei

MAP P.78, POCKET MAP J2
Schönhauser Allee 36 (entrance on Sredzkistr.) Ⓤ Eberswalder Str. or trams M12, M1, M10 ☎ 030 44 35 21 70, Ⓦ kulturbrauerei.de. Open 24hr year round. Free for main complex, price varies for specific venues.

This lovely, sprawling, red-and-yellow brick complex dates to 1842, when it was a small brewery and pub. It was expanded to its current size after 1880. Since the late 1990s, it's been one of Prenzlauer Berg's major commercial hubs, with offices, bars, restaurants, clubs and an eight-theatre cinema (Kino in der KulturBrauerei; ☎ 018 05 11 88 11, Ⓦ cinestar.de). As well as the cinema and shops, the weekly Street Food market (every Sunday) and Scandinavian Christmas market (end

of November to end of December) are worth a visit, as is the **Museum in der Kulturbrauerei** (Knaackstr. 97; ☎ 030 46 77 77 911; free) – opened 2013 – whose permanent exhibition, "Everyday Life in the GDR", documents East German cultural history. The Kesselhaus concert hall hosts some decent indie rock and pop shows. You can also pick up guided cycle tours (March–Nov; ☎ 030 43 73 99 99, Ⓦ berlinonbike.de).

Museum Pankow

MAP P.78, POCKET MAP J3
Prenzlauer Allee 227–228
Ⓤ Senefelderplatz ☎ 030 90 29 53 917.
Tues–Sun 10am–6pm. Free.

Spread across the first floor of a former school, this small but lively museum documents the history of the district and its working-class inhabitants from the nineteenth century to today. The permanent exhibition consists mainly of photos and texts (German only) displayed along corridors, though a couple of large rooms and a separate building across the courtyard occasionally host more modern, multimedia exhibitions on themes such as the evolution of lesbian, gay and transgender life in the area.

Zeiss-Grossplanetarium

MAP P.78, POCKET MAP K1
Prenzlauer Allee 80 Ⓢ Prenzlauer Allee
☎ 030 42 18 45 10. For opening hours and prices see Ⓦ www.planetarium.berlin.

A massive building set back from bustling Prenzlauer Allee, the Zeiss Planetarium was built in 1987. At the time, it was one of Europe's largest and most modern stellar theatres, with a giant, golf-ball-esque silver dome measuring 23m across. Reopened in early 2016, its auditorium still contains a digital projection of Earth's starry skies into the roof, but the program of astronomical, science, film and music events are more cutting edge, as well as entertaining and educational. Many of the shows are multilingual too (English, Spanish, French).

PRENZLAUER BERG AND WEDDING

Shops

Flagshipstore

MAP P.78, POCKET MAP H2

Oderberger Str. 53 ⓤ Eberswalder Str. ⓣ 030 43 73 53 27, ⓦ www.flagshipstore-berlin.de. Mon–Fri noon–8pm, Sat from 11am

Representing dozens of Berlin's fashion labels and international designers, Flagshipstore offers a vast range of urban clothing and accessories for women and men.

Goldhahn & Sampson

MAP P.78, POCKET MAP J1

Dunckerstr. 9 ⓤ Eberswalder Str. ⓦ www .goldhahnundsampson.de. Mon–Fri 8am–8pm, Sat 9am–8pm.

A foodies' paradise that houses a vast spread of condiments, spices and other tasty delicacies from all over the world, plus cookbooks and utensils. It holds regular wine tasting and cookery courses, and there is a second location at Wilmersdorfer Str. 102 (ⓤWilmersdorfer Str.).

Lunettes Selection

MAP P.78, POCKET MAP K1

Dunckerstr. 18 ⓤ Eberswalder Str. ⓣ 030 44 71 80 50, ⓦ lunettes-selection.de. Tues & Fri noon–8pm, Sat noon–6pm.

Vintage eyewear fanatics will adore this small space, which stocks original frames from brands like

Mundo Azul

Alain Mikli and Christian Dior, plus in-house designs by Uta Geyer.

Mundo Azul

MAP P.78, POCKET MAP J2

Choriner Str. 49 ⓤ Senefelderplatz ⓣ 030 49 85 38 34. Mon & Tues 2am–6pm, Wed– Fri 10am–7pm, Sat 10am–4pm.

"Blue world" is a children's and illustration bookstore that stocks beautiful books in French, Spanish, German and English, and also runs events and exhibitions.

Noodles, Noodles & Noodles

MAP P.78, POCKET MAP J2

Schönhauser Allee 156 ⓤ Eberswalder Str. ⓣ 030 44 04 54 93, ⓦ noodles.de. Mon–Fri 10am–7pm, Sat noon–4pm.

Despite its slightly under-the-radar location, this store is worth seeking out for its handsome furniture, made using old-school artisanal techniques and high-quality materials – built to last.

OYE

MAP P.78, POCKET MAP J2

Oderberger Str. 4 ⓤ Eberswalder Str. ⓣ 030 66 64 78 21. Mon–Sat noon–8pm, Wed till 10pm

Originally catering for collectors of Latin, soul and funk vinyl, OYE now covers an impressive range of styles, from Afrobeat to Berlin club staples house and techno.

St George's Bookshop

MAP P.78, POCKET MAP J2

Wörther Str. 27 ⓤ Eberswalder Str. or tram #M2 to Marienburger ⓣ 030 81 79 83 33, ⓦ www.saintgeorgesbookshop.com. Mon– Fri 11am–8pm, Sat 11am–7pm.

Founded in 2003 by British twins Paul and Daniel, this delightful shop sells a fine selection of new and used English-language books. There's a sofa to chill on, free wi-fi and they'll buy your used books.

Supalife Kiosk

MAP P.78, POCKET MAP J1

Raumerstr. 40 ⓤ Eberswalder Str. ⓣ 030 44 67 88 26, ⓦ supalife.de. Mon–Sat noon–7pm.

This small boutique sells the wares of Berlin urban artists, from comics and fanzines to silkscreen prints and paintings. They're well connected to some of the city's best-known artists so expect special one-offs too.

Thatchers

MAP P.78, POCKET MAP H2
Kastanienallee 21 Ⓤ Eberswalder Str.
Ⓣ 030 24 62 77 51. Mon–Sat 11am–7pm.
Upmarket fashion store for women who like their dresses, skirts and shirts classy and sexy without ever being over the top. A perfect place to pick up sensual evening dresses, sophisticated club wear and also savvy gifts.

Restaurants

The Bird

MAP P.78, POCKET MAP H1
Am Falkplatz 5 Ⓤ/Ⓢ Schönhauser Allee
Ⓣ 030 51 05 32 83, Ⓦ thebirdinberlin.com.
Mon–Thurs 6–11pm, Fri 4pm–midnight, Sat noon–midnight, Sun noon–11pm. Cash only.
This no-nonsense New York-style steakhouse is famed for its large and tasty burgers, spicy chicken wings and casual ambience. With the neon bar, exposed brickwork and US accents it's a bit like being on the set of *Cheers*. A great place to fill up cheaply and sip on a cold beer.

Chez Maurice

MAP P.78, POCKET MAP L3
Bötzowstr. 39 Ⓢ Greifswalder Str. Ⓣ 030 42 50 506, Ⓦ chez-maurice.com. Daily from 5pm
One of the finer dining spots in the quietly upmarket Bötzowviertel, *Maurice* is an intimate, rustic place offering high-quality seasonal French dishes – they'll even take requests with enough notice – and an expansive wine list (over two hundred from France alone).

Chutnify

MAP P.78, POCKET MAP J2
Szredki Str. 43 Ⓤ Eberswalderstr. Ⓣ 030 44 01 07 95, Ⓦ chutnify.com. Daily noon–11pm.
Single-handedly challenging Berlin's dire reputation for mediocre, spice-avoiding Indian food, *Chutnify* specializes in South Indian street food with an emphasis on delicious *dosas*, crispy lentil crêpes and spicy *chai* teas. Designed by owner Aparna Aurora, it looks good too, with colourful furnishings and outside seating in summer. A second branch can be found at Pflügerstr.25 (same opening times).

Gugelhof

MAP P.78, POCKET MAP J2
Knaackstr. 37, cnr Kollwitzplatz
Ⓤ Senefelderplatz/Eberswalder Str. Ⓣ 030 44 29 229, Ⓦ www.gugelhof.com. Mon & Wed–Fri from 5pm, Sat & Sun from 10am.
A Kollwitzplatz classic, *Gugelhof* has been serving consistently good Alsatian food since the Wall fell, and counts Bill Clinton among its many dignified diners. It's a surprisingly down-to-earth place, with friendly staff and robust yet refined cuisine that includes *Flammkuchen* (*tarte flambée*) and pork knuckle. Reservations recommended.

Lucky Leek

MAP P.78, POCKET MAP J2
Kollwitzstr. 54 Ⓤ Senefelderplatz Ⓣ 030 66 40 87 10, Ⓦ lucky-leek.com. Wed–Sun 6–10pm.
This high-end vegan spot occupies a smart space inside an old building on one of Prenzlauer Berg's loveliest streets. The menu is inventive and service excellent, but you'll certainly pay above average for the experience. Mains around €18; five-course menu €59.

Mao Thai

MAP P.78, POCKET MAP J2
Wörther Str. 30 Ⓤ Eberswalder Str. Ⓣ 030 44 19 261, Ⓦ maothai.de. Daily noon–11.30pm.
Don't be put off by the beaming Buddhas in the window – there's a refreshing lack of garish decoration inside this reliable neighbourhood Thai restaurant. Decent service and a tasty range of classics – *tom ka gai*, spring rolls, glass noodle salads – make this a popular place.

Maria Bonita

MAP P.78, POCKET MAP J2

Danziger Str. 33 Ⓤ Eberswalder Str. Ⓦ mariabonita.de. Daily noon–11pm, Fri & Sat until 10.30pm.

Tucked away amidst the slew of *imbisses* and kebab shops that make up much of this part of Danziger Strasse, *Maria Bonita* stands out for its above-average street-style Mexican food. You couldn't swing an enchilada inside, but the burritos, tacos and *quesadillas* – and the guacamole for that matter – are well worth trying.

Marienburgerie

MAP P.78, POCKET MAP K2

Marienburger Str. 47; tram #M2 to Marienburger Str. Ⓣ 030 30 34 05 15, Ⓦ marienburgerie.de. Mon–Fri 11am–10pm, Sat & Sun 1–10pm.

This diminutive but buzzy burger hangout lures locals back again and again with huge, delicious beef, chicken, fish or vegetable burgers (the Marienburger is almost too big to eat in one sitting). Organic options also available.

Pappa e Ciccia

MAP P.78, POCKET MAP H2

Schwedter Str. 18 Ⓤ Senefelderplatz Ⓣ 030 61 62 08 01, Ⓦ pappaeciccia.de. Mon–Sun 6pm–midnight

Bored of the usual Berlin brunch formula? Check out the weekend brunch at this smart-casual Italian restaurant, where chefs dole out freshly made antipasti and other scrumptious dishes, and diners gather on the long communal tables outside. It's all organic and there are decent vegetarian and vegan options. Ice cream, cakes and more on offer at the adjacent organic deli.

Pasternak

MAP P.78, POCKET MAP J2

Knaackstr. 22–24 Ⓤ Senefelderplatz Ⓣ 030 44 13 399, Ⓦ restaurant-pasternak.de. Daily 9am–1am.

This long-standing Russian/Jewish restaurant, named after the author of *Doctor Zhivago*, is best known for its incredible Sunday brunch

(9am–3pm, €13.90): a regal spread of blini, caviar, fish and much more; it's so popular you'll need to get there early (no reservations). The same proprietors run a decent Israeli restaurant over the road (directly opposite the synagogue) called – get it? – *Masel Topf* (Ⓣ 030 443 17 525, Ⓦ restaurant-maseltopf.de).

Sasaya

MAP P.78, POCKET MAP J1

Lychener Str. 50 Ⓤ / Schönhauser Allee Ⓣ 030 44 71 77 21. Mon & Thurs noon–3pm & 6–11.30pm.

Bucking the trend for catch-all pan-Asian menus, *Sasaya* focuses on serving traditional and innovative Japanese food. The quality and freshness of the ingredients is high, the food is delicious and service is swift – a serious contender for best sushi spot in the city.

Weinstein

MAP P.78, POCKET MAP J1

Lychener Str. 33 Ⓤ Eberswalder Str. Ⓣ 030 44 11 842, Ⓦ weinstein.eu. Mon–Sat 5pm–2am, kitchen 6–11.30pm.

This intimate wine bar and restaurant, all sturdy wooden tables and wine barrel decoration, is a bit of a local secret. The food has a strong emphasis on local produce and German wines, as well as imported high-quality products like Allgäu cheese and Iberian ham. Mains start at €13.50, and from Monday to Wednesday you can get eight small courses for €59.

Zula

MAP P.78, POCKET MAP J2

Husemann Str. 10 Ⓤ Senefelderplatz Ⓣ 030 41 71 51 00, Ⓦ zulaberlin.com. Daily from 11am.

The humble chickpea dish reaches superlative status at this cosy, Israeli-run hummus spot. Visitors can stick with a traditional hummus plate or try out the *hummus shakshuka* and even *hummus goulash* – all of it is delicious. Home-made pitta bread and a nice wine list seal the deal.

Snacks

Konnopke's Imbiss

MAP P.78, POCKET MAP J1
Schönhauser Allee 44b ⓤ Eberswalder Str.
ⓣ 030 44 27 765, ⓦ www.konnopke-imbiss.
de. Mon–Fri 10am–8pm, Sat noon–8pm.
This legendary stand has been
serving up Berlin street snacks –
Currywurst, pommes frites, Bratwurst
– since 1930. Incredibly it's been
run by the same family all that
time – perfect for a quick bite. It's
perfect for a quick bite any time of
day; if you want to feel like a local,
eat your food standing up at one of
the tables outside.

Zula

Cafés and bars

Anna Blume

MAP P.78, POCKET MAP J2
Kollwitzstr. 83 ⓤ Eberswalder Str. ⓣ 030
44 04 87 49, ⓦ www.cafe-anna-blume.de.
Daily 8am–2am.
Part flower shop, part café and
part bakery, this Art Deco classic –
named after a Kurt Schwitters poem,
whose lines are elegantly inscribed
on the walls inside – is one of the
area's best known cafés. Slide into
one of the red leather banquettes and
sample one of their superb cakes, or
come early at the weekend and try a
refined tiered breakfast platter.

Ataya Café

MAP P.78, POCKET MAP K1
Zelter Str. 6 ⓢ Prenzlauer Allee ⓣ 030 33 02
10 41, ⓦ atayacaffe.de. Tue–Thurs & Sun
11am–6pm, Fri & Sat 11am–4pm & 6–10pm.
This Sardinian-Senegalese café base
their food on seasonal, fresh and
plant-based ingredients and influences
– as a bonus, they work from a
plastic-free kitchen. With colourful
décor featuring African style prints,
they offer anything from sandwiches
and pastas to baked goods.

Badfish

MAP P.78, POCKET MAP J1
Stargarder Str. 14 ⓤ/ⓢ Schönhauser Allee

ⓣ 030 547 147 88, ⓦ badfishbarberlin.
com. Daily 5pm–late.
This New York-style neighbourhood
bar has become an in-spot for
expats and natives alike. Smokey
and boisterous (especially at
weekends), and with a hip selection
of sounds on the jukebox, friendly
staff and an excellent array of craft
beers, whiskeys and shots, it makes
for an almost guaranteed fun night
out. "Angry hour" between 5–7pm
and free popcorn at all times.

Becketts Kopf

MAP P.78, POCKET MAP J1
64 ⓤ/ⓢ Schönhauser Allee ⓣ 030 44 03
58 80. Mon–Thurs & Sun 7pm–2am, Fri &
Sat 7pm–4am.
It's easy to walk straight past this
deliberately clandestine cocktail bar
– but you'd be missing out. Look out
for the glowering head of Mr Beckett
staring at you from the darkness,
and enter to find a sophisticated and
intimate space with one of the best
cocktail lists in town.

Bekarei

MAP P.78, POCKET MAP J1
Dunker Str. 23 ⓢ Prenzlauer Allee
ⓣ 030 34 62 22 30, ⓦ bekarei.com. Daily
7am–6.30pm.

Kapitalist

This Greek-Portuguese bakery is a firm local favourite thanks to its freshly baked breads, pretzels, cakes and pastries. The interior is colourfully retro, the staff are friendlier than usual and menu items of note include pancakes, flakey *tiropitakia* and *pastel de nata*. Note that it gets particularly busy with families at weekends.

Bonanza Coffee Heroes

MAP P.78, POCKET MAP H2
Oderberger Str. 35 Ⓤ Bernauer Str./
Eberswalder Str. ☎ 030 20 84 88
020, Ⓦ bonanzacoffee.de. Mon–Fri
8.30am–6pm, Sat & Sun 10am–6pm.
Coffee connoisseurs flock to *Bonanza* to sample the wares of their famed baristas: perfect lattes and flat whites knocked up on a fancy Slayer Espresso machine. Single origin filter coffees also served, and there is a second location in Kreuzberg (Adalbertstr. 70).

Café November

MAP P.78, POCKET MAP J2
Husemannstr. 15 Ⓤ Senefelderplatz/
Eberswalder Str. ☎ 030 44 28 425, Ⓦ www.
cafe-november.com. Mon–Fri from 2pm,
Sat & Sun from 10am.
Café November is an appealing, gay-friendly but mixed café that sells good cakes, soups and mains. There's a breakfast buffet until 3pm on Saturdays and 4pm on Sundays, free wi-fi and the outside patio is great in the summer.

Frau Krüger

MAP P.78, POCKET MAP H1
Kopenhagener Str. 37 Ⓤ Schönhauser
Allee ☎ 03012 09 85 04, Ⓦ www.cafe-
fraukrueger.de. Daily 9am–8pm.
A simple but friendly and cute café just off Mauerpark, one of the best places to come after a day in the park or when you are ready to get some of their famous frozen yoghurt, having spent the morning at the flea market. The friendly staff makes having coffee, cake, breakfast or brunch here even nicer.

Herman

MAP P.78, POCKET MAP F10
Schönhauser Allee 173 Ⓤ Senefelderplatz
☎ 30 44312854. Sun & Mon 6pm–midnight,
Tues–Thurs 6pm–1am, Fri & Sat 6pm–2am.
Located along the busy section of Schönhauser Allee that links Mitte with Prenzlauer Berg, this Belgian-themed bar – run by welcoming and knowledgeable owner Bart Neirynck – has an incredibly broad selection of beers. It's a great place to start the night, but chances are you'll end up staying for longer than planned.

Kapitalist

MAP P.78, POCKET MAP J2
Oderberger Str. 2 Ⓤ Eberswalder Str.
☎ 030 47 37 44 860. Mon–Fri 1pm–open
end, Sat & Sun 11am–open end.
Kapitalist is a much less anti-establishment place than its beaten-up facade suggests – in fact it's completely harmless, drawing a friendly, bubbly crowd of locals who come for coffees and people-watching in the day and beer and wine at night.

Kauf Dich Glücklich

MAP P.78, POCKET MAP H2
Oderberger Str. 44 Ⓤ Bernauer Str./
Eberswalder Str. ☎ 030 48 62 32 92
Ⓦ www.kaufdichgluecklich.de. Mon–Thurs

10am–10.30pm, Fri & Sat 10am–12.30am, Sun 10am–10.30pm.

Come here for waffles, ice cream – and a spot of cutely kitsch capitalism. "Buy yourself happy" is an irrepressibly cheerful place where you can not only get great coffee and sweet treats, but also buy any of the secondhand furniture – tables, chairs, lamps, sunglasses – you see around you.

Kiezkind Berlin

MAP P.78, POCKET MAP J1
Helmholtzplatz ⓤ Eberswalderstr. ☎ 030 40 05 78 50, ⓦ www.mein-kiezkind.de. Mon–Fri noon–6pm, Sat & Sun 10am–6pm.
Located right on leafy Helmholtzplatz, this large, family-oriented café is an ideal place to take a break with the little ones. Inside, they can play with the abundant toys or in the sandpit, or ride around on the tricycles outside while you enjoy a well-made latte and slice of cake from the counter. Regular family-friendly flea markets also.

Liebling

MAP P.78, POCKET MAP J1
Raumerstr. 36 ⓢ Prenzlauer Allee/ ⓤ Eberswalder Str. ☎ 030 91 45 37 10. Mon–Thurs 8.30am–2am, Fri till 3am, Sat & Sun 10am till late.
There's no sign on this café/bar, but you'll find it right on the corner of Dunckerstrasse and Raumerstrasse. Inside is a subtly cool interior, great cakes and decent lunch options (soups, quiches). The good wine and beer, and the *au courant* music on the system, makes it popular in the evenings too.

Meierei

MAP P.78, POCKET MAP J2
Kollwitz Str. 42 ⓤ Senefelderplatz ☎ 030 92 12 95 73, ⓦ www.meierei.net. Mon–Fri 7.30am–5pm, Sat 9am–5pm, Sun 10am–5pm.
This itsy café-cum-deli in leafy Kollwitzstrasse offers a taste of the high life. Styled around a mountain hut interior, with Alpine landscapes painted on the walls, the organic Swiss and Austrian cuisine – from

Weisswürst (veal sausage) to apple *Strudel* – is best enjoyed at one of the large outdoor tables.

Metzer Eck

MAP P.78, POCKET MAP F10
Metzer Str. 33 ⓤ Eberswalder Str. ☎ 030 44 27 656, ⓦ www.metzer-eck.de. Mon–Fri 4pm–1am, Sat 6pm–1am.
The oldest inn in Prenzlauer Berg (1913) inevitably packs plenty of old-school charm. It's faded slightly since its days as a major meeting point for Prenzlauer Berg's more bohemian contingent in the GDR, but still serves a decent Pilsner and delicious *Bolettes* (meatballs) and *Bockwurst*.

Morgenrot

MAP P.78, POCKET MAP H2
Kastanienallee 85 ⓤ Eberswalder Str. ☎ 030 44 31 78 44, ⓦ cafe-morgenrot. de. Tues–Thurs 10am–1am, Fri & Sat 11am–3am, Sun 11am–midnight.
Kastanienallee's best-known alternative café is located right next to an immense squat (one of the last in the area). Despite the anticapitalist slogans and punk aura, it's a friendly, open place that serves up a good weekend breakfast (vegetarian) for which you pay between €4 and €7, depending on your income.

No Fire No Glory

MAP P.78, POCKET MAP J2
Ryke Str. 45 ⓤ Eberswalder Str. ☎ 030 288 83 92 33, ⓦ www.nofirenoglory.de. Daily 9am–5pm.
This trendy café specializes in quality roasted coffee (they use blends by Bonanza Coffee Roasters and The Coffee Collective), changing depending on the season. The baristas will be able to find the best blend for you without even trying. Also serves delicious sandwiches, homemade cakes and a mean brunch (daily till 2pm).

Prater

MAP P.78, POCKET MAP J2
Kastanienallee 7–9 ⓤ Eberswalder Str. ☎ 030 44 85 688, ⓦ www.pratergarten.de. Beer garden April–Sept daily from noon;

restaurant year-round Mon–Sat 6–11pm, Sun noon–11pm.

Dating back to 1837, *Prater* is the city's oldest beer garden and remains a fantastic place for a taste of traditional Berlin boozing, especially during summer when people swarm around the long tables and snack kiosks. During winter, it's all about feasting on home-made Berlin cuisine inside the classic interior.

Salt N Bone

MAP P.78, POCKET MAP J1
Schliemannstr. 3 Ⓢ Schönhauser Allee
Ⓣ 030 91 44 88 85, Ⓦ saltnbone.de. Bar:
Mon–Fri from 6pm, Sat & Sun from 5pm,
Restaurant: Mon–Fri from 6–11pm, Sat
5–11pm, Sun 5–10pm.

The gastropub scene has well and truly arrived in Berlin with this place, where Sunday roasts and modern bar food are served up alongside local craft beers, very good cocktails, and a decent gin and tonic selection. Friendly staff and a largely expat clientele.

Saphire Bar

MAP P.78, POCKET MAP L3
Bötzowstr. 31 Ⓢ Greifswalder Str. Ⓣ 030 25
56 21 58, Ⓦ saphirebar.de. Mon–Thurs &
Sun 8pm–2am, Fri & Sat 8pm–4am.

The *Saphire Bar* mixes together its whisky and cocktail bar credentials as well as it mixes its drinks, with two elegant lounges to enjoy a cultivated yet unpretentious evening in.

Schwarzsauer

MAP P.78, POCKET MAP J2
Kastanienallee 13 Ⓤ Eberswalder Str.
Ⓣ 030 44 85 633. Daily 9am–4am.

"Black and Sour" lives up to its name with its moody service, average food and smoky, plain interior. Still, it has a certain Berlin-esque atmosphere that makes it decidedly popular.

Scotch & Sofa

MAP P.78, POCKET MAP F10
Kollwitzstr. 18 Ⓤ Senefelderplatz Ⓣ 030
68 00 42 03, Ⓦ www.scotch-sofa.de. Daily
from 6pm–2am.

This quietly hip neighbourhood bar is a fine spot for sinking into a granny-style sofa, sipping on a cocktail and having a *tête-à-tête*. They always play interesting music – everything from Elvis to rap – and smokers and ping-pong fans can indulge their passions downstairs.

Sgaminegg

MAP P.78, POCKET MAP J1
Seelower Str. 2 Ⓤ/Ⓢ Schönhauser Allee
Ⓣ 030 44 73 15 25, Ⓦ www.sgaminegg.de.
Tues–Fri 8.30am–6pm, Sat 9.30am–6pm.

There are a dearth of decent cafés north of Stargarderstrasse, but *Sgaminegg* is an absolute treasure thanks to delicious coffees, home-made lunches – couscous, lentil and south German dishes – and a little shop that sells local produce.

Suicide Sue

MAP P.78, POCKET MAP J2
Dunckerstr. 2 Ⓤ Eberswalder Str. Ⓣ 030
64 83 47 45, Ⓦ suicidesue.com. Mon–Fri
8am–6pm, Sat 9am–7pm, Sun 10am–7pm.

This local fave features crumpled leather armchairs, chunky wooden tables and a street-facing espresso bar. The food is tasty too: breakfast spans croissants and scrambled eggs (served in a tiny frying pan), but the real speciality is the *Stullen* – thick slices of home-made bread with toppings you mix and match yourself.

Vagabund Brauerei

POCKET MAP C1
Antwerpener Str. 3 Ⓢ Seestrasse Ⓣ 030 52
66 76 68, Ⓦ www.vagabundbrauerei.com.
Mon–Fri from 5pm, Sat & Sun from 1pm.

One of Europe's first crowd-sourced breweries, *Vagabund* is run by three American friends with a highly infectious passion for craft beer. As well as their own excellent brews, they sell classic Belgian ales and lager from family breweries in southern Germany, all in a welcoming, unpretentious atmosphere that draws locals and expats alike.

Wohnzimmer

MAP P.78, POCKET MAP J1
Lettestr. 6 ⓤ Eberswalder Str. ☎ 030 44
55 458, ⓦ www.wohnzimmer-bar.de. Daily
2pm–late.

This retro, elegant "living room" is
a local institution. One of the first
spots to champion flea-market chic,
it serves as both a daytime café and
amiable bar later on. At weekends
a cocktail bar magically pops up
between its two rooms.

ZAZA

MAP P.78, POCKET MAP J2
Kastanienallee 12 ⓤ Eberswalder Str.
☎ 030 44 03 11 85, ⓦ www.zazabar.de.
Daily from 4pm

Stylish, modern cocktail bar, mixing
some of the most delicious cocktails
around for a very fair price. In
need of a snack? ZAZA offers great
sushi and other Asian finger foods
to enjoy with their large cocktail
selection. They have Happy Hour
every day from 6–8pm, when all
cocktails are €5; make sure to try
the ZAZA special drink.

Zuckerfee

MAP P.78, POCKET MAP J1
Greifenhagener Str. 15 ⓤ/Ⓢ Schönhauser
Allee ☎ 030 52 68 61 44, ⓦ zuckerfee-
berlin.de. Tues–Sun 10am–6pm.

"Sugar Plum Fairy" is an apt name
for this delightful place, tucked
down a quiet street. The interior is
dotted with tasteful ornamentation,
while the menu features delicious
waffles, cakes and uniquely
presented breakfasts and lunches
(book ahead at weekends).

Clubs and venues

Ausland

MAP P.78, POCKET MAP J1
Lychener Str. 60 Ⓢ Prenzlauer Allee ☎ 030
44 77 008, ⓦ ausland-berlin.de.

One for the experimentalists,
Ausland is a nonprofit club
committed to promoting music,
performance and related events.
You can find anything from free

Suicide Sue

jazz and sound-art gigs to movies
and installations, all of which take
place in an undecorated bunker in
front of an apartment block. Door
fees go directly to the artists.

Duncker

MAP P.78, POCKET MAP K1
Dunckerstr. 64 Ⓢ Prenzlauer Allee ☎ 030
44 59 509, ⓦ dunckerclub.de. Mon from
10pm, Thurs from 9pm, Fri & Sat from
11pm. Entry fee varies but free Thurs.

Duncker touches the musical parts
other Prenzlauer Berg clubs don't
reach, thanks to a mix of new wave
and indie nights and particularly
its weekly "Dark Mondays" – one
of the city's few goth/industrial
nights. Aptly enough, it's located in
a striking neo-Gothic church.

Panke

POCKET MAP E1
Gerichtstr. 23 Ⓢ Wedding ☎ 0163 831
4755, ⓦ www.pankeculture.com. Wed–Sat
from 6pm. Admission varies.

This alternative cultural hub, run
by a group of Lithuanian friends, is
hidden away in a network of run-
down industrial courtyards. Expect
underground DJ nights, which veer
from hip-hop and soul to world and
funk (never techno), plus film and
art nights and a decent bar and café.

Friedrichshain

Though part of an ensemble of former East inner-city areas, Friedrichshain has developed a slightly differently mien than that of neighbouring Mitte and Prenzlauer Berg. A magnet for lefties, anarchists and students, it has managed to resist the same levels of gentrification thanks to an organized squatter scene, activist demos and the occasional car-burning frenzy. That said, its defiantly unkempt environs have succumbed to an invasion of bars and cafés around Boxhagener Platz, and an encroaching media presence along the river. It's most popular for bar-hopping, clubbing and cheap midnight snacking, but the area does offer some heavyweight public monuments, the world-famous East Side Gallery and the imposing Karl-Marx-Allee among them. It's also home to – indeed named after – the lovely, sprawling Volkspark Friedrichshain.

Volkspark Friedrichshain

MAP P.92, POCKET MAP K3
Ⓤ Strausberger Platz/Weberweise.
Established 150 years ago to commemorate the centenary of Frederick the Great's accession to the throne, Volkspark

Friedrichshain is one of Berlin's oldest parks. Casually straddling the boroughs of Prenzlauer Berg and Friedrichshain, it's a sprawling place featuring lots of recreational opportunities (tennis courts, volleyball nets and climbing

Volkspark Friedrichshain

Karl-Marx-Allee

walls) and a wealth of impressive monuments. Highlights include the **Märchenbrunnen**, a neo-Baroque fountain built at the turn of the twentieth century, memorials to Frederick the Great, the German antifascist groups of World War II and a **peace bell** given to East Berlin by Japan. The park's two main hills (the 78m Grosse Bunkerberg and the 48m Kleine Bunkerberg) were constructed with rubble from the war. The park also has a café and a summertime open-air cinema.

East Side Gallery

MAP P.92, POCKET MAP L6
Mühlenstr. 1 ⓤ Warschauer Str. ☏ 030 25 17 159, ⓦ eastsidegallery-berlin.com. 24hr.
This 1.3km-long section of the Berlin Wall by the Spree is purportedly the largest open-air gallery in the world and one of the city's best-known landmarks. Painted in 1990 (on the east side) when the Wall fell, the gallery features works from over a hundred artists from all over the world. Over the years it has fallen victim to vandalism and erosion, hence a controversial decision to repaint it in time for the twentieth-anniversary celebrations in 2009. The East Side Gallery made the news again in 2013 when a section was removed to make way for some luxury apartments; the resulting outcry drew ten thousand protesters and an impromptu appearance by David Hasselhoff. Since 2016 a **museum** close to the Oberbaumbrücke (see page 93) end of the Wall (Mühlenstr. 78-80 ☏ 030 94 51 29 00, ⓦ thewallmuseum. com; daily 10am–7pm; €12.50), tells the story of the Wall years through a multimedia presentation that includes over 100 screens, interactive displays, original newsreel footage and filmed interviews with border guards.

Karl-Marx-Allee

MAP P.92, POCKET MAP L5
ⓤ Frankfurter Tor/Strausberger Platz.
The monumental Karl-Marx-Allee, as the name suggests, is a thoroughly Communist

phenomenon. Built between 1952 and 1960, the imposing 89m-wide, 2km-long street – book-ended by German architect Hermann Henselmann's tiered "wedding cake" towers at Frankfurter Tor and Strausberger Platz – was originally named Grosse Frankfurter Strasse and later Stalinallee. The idea was to build luxurious apartments for workers (they were inevitably doled out to party officials) as well as a leisure area featuring shops, restaurants, cafés and the still-standing Kino International. On June 17, 1953, the street was the focus of worker demonstrations; at least 125 people died in the brutal suppression by Soviet forces that followed. Since reunification most of the buildings have been restored and the apartments converted into upmarket flats and offices. The vast dimensions of the street and its run of blocky

Soviet architecture make it a fantastic place for a stroll. Stop off at *Café Sybille* (see page 97), which hosts a small but insightful museum on the street's history.

Computerspielemuseum

MAP P.92, POCKET MAP L5
Karl-Marx-Allee 93a Ⓤ Weberwise Ⓣ 030 60 98 85 77, Ⓦ computerspielemuseum.de. Daily 10am–8pm. €9.

The world's first-ever computer games museum is a fun and highly interactive tribute to gaming, featuring pretty much every kind of arcade machine and games console ever made, from the pioneering Nimrod (1951) and legendary PONG (1972), right up to contemporary classics like Tomb Raider. There are plenty of opportunities to punch keyboards and waggle joysticks – and even get a jolly old electric shock via the two-player "Pain Station".

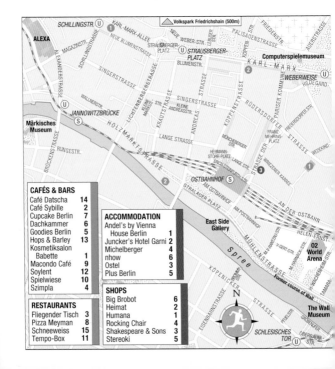

CAFÉS & BARS

Café Datscha	14
Café Sybille	2
Cupcake Berlin	7
Dachkammer	6
Goodies Berlin	5
Hops & Barley	13
Kosmetiksalon Babette	9
Macondo Café	9
Soylent	12
Spielwiese	10
Szimpla	4

RESTAURANTS

Fliegender Tisch	3
Pizza Meyman	8
Schneeweiss	15
Tempo-Box	11

ACCOMMODATION

Andel's by Vienna House Berlin	1
Juncker's Hotel Garni	2
Michelberger	4
nhow	6
Ostel	3
Plus Berlin	5

SHOPS

Big Brobot	6
Heimat	2
Humana	1
Rocking Chair	4
Shakespeare & Sons	3
Stereoki	5

Boxhagener Platz market

MAP P.92, POCKET MAP A17
Boxhagener Platz ⓤ **Samariterstr.**
ⓦ **boxhagenerplatz.org.** Farmers' market:
Sat 9.30am–3.30pm. Flea market: Sun
10am–6pm.

The Sunday flea market at
Boxhagener Platz is a popular place
for locals and tourists alike. While
not as large as Mauerpark (see page
76), you can find vinyl, vintage
fashion, old crockery and more.

Oberbaumbrücke

MAP P.92, POCKET MAP M7
ⓤ **Warschauer Str.**

This attractive, Spree-spanning
landmark connects the districts
of Friedrichshain and Kreuzberg,
today officially part of the same
borough but previously divided by
the Berlin Wall. The double-decker
bridge (and its name) dates back
to the eighteenth century when it
was originally constructed – from
wood – and acted as a gateway to

Oberbaumbrücke

the city. A new version opened
in 1896, designed by architect
Otto Stahn in brick gothic style.
In 1945 the bridge was partly

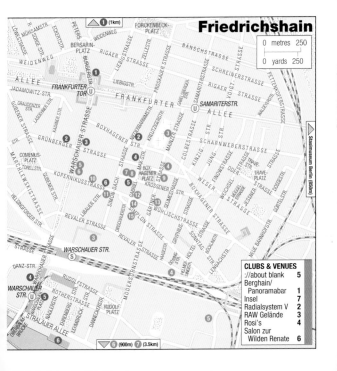

Friedrichshain

CLUBS & VENUES
://about blank   5
Berghain/
    Panoramabar   1
Insel   7
Radialsystem V   2
RAW Gelände   3
Rosi's   4
Salon zur
    Wilden Renate   6

Stasi Museum

destroyed by the Wehrmacht to stop the Red Army crossing it, and afterwards ended up straddling the American and Soviet sectors. When the Berlin Wall went up in 1961, the bridge became part of East Berlin's border with West Berlin; when it fell in 1989, the bridge was restored to its former appearance with a new steel middle section designed by Spanish architect Santiago Calatrava. Today the bridge stands as a symbol of unity between Friedrichshain and Kreuzberg (and is the site of a friendly "water battle" in summer). Look out for the neon *Stone Paper Scissors* installation by Thorsten Goldberg – a political statement about the apparent arbitrariness of decisions to grant immigration or asylum status.

Stasi Museum

MAP P.92, POCKET MAP M5
Ruschestr. 103, Haus 1, Lichtenberg
ⓤ Magdalenenstr. ☎ 030 55 36 854,
ⓦ www.stasimuseum.de. Mon–Fri
10am–6pm, Sat & Sun 11am–6pm. €6

(reductions for groups), public tours every Thurs–Mon (English tours start 3pm).
East Germany's State Security Service – Stasi – struck terror into East Germans, using dark and dastardly spying methods to unveil any potential signs of rebellion. This museum – in Lichtenberg, just east of Friedrichshain – used to be the Stasi headquarters: it was stormed and taken over when the Wall fell by an indignant group of people, many of whose lives had been affected by years of abuse, and members of this group still run the museum today. Following extensive renovations, the main building of the campus (Haus 1, which housed the Minister of State Security among others) reopened in 2012 and the exhibition "State Security in the SED Dictatorship" has been on permanent display since 2015. Visitors can see Stasi chief Erich Mielke's ridiculously immense desk (and equally large number of telephones) and the complex filing system that includes samples of body odours.

Shops

Big Brobot

MAP P.92, POCKET MAP A16
Kopernikusstr. 19 ⓤ/Ⓢ Warschauerstr.
ⓣ 030 74 07 83 88. Mon–Fri 11am–8pm,
Sat 11am–6pm.
Friendly and vaguely trashy store
where you can browse rare toys, art
books and streetwear.

Heimat

MAP P.92, POCKET MAP A16
Niederbarnimstr. 17 ⓤ Samariterstr. ⓣ 030
74 69 99 14, ⓦ mein-heimat-laden.de.
Mon–Fri noon–7pm, Sat noon–6pm.
Specializes in stylish T-shirts,
bags and accessories. Robots,
bicycles, strange animals and other
hipster designs appear on almost
every item.

Humana

MAP P.92, POCKET MAP A16
Frankfurter Tor 3 ⓤ Frankfurter Tor ⓣ 030
422 2018. Mon–Sat 10am–8pm.
This immense five-storey
warehouse, part of a grand Soviet
"worker palace", brims with
secondhand clothes. The top floor
has the best vintage gear.

Rocking Chair

MAP P.92, POCKET MAP A17
Gabriel-Max-Str. 13 ⓤ Samariterstr./
Frankfurter Tor ⓣ 030 29 36 42 91,
ⓦ rockingchair-berlin.de. Mon–Fri
noon–7pm, Sat 10am–4pm.
This charming vintage store is a
great place for anything from a
Hawaiian shirt to a retro handbag.
Also open sunny Sundays.

Shakespeare & Sons

MAP P.92, POCKET MAP A16
Warschauerstr. 74 ⓤ/Ⓢ Warschauerstr.
ⓦ shakespeareandsons.com. Mon–Sun
8am–8pm.
One of the city's best English-
language bookshops, this is a
welcoming space filled with literary,
sci-fi and academic classics, as well
as a great selection of kids' books,
French-language titles and Berlin-

themed tomes. Inside, *Fine Bagels*
serves up some of the best bagels
in town.

Stereoki

MAP P.92, POCKET MAP A17
Gabriel-Max-Str. 18 ⓤ/Ⓢ Warschauerstr.
ⓣ 030 53 79 4667, ⓦ stereoki.com. Mon–
Fri 11.30am–8pm, Sat 11am–7pm.
This slick, white-walled men's
fashion store carries shoes,
trainers, wallets, bags, hats,
tees and more by brands like
Adidas and New Balance,
Herschel Supply and Element
Emerald Collection.

Restaurants

Fliegender Tisch

MAP P.92, POCKET MAP B16
Mainzer Str. 10 ⓤ Samariterstr. ⓣ 030
29 77 64 89, ⓦ fliegender-tisch.de. Daily
from 5pm.
"The flying table" is a small, cosy
place with just a few wooden
tables. It's justly popular thanks
to tasty Italian staples like thin-
crust pizza and risotto for decent
prices (€7–8).

Pizza Meyman

MAP P.92, POCKET MAP A17
Warschauer Str. 80 ⓤ Frankfurter Tor
ⓣ 030 64 49 68 80, ⓦ pizzeria-meyman.
de. Mon–Thurs & Sun noon–2am, Fri & Sat
noon–3am.
This unassuming restaurant is
great for late-night cravings or
for a break between bar hops.
Ingredients are fresh, prices are
reasonable (€5.50–7.90 for a
main), and there's usually a table
free. Pasta dishes and salads as well
as pizza.

Schneeweiss

MAP P.92, POCKET MAP A17
Simplonstr. 16 ⓤ Warschauer Str. ⓣ 030
29 04 97 04, ⓦ schneeweiss-berlin.de.
Summer hours: Mon–Fri 11.45pm–4pm
& 5.30–1am, regular hours: Mon–Fri
6pm–1am, Sat & Sun 10am–1am (kitchen
closes 11pm).

One of Friedrichshain's few upmarket restaurants, "Snow White" is an understated place with a minimalist design and a menu that it describes as "Alpine" – Italian, Austrian and south German recipes such as Schnitzel and pasta. There's a decent weekend brunch (10am–3pm), a fireplace lounge and a low-key bar vibe come evening.

Tempo-Box

MAP P.92, POCKET MAP A16
Simon-Dach Str. 15–16 Ⓢ Warschauer Str. ⓣ 030 74 07 88 61, ⓦ tempo-box.de. Sun–Thu 9am–midnight, Fri & Sat until 3am.

This modern restaurant serves everything from eggy breakfasts to Argentinian rump steak, all set in the middle of Friedrichshain – during summer times you can enjoy watching the streets of Berlin from their sunny terrace. Mondays and Tuesdays are known

as 'Burgertage' (Burger day), where you can get a burger for €8.90 and vegetarian dishes for €7.50. Make sure to get in before the daily Happy Hour (5–8pm) is over, as there over 160 cocktails to choose from.

Cafés and bars

Café Datscha

MAP P.92, POCKET MAP A17
Gabriel-Max-Str. 1 Ⓤ Samariterstr. ⓣ 030 70 08 67 35, ⓦ cafe-datscha.de. Mon–Sat 10am–1am

Built in the style of a traditional Russian home – wood furniture, tall ceilings – albeit a fairly smart one, *Datscha* offers a rich spread of Russian and Ukrainian dishes like *borscht*, *blini* and *solyanka* (a spicy, sour soup). There's a daily changing lunch menu (€8) and Sunday brunch (10am–3pm; €12.40).

Big Brobot

Café Sybille

MAP P.92, POCKET MAP L5
Karl-Marx-Allee 72 ⓊStrausberger Platz
☎ 030 29 35 22 03, ⓦcafe-sibylle.de. Mon
11am–7pm, Tues–Sun 10am–7pm.
It's worth a stop at *Café Sybille*
not just for the ice cream, cakes
and coffee, but because it also
hosts a small museum about the
history of Karl-Marx-Allee, with
propaganda posters, socialist
statues and other exhibits to
browse while your drinks are
made. The restaurant closed in
2018, which led to many upset
Berliners. Luckily, a new owner
was found and the café reopened
its doors in 2019.

Cupcake Berlin

MAP P.92, POCKET MAP A17
Krossener Str. 12 ⓈSamariterstr. ☎ 030
25 76 86 87, ⓦcupcakeberlin.de. Daily
10am–8pm.
The city's first outlet dedicated
to cupcakes, all home-made by
American owner, Dawn, for sale
in a café that's every bit as sweet
and retro as her cakes. Brownies,
fantastic New York cheesecake
and apple pie are also available (all
around €2.80). There's a second
Cupcake Kreuzberg at Köpenicker
Str. 4.

Dachkammer

MAP P.92, POCKET MAP A17
Simon-Dach-Str. 39 Ⓢ/ⓊWarschauerstr.
☎ 030 29 04 90 54, ⓦdachkammer.com.
Daily 1pm until late.
The largest and possibly most
sociable place on the strip –
the combination of rustic bar
downstairs and retro bar upstairs
has made this a local classic.

Goodies Berlin

MAP P.92, POCKET MAP A17
Warschauer Str. 69 ⓊFrankfurter Tor
☎ 176 72 50 33 39, ⓦgoodies-berlin.
de. Mon–Fri 7.30am–7pm, Sat & Sun
9am–7pm.
Goodies is a tiny, wholesome café
serving home-made baked goods,
sandwiches, bagels, daily-changing
organic soup, plus salads and vegan
options. Free wi-fi and a children's
area. Cash only.

Hops & Barley

MAP P.92, POCKET MAP A17
Wühlischstr. 22/23 ⓈSamariterstr. or
Ⓢ/ⓊWarschauerstr. ☎ 030 29 36 75 34,
ⓦhopsandbarley-berlin.de. Mon–Fri 5pm
till late, Sat & Sun 3pm till late.
This unassuming wood-and-tiles
brewpub attracts a diverse crowd
that ranges from international
hipsters to elderly locals. Five
draft beers (three standard and
two experimental ones) that are
produced on-site, supplemented by
simple snacks such as sausages and
brewer's grain bread.

Kosmetiksalon Babette

MAP P.92, POCKET MAP K4
Karl-Marx-Allee 36 ⓊSchillingstr. ☎ 017
63 83 88 943, ⓦwww.barbabette.com.
Daily from 6pm.
This glass box, once a GDR
cosmetics shop, is now a chic
and lively bar. At night, the
only identifying marker is the
warm glow of the cube's interior
lights. The ground floor is
sparsely furnished, while the
former treatment rooms upstairs
occasionally have book readings
and performances.

Macondo Café

MAP P.92, POCKET MAP A17
Gärtnerstr. 14 ⓊSamariterstr. ☎ 030 54
73 59 43. Mon–Fri noon–late, Sat & Sun
from 10am.
Kitted out with fraying vintage
furniture, this local chill-out spot
offers a good selection of books
and board games and a great
atmosphere for lounging. Serves
brunch at weekends.

Soylent

MAP P.92, POCKET MAP A17
Gabriel-Max-Str. 3. ⓈSamariterstr. ☎ 030
29 36 94 63, ⓦcafesoylent.eu. Mon–Sun
6pm–late
One of the locals' favourites in this
area, the bar has a vintage living

room feel with walls covered in graffiti and psychedelic murals – which can spark some interesting converstations. A great selection of German beers, ales and crowd pleasing-cocktails.

Spielwiese

MAP P.92, POCKET MAP A17
Kopernikusstr. 24 ◎ Warschauer Str.
☎ 030 28 03 40 88, ◐ spielwiese-berlin.de. Mon 5–11pm, Thurs & Fri 6pm–midnight, Sat 3pm–midnight, Sun 3–8pm.

This café and games publisher stocks over 1800 games, from chess to Risk. For a small fee (€1/person), you can play games in the café or rent them (€1–3/day) to take home.

Szimpla

MAP P.92, POCKET MAP B17
Gärtnerstr. 15 ◎ Warschauer Str/
◎ Samariterstr. ☎ 030 66 30 85 23, ◐ szimpla.de. Sun & Mon 9am–midnight, Tue & Wed 9am–1am, Thurs–Sat 9am–2am

From breakfast, brunch, cocktails and beer, Szimpla will be able to satisfy every need. The name comes from a famous bar in Budapest, which made its way to Berlin. It's located on the corner of Boxhagener Platz, which makes it a great location for a Sunday brunch after some flea market shopping.

Clubs and venues

://about blank

MAP P.92, POCKET MAP M7
Markgrafendamm 24c ◎ Ostkreuz
◐ aboutparty.net. Club Thurs–Sun midnight till late; from 7pm for midweek live shows. €10–14.

Set inside a nondescript concrete block, this is one of the city's better underground clubs, with two main dancefloors, lots of nooks and crannies, and a garden where DJs spin in the summer. The dominant music policy is house and techno with occasional

forays into related electronic genres plus live concerts.

Berghain/Panoramabar

MAP P.92, POCKET MAP L6
Am Wriezener Bahnhof ◎ Ostbahnhof
☎ 030 29 36 02 10, ◐ berghain.de. Fri & Sat midnight–late. €12–18.

A strong contender for best club in the city, if not the world, this former power station attracts techno fans from all over the globe for its fantastic sound system, purist music policy and awe-inspiring industrial interior. The best time to arrive is after 5am on Saturday morning; the club runs till Sunday evening. In 2017, the club opened up the ground floor for more experimental sounds.

Insel

MAP P.92, POCKET MAP M7
Alt-Treptow 6, Treptow ◎ Plänterwald
☎ 030 80 96 18 50, ◐ inselberlin.de. Tues–Fri noon till late, Sat & Sun 3pm till late.

Reliable venue for thrash/punk gigs and club nights, on a Spree island that's part of Treptower Park. Occasional outdoor raves on the large terrace in summer.

Radialsystem V

MAP P.92, POCKET MAP K6
Holzmarktstr. 33 ◎ Ostbahnhof ☎ 030 28 87 88 588, ◐ radialsystem.de. Ticket office Mon–Fri 10am–7pm, Sat noon–7pm. For evening performances, the box office opens one hour before the show.

This sprawling space, housed in a former pumping station on the Spree, was retrofitted and reopened as a space for the arts in 2006, with a glass extension added. As well as visual and performing arts exhibitions, it hosts events ranging from opera concerts to relaxed jam sessions.

RAW Gelände

MAP P.92, POCKET MAP A17
Revaler Str. 99 ◎/◎ Warschauerstr.
◐ rawcc.org. Entry prices and opening times vary.

Berghain/Panoramabar

Sprawling, heavily graffitied ensemble of former train yard buildings, now one of the city's most alternative clubbing and cultural complexes. There are several shabby-chic bars and clubs, including the laidback Crack Bellmer (Ⓦ crackbellmer. de) and the more upbeat electro and techno clubs Cassiopeia (Ⓦ cassiopeia-berlin.de) and Suicide Circus (Ⓦ suicide-berlin .com). Urban Spree (Ⓦ urbanspree.com), a beer garden that often has DJs and live music into the night, is at the Warschauer Strasse side, and there's even a chic outdoor pool with a club and concert space called Haubentauscher (Ⓦ haubentaucher.berlin).

Rosi's

MAP P.92, POCKET MAP B17
Revaler Str. 29 Ⓤ Warschauer Str. Ⓦ rosis-berlin.de. Thurs–Sat from 11pm.

Nothing more – or less – than a derelict industrial shack, decorated with secondhand furniture, graffiti and ping-pong tables, *Rosi's* puts on some very decent indie, punk and electronic nights. Best in summer when the beer garden is open for barbecues.

Salon zur Wilden Renate

MAP P.92, POCKET MAP M7
Alt-Stralau 70 Ⓢ Treptower Park. ⓘ 030 25 04 14 26 Ⓦ renate.cc.
Located near the train tracks that run towards Treptower Park, *Renate* is an artist-run event space in a semi-derelict house with three floors, a cocktail bar and flamboyant decor that changes with each party. The music is good and the crowd is mixed. Open-air sister club, *Else*, just across the bridge, hosts open-air parties and has a beer garden open from Wed–Sun.

West Kreuzberg

The western section of Kreuzberg is centred on the main streets of Gneisenaustrasse and Bergmannstrasse, and pretty Viktoriapark. Once one of the poorest areas in Berlin, it's now one of its most bourgeois and bohemian and lies in sharp contrast to the more scruffy, multicultural part of the district to the east. Indeed, walking along café- and boutique-lined streets like Bergmannstrasse you're reminded of the gentrified environs of Prenzlauer Berg. At the end of this street is Viktoriapark, whose Iron Cross monument gives the district its name, and nearby is Chamissoplatz, which hosts a popular organic farmers' market every Saturday morning.

Mauermuseum – Museum Haus am Checkpoint Charlie

MAP P.102, POCKET MAP C15
Friedrichstr. 43–45 ⓤ Kochstr. ☏ 030 25 37 250, ⓦ mauermuseum.de. Daily 9am–10pm. €14.50.

"Checkpoint C" (or "Checkpoint Charlie" as it was called by the Western Allies) was the best-known Berlin Wall crossing point between East and West Berlin during the Cold War. Today it's one of the key places to learn about life in Berlin during the division. The museum – founded in 1962 by Dr Rainer Hildebrandt – is marked by the well-known "YOU ARE NOW LEAVING THE AMERICAN SECTOR" sign that remains outside the building alongside stone-faced (mock) guards, and a replica of the checkpoint (the original is in the Allied Museum in Dahlem). One of the most

Checkpoint Charlie

visited museums in Berlin, its exhibitions focus mostly on the creative ways East Berliners tried to escape – hot-air balloons, vehicles with special compartments, even a one-man submarine. There are also exhibits on the concept of freedom and nonviolent protest in general, including the Charter 77 typewriter and Mahatma Gandhi's diary.

Topography of Terror

MAP P.102, POCKET MAP F6
Niederkirchnerstr. 8 ①/Ⓢ Potsdamer Platz
☎ 030 25 45 09 50, Ⓦ www.topographie.de.
Daily 10am–8pm. Free.

From 1933–1945, the headquarters of the Gestapo, their "house prison" and the Reich Security main office stood on this site, making it one of the most notorious locations of Nazi brutality. It's now called the Topography of Terror (Topographie des Terrors) documentation centre, and though many of the buildings were destroyed in World War II, visitors can walk around the largely open-air museum, where exhibits display the history of the site, and explore the events of the Holocaust. A documentation centre focuses on the central institutions of the SS and police in the Third Reich and their crimes. The displays are graphic, so families with children should exercise caution. An audio-guide is available.

Martin-Gropius-Bau

MAP P.102, POCKET MAP F6
Niederkirchnerstr. 7 ①/Ⓢ Potsdamer Platz
☎ 030 25 48 60, Ⓦ gropiusbau.de. Wed–Mon 10am–7pm. Prices vary from €10–15.

Envisioned as an applied arts museum, the stunning Martin-Gropius-Bau has evolved into one of Berlin's major contemporary art venues. The ornate, Renaissancestyle building was badly damaged during World War II, and rebuilt 1978–81. It draws big-name international displays on art and history, such as retrospectives of Frida Kahlo and Méret Oppenheim and exhibitions by the likes of Ai Weiwei.

Deutsches Technikmuseum

Anhalter Bahnhof

MAP P.102, POCKET MAP F7
Askanischer Platz 6 ① Mendelssohn-Bartholdy-Park ☎ 030 50 58 68 30. Free.

This haunting landmark is a remnant of the Anhalter Bahnhof, once one of Berlin's busiest railway stations. The terminus opened in 1841, but its notoriety stems from World War II when it was one of the three stations used to deport Jews to Theresienstadt (or Terezín), and from there to the death camps. Nearly ten thousand Jews were deported from here, usually in groups of fifty to a hundred; the last train left on March 27, 1945. Though badly damaged in World War II, it was only closed in 1952. Today, all that remains is a portion of the entrance facade and a commemorative plaque, though an S-Bahn station shares its name.

Deutsches Technikmuseum

MAP P.102, POCKET MAP F7
Trebbiner Str. 9 ① Gleisdreieck ☎ 030 90 25 40, Ⓦ www.sdtb.de. Tues–Fri 9am–5.30pm, Sat & Sun 10am–6pm. €8.

Opened in 1982 in the former goods depot of the Anhalter

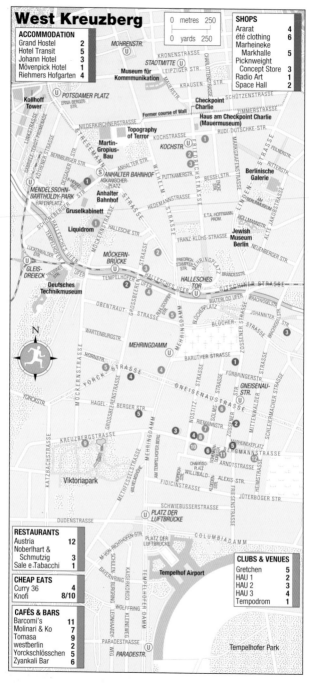

WEST KREUZBERG

West Kreuzberg

| 0 metres | 250 |
| 0 yards | 250 |

ACCOMMODATION
Grand Hostel	2
Hotel Transit	5
Johann Hotel	3
Mövenpick Hotel	1
Riehmers Hofgarten	4

SHOPS
Ararat	4
été clothing	6
Marheineke Markhalle	5
Picknweight Concept Store	3
Radio Art	1
Space Hall	2

RESTAURANTS
Austria	12
Noberlhart & Schmutzig	3
Sale e Tabacchi	1

CHEAP EATS
| Curry 36 | 4 |
| Knofi | 8/10 |

CAFÉS & BARS
Barcomi's	11
Molinari & Ko	7
Tomasa	9
westberlin	2
Yorckschlösschen	5
Zyankali Bar	6

CLUBS & VENUES
Gretchen	5
HAU 1	2
HAU 2	3
HAU 3	4
Tempodrom	1

Map labels:
MOHRENSTR. · KRONENSTRASSE · STADTMITTE · LEIPZIGER STR. · Museum für Kommmunikation · KRAUSEN- · Kollhoff Tower · POTSDAMER PLATZ · ERNA-BERGER-STR. · Checkpoint Charlie · Haus am Checkpoint Charlie (Mauermuseum) · Former course of Wall · NIEDERKIRCHNERSTRASSE · Topography of Terror · KOCHSTRASSE · RUDI-DUTSCHKE-STR. · STRESEMANNSTR. · Martin-Gropius-Bau · KOCHSTR. · ANHALTER STR. · Berlinische Galerie · ANHALTER BAHNHOF · PUTTKAMERSTR. · BESSELSTR. · MENDELSSOHN-BARTHOLDY-PARK · ASKANISCHER PLATZ · Anhalter Bahnhof · HEDEMANNSTRASSE · E.T.A.-HOFFMANN-PROM. · HOLLMANNSTR. · Gruselkabinett · Jewish Museum Berlin · Liquidrom · FRANZ-KLÜHS-STRASSE · NEUENBURGER STR. · LUCKENWALDER STR. · MÖCKERN-BRÜCKE · FRIEDRICH-STAMPFER-STR. · MEHRINGPLATZ · BRANDESSTR. · GLEIS-DREIECK · TEMPELHOFER UFER · HALLESCHES TOR · GITSCHINER STRASSE · Deutsches Technikmuseum · OBENTRAUT-STRASSE · GROSSBEERENSTRASSE · WATERLOO-UFER · BLÜCHERPLATZ · BLÜCHER-STRASSE · JOHANNITER · WARTENBURGSTR. · MEHRINGDAMM · BARUTHER STRASSE · FÜRBRINGERSTR. · HORNSTR. · YORCK-STRASSE · GNEISENAUSTRASSE · GNEISENAU-STR. · YORCKSTR. · HAGEL- · BERGER STR. · NOSTITZ · SOLMS- · RIEMANNSTR. · ZOSSENER STR. · KREUZBERGSTRASSE · MARHEINEKEPLATZ · BERGMANNSTRASSE · Viktoriapark · AM TEMPELHOFER BERG · CHAMISSO PLATZ · WILLIBALD- · ARNDTSTRASSE · FIDICINSTRASSE · ALEXIS-STR. · JÜTERBOGER STR. · SCHWIEBUSSERSTRASSE · DUDENSTRASSE · PLATZ DER LUFTBRÜCKE · COLUMBIADAMM · M-VON-RICHTHOFEN-STR. · Tempelhof Airport · KAISERKORSO · WOLFFRING · PARADESTRASSE · PARADESTR. · Tempelhofer Park

Bahnhof, the German Technology Museum presents a comprehensive (some might say overwhelming) overview of German technology. The vast collection includes trains, planes, computers, radios, cameras and more. There's a strong emphasis on rail, with trains from 1835 to the present day, but there are also maritime and aviation halls and exhibits on the industrial revolution, the computer and space age, and the pharmaceutical and chemical industry. A new exhibition on information and communication networks and the history of mobility is housed in the annexe on Ladestrasse. Much of the museum is based on life-sized reproductions and actual machines, though the Science Center Spectrum annexe at Möckernstrasse 26 is more interactive.

Jewish Museum Berlin

MAP P.102, POCKET MAP G7
Lindenstr. 9–14 ⓤ Hallesches Tor/Kochstr. ☏ 030 25 99 33 00, ⓦ www.jmberlin.de. Daily 10am–8pm. €6.

Daniel Libeskind's Jewish Museum (Jüdisches Museum) is a must-see, both historically and architecturally. The stark, zinc-covered building has been thoughtfully designed, with each element symbolizing various aspects of the historical Jewish experience over some two thousand years. The process of moving through the building – which really is a work of art – is an experience in itself, not least thanks to its five vertical voids and walls of dark concrete. Guided tours are available and the restaurant serving traditional Jewish cuisine (though not kosher) is very good. Note that the permanent exhibition is closed until 2020, when a new permanent exhibition and children's museum will be added.

Berlinische Galerie

MAP P.102, POCKET MAP H7
Alte Jakobstr. 124–128 ⓤ Hallesches Tor/Kochstr. ☏ 030 78 90 26 00, ⓦ www.

berlinischegalerie.de. Daily except Tues 10am–6pm. €10, €6 first Mon of the month; special exhibition prices vary; combined ticket with Jewish Museum available. Guided tours in English first Mon of month at 3pm.

Founded in 1975 as a private institution, the Berlinische Galerie was once part of the Martin-Gropius-Bau before moving to its current premises in 2004. Its mission is to showcase art made in Berlin, bringing together fine art, photography and architecture. The permanent exhibition includes works from 1870 to the present day, spanning major movements such as the Secessionists, Fluxus, Dada and the Expressionists, with works by Max Liebermann, Otto Dix, Georg Grosz and Hannah Höch. A spacious hall also hosts temporary exhibitions and there are tours, occasional lectures and film screenings.

Berlin Story Museum & Hitler Documentation

MAP P.102, POCKET MAP F7
Schöneberger Str. 23a ⓤ Mendelssohn-Bartholdy-Park ☏ 030 20 45 46 73, ⓦ berlinstory.de. Daily 10am–7pm (last admission 5.30pm). €6 (museum), €12 (Hitler Documentation).

The Memory Void, Jewish Museum Berlin

Tempelhofer Park

This attraction, set inside a WW2 bunker, features 800 years of Berlin history (free audioguide included) in the Berlin Story Museum, plus a more controversial exhibition about Adolf Hitler's life and WW2 that includes a reconstruction of his living and working rooms from the original "Führerbunker" near Potsdamer Platz.

Viktoriapark

MAP P.102, POCKET MAP F9
Between Kreuzbergstr., Dudenstr., Katzbachstr. and Methfesselstr.
Ⓤ Yorckstr./Mehringdamm. Open 24hr.
Famous for hosting Berlin's highest peak, "Vikky Park" is one of the most popular in the city. A multitude of pathways winds around and up the hill to give visitors stunning panoramic views, and there are playgrounds, landscaped rose gardens, a tumbling waterfall and even vineyards to enjoy and explore; the well-known *Golgatha* beer garden provides shade and sustenance.

Tempelhofer Park

MAP P.102, POCKET MAP G9
Columbiadamm 192 Ⓤ Südstern
Ⓦ tempelhofer-park.de. Park daily sunrise to sunset (see website for exact times); free. Airport tours (2hr) Wed–Sun 1.30pm.

€15. Booking: Ⓦ www.thf-berlin.de, ☎ 030 200 03 7441.
The largest park in continental Europe, Tempelhofer Park is the site of the now defunct Tempelhof airport, an immense building created by the Nazis (the terminal was designed to resemble an eagle) which became famous for the 1948–49 Berlin Airlift. Tours of the airport building, which stages events through the year, relate the story. The huge space surrounding the airport doesn't boast any actual attractions but is still a great place to go cycling, walking, roller-skating – or to enjoy a picnic (which can be purchased on site).

Liquidrom

MAP P.102, POCKET MAP F7
Möckernstr. 10 Ⓤ Möckernbrücke ☎ 030 25 80 07 820, Ⓦ liquidrom-berlin.de.
Mon–Thurs & Sun 9am–midnight, Fri & Sat 9am–1am.
This designer spa features saunas, slightly cramped chill-out areas and a large, domed flotation pool where you can drift and listen to soft electronic music, sometimes mixed live by DJs, as well as readings and live concerts. A range of massage treatments are also available. A two-hour sauna and thermal bath is €20.

Shops

Ararat

MAP P.102, POCKET MAP G9
Bergmannstr. 9 ⓤ Gneisenaustr. ☎ 030 69 35 080, ⓦ ararat-berlin.de. Mon–Sat 10am–8pm.

It's easy to lose yourself in here, surrounded by prints and picture frames; over the road at no. 99, another branch sells postcards and gifts.

été clothing

MAP P.102, POCKET MAP G9
Bergmannstr. 18 ⓤ Gneisenaustr. ☎ 030 32 89 55 43, ⓦ ete-clothing.de. Mon–Sat 11am–8pm.

With shirts and hoodies from trusted brands like RVLT, Volcom and Iriedaily, and a decent range of sneakers, this is a good stop for streetwear in Kreuzberg.

Marheineke Markhalle

MAP P.102, POCKET MAP G9
Marheinekeplatz 15 ⓤ Gneisenaustr. ⓦ meine-markthalle.de. Mon–Fri 8am–8pm, Sat 8am–6pm.

This popular covered market hall is an excellent place for grocery shopping as well as for breakfasts and lunches. Stalls often emphasize organic and regional products. You'll also find crêpes and tapas, as well as regular art exhibitions and events.

Picknweight Concept Store

MAP P.102, POCKET MAP G9
Bergmannstr. 102 ⓤ Mehringdamm ☎ 030 69 43 348, ⓦ picknweight.de. Mon–Sat 11am–7pm.

A retro paradise with secondhand clothes spanning the 1960s to 1980s – particularly good on the 1970s.

Radio Art

MAP P.102, POCKET MAP G8
Zossener Str. 2 ⓤ Mehringdamm ☎ 030 69 39 435, ⓦ radio-art.de. Thurs & Fri noon–6pm, Sat 10am–1pm.

A visually satisfying shop for radio lovers, its shelves brimming with vintage (and some modern) radio sets and record players.

Space Hall

MAP P.102, POCKET MAP G8
Zossener Str. 33 ⓤ Gneisenaustr. ☎ 030 69 47 664. Mon–Wed & Fri–Sat 11am–8pm, Thurs till 10pm.

This excellent two-store, multi-roomed record shop offers a large CD collection at no. 33 (rock, pop, electronic, rap) and DJ-friendly vinyl at no. 35.

Restaurants

Austria

MAP P.102, POCKET MAP G9
Bergmannstr. 30, on Marheineke Platz ⓤ Gneisenaustr. ☎ 030 69 44 440, ⓦ austria-berlin.de. Mon 6–midnight, Tues–Sun noon–midnight.

Austria serves classic Austrian dishes, using organic ingredients, in a hunting lodge-style interior. The huge Schnitzel is justly famous (mains €13.50–20.80).

Nobelhart & Schmutzig

MAP P.102, POCKET MAP G6
Friedrichstr. 218 ⓤ Kochstr./ Checkpoint Charlie ☎ 030 25 94 06 10, ⓦ nobelhartundschmutzig.com. Tues–Sat 6.30–10.30pm.

Founded by sommelier Billy Wagner, formerly of *Weinbar Rutz* (see page 35) and chef Micha Schäfer, this chic spot offers delicious, creative food, fiercely committed to a local and seasonal ethos.

Sale e Tabacchi

MAP P.102, POCKET MAP G6
Rudi-Dutschke-Str. 23 ⓤ Kochstr. ☎ 030 25 21 155, ⓦ www.sale-e-tabacchi.de. Daily 10am–11.30pm.

Located towards the Mitte end of Kreuzberg, "Salt and Tobacco" has a more classic feel than most restaurants in the area. It's known for its excellent seafood dishes (tuna €26, monkfish €24) and Italian wines; the menu changes daily. The interior is large and airy and there's a garden out back.

Cheap eats

Curry 36

MAP P.102, POCKET MAP G8

Mehringdamm 36 ⓤ Mehringdamm ⓣ 030 25 17 368. Daily 9am–5pm.

Everyone in Berlin has a favourite place to eat *Currywurst* – sausage doused in curry sauce – but *Curry 36* is cited more often than most (along with *Konnopke's*, see page 85); its popularity alone guarantees it's a buzzy place to grab a snack (around €1.50).

Knofi

MAP P.102, POCKET MAP G9

Bergmannstr. 11 & 98 ⓤ Gneisenaustr. ⓣ 030 69 56 43 59 (no. 11), ⓣ 030 69 45 807 (no. 98). Daily 8am–midnight (no. 11); daily 9am–midnight (no, 98).

There are two *Knofis* opposite each other. At no. 11 you'll find a small deli-style restaurant serving tasty Turkish food. Over the road is a Turkish deli.

Cafés and bars

Barcomi's

MAP P.102, POCKET MAP G9

Bergmannstr. 21 ⓤ Gneisenaustr. ⓣ 030 69 48 138, ⓦ www.barcomis.de. Mon–Fri 8am–9pm, Sat & Sun 9am–9pm.

Not quite as cosy as its Mitte branch (see page 36), but you can find excellent quality coffee – *Barcomi's* roasts its thirteen coffee varieties here, hence the decorative coffee sacks and delicious odour – as well as handmade breads, pastries, soups and sandwiches.

Molinari & Ko

MAP P.102, POCKET MAP G9

Riemannstr. 13 ⓤ Gneisenaustr. ⓣ 030 69 13 903, ⓦ www.molinari-ko.de. Mon–Fri 8am–midnight, Sat & Sun 9am–midnight.

This welcoming Italian café/bar/ restaurant, hidden away on a residential street, offers a menu of breakfast and snacks, pasta and pizza. A decent wine and beer selection make it a good choice for evenings, too.

Tomasa

MAP P.102, POCKET MAP F9

Kreuzbergstr. 62 ⓤ Mehringdamm ⓣ 030 81 00 98 85, ⓦ www.tomasa.de. Sun–Wed 9am–midnight, Thurs–Sat 9am–1am.

This old-school villa, on the edge of Viktoriapark, is a particularly pleasant place for a relaxed breakfast or lunch. The classic interior, good seasonal menu (from tapas to pasta and German dishes) and friendly service attract a mixed clientele, families included. Sunday brunch is very popular.

westberlin

MAP P.102, POCKET MAP G6

Friedrichstr. 215 ⓤ Kochstr. ⓣ 030 25 92 27 45, ⓦ westberlin-bar-shop.de. Mon–Fri 8.30am–7pm, Sat & Sun 10am–6pm.

This handsome haven is part chic media hangout and part café. Occupying a grittier part of Friedrichstrasse that's only just starting to come to life, you can sip on a locally roasted flat white while working away on your laptop or enjoying a delicious cake, sandwich or quiche. They also have a decent selection of fashion and style magazines as well as Berlin guides.

Yorckschlösschen

MAP P.102, POCKET MAP F8

Yorckstr. 15 ⓤ Mehringdamm ⓣ 030 21 58 070, ⓦ www.yorckschloesschen.de. Mon–Sat 5pm–3am, Sun 11am–3am.

This place has been a Kreuzberg institution for over a hundred years, though it doesn't seem to have been updated since the 1970s. The menu is mostly basic and local – meatballs and *Leberkäse* (meatloaf) – and the service gruff, but the tree-shaded garden is a very pleasant place to eat. Live jazz, blues and country bands play most days (Wed–Sat 9pm, Sun 2pm).

Zyankali Bar

MAP P.102, POCKET MAP G8

Gneisenaustr. 17 ⓤ Gneisenaustr. ⓣ 030 68

Radio Art

83 01 70, ⓦ zyankali.de. Daily from 4pm.
This unique "herbal clinic" bar
has an incredible range of strange
and surprising cocktails (often
with home-made ingredients),
occasional DJs and a "play area"
with football and pinball, and a
beer garden with plenty of seating.
Alcohol-infused ice-cream (summer
only) and snacks like *dim sum* and
Hawaiian toast are also served.

Clubs and venues

Gretchen

MAP P.102, POCKET MAP G8
Obentrautstr. 19-21 ⓤ Hallesches Tor
ⓣ 030 25 92 27 02, ⓦ gretchen-club.de.
Opening times and admission varies.
Named after a murderous character
in Goethe's *Faust*, this alternative
club space offers a handsome
interior that's all columns and
vaulted ceilings, and a mix of
electronic sounds (drum 'n' bass,

dubstep, trip hop). A refreshing
alternative to the usual Berlin
"techno-shack" formulas.

Hebbel am Ufer

MAP P.102, POCKET MAP G7
HAU1 Stresemannstr. 29; HAU2 Hallesches
Ufer 32; HAU3 Tempelhofer Ufer 10
ⓤ Hallesches Tor ⓣ 030 25 90 04 27,
ⓦ www.hebbel-am-ufer.de.
These three neighbouring venues
of HAU Hebbel am Ufer – HAU1,
HAU2 and HAU3 – are *the* places
for ground-breaking theatre, the
occasional concert and more.

Tempodrom

MAP P.102, POCKET MAP F7
Möckernstr. 10 ⓤ Möckernbrücke ⓣ 030
74 73 70 (ⓣ 1806 554 111 – ticket hotline),
ⓦ www.tempodrom.de.
A giant tent-like arena in the
heart of Berlin, Tempodrom puts
on concerts, shows, plays, galas,
conferences, fashion shows – you
name it, Tempodrom's hosted it.

East Kreuzberg

An isolated section of West Berlin throughout the Cold War, Kreuzberg has since grown into one of Berlin's most colourful districts – a magnet for left-wing anarchists, LGBT culture, Turkish immigrants (it's sometimes called Little Istanbul) and, increasingly, hipsters and tourists. Despite being a coherent borough (nowadays part of Kreuzberg-Friedrichshain), Kreuzberg is still largely considered two distinct halves roughly coterminous with the former postal codes: SO 36 and SW 61 in the eastern and western sides respectively. Much of the eastern part of Kreuzberg abutted the wall on the West side and was strongly associated with Berlin's squatter and anarchist scenes. Though the area has gentrified somewhat since those heady days, it maintains a grungy, vibrant feel that spreads out from Schlesisches Tor down to Kottbusser Tor and beyond, fuelled by an ever-expanding series of excellent independent bars, clubs and restaurants.

Museum der Dinge
MAP P.108, POCKET MAP J7

Oranienstr. 25 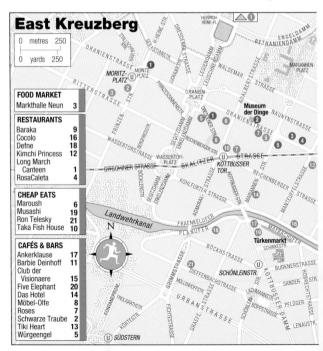 Kottbusser Tor ☏ 030 92 10 63 11, Ⓦ www.museumderdinge.de.

East Kreuzberg

| | metres | 250 |
| 0 | yards | 250 |

FOOD MARKET
Markthalle Neun ... 3

RESTAURANTS
Baraka ... 9
Cocolo ... 16
Defne ... 18
Kimchi Princess ... 12
Long March
  Canteen ... 1
RosaCaleta ... 4

CHEAP EATS
Maroush ... 6
Musashi ... 19
Ron Telesky ... 21
Taka Fish House ... 10

CAFÉS & BARS
Ankerklause ... 17
Barbie Deinhoff ... 11
Club der
  Visionaere ... 15
Five Elephant ... 20
Das Hotel ... 14
Möbel-Olfe ... 8
Roses ... 7
Schwarze Traube ... 2
Tiki Heart ... 13
Würgeengel ... 5

Mon & Thurs–Sun noon–7pm. €6.
A museum dedicated to the somewhat ambiguous culture of "things" could have gone either way. In fact it succeeds by presenting an interesting array of implements – around 25,000 to be precise. Everyday houseware, furniture and knick-knacks are mixed with the unusual, spanning the nineteenth century to the present day. Located on the top floor of a Kreuzberg apartment block, the museum is a design-fiend's dream, with exhibits including Manoli ashtrays, Art Deco fondue sets and World War II memorabilia, all inside a room that's modern and well organized. One of the latest attractions is the modular "Frankfurt Kitchen" designed by Viennese architect Margarete Schütte-Lihotzky in 1926 – the model for the fitted kitchen of today. The exhibition texts are in German and English, and you'll also find a colourful and nicely curated giftshop near the entrance.

Ramones Museum

MAP P.108, POCKET MAP L7
Oberbaumstr. 5 ⓤ Schlesisches Tor ☏ 030 61 28 53 99, ⓦ ramonesmuseum.com.
Daily 10am–10pm. €4.50 (concerts vary but mostly free).

Berlin's own shrine to the American proto-punks, the Ramones Museum was started by music editor Flo Hayler two decades ago. Back then the collection amounted to a few signed posters and some T-shirts, but today it has expanded to over three hundred items of memorabilia. It's certainly an eclectic assortment, ranging from childhood photos of the group to gig set lists and flyers. The museum also hosts film screenings, the odd acoustic show from artists as well known as Fran Healy from Travis and special events. There's a decent café (*Mania*) inside selling coffee, beer and snacks.

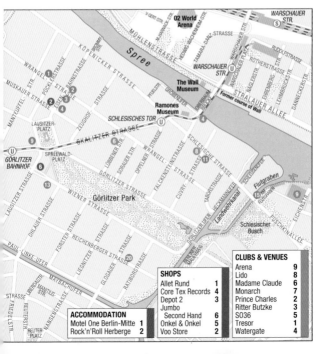

SHOPS

Allet Rund	1
Core Tex Records	4
Depot 2	3
Jumbo Second Hand	6
Onkel & Onkel	5
Voo Store	2

CLUBS & VENUES

Arena	9
Lido	8
Madame Claude	6
Monarch	7
Prince Charles	2
Ritter Butzke	3
SO36	5
Tresor	1
Watergate	4

ACCOMMODATION

Motel One Berlin-Mitte	1
Rock'n'Roll Herberge	2

Shops

Allet Rund

MAP P.108, POCKET MAP J7

Dresdener Str. 16 ⓤ Kottbusser Tor ⓣ 030 27 01 48 36. Mon–Fri noon–7pm, Sat noon–5pm.

Joachin Semrau offers fair-trade, Kreuzberg-made designs for sizes 42 to 60, using European fabrics.

Core Tex Records

MAP P.108, POCKET MAP K7

Oranienstr. 3 ⓣ Görlitzer Bahnhof ⓣ 030 61 28 00 50, ⓦ coretexrecords.com. Mon–Sat 11am–8pm.

The best place for punk or hardcore music, plus T-shirts, accessories, books and concert tickets.

Depot 2

MAP P.108, POCKET MAP K7

Oranienstr. 9 ⓤ Görlitzer Bahnhof ⓣ 030 61 14 655, ⓦ www.depot2.de. Mon–Sat 11am–8pm.

An ice-cool assortment of street-oriented fashions, including Vans and other stylish footwear.

Jumbo Second Hand

MAP P.108, POCKET MAP K7

Wiener Str. 63 ⓤ Görlitzer Bahnhof. Mon–Sat 10am–8pm.

A quantity-over-quality secondhand clothes and accessories store. It's worth trying to bargain.

Onkel & Onkel

MAP P.108, POCKET MAP K7

Oranienstr. 195 ⓤ Kottbusser Tor ⓣ 033 203 26 90 14. Mon–Sat 10am–6pm.

A magazine shop that specializes in graphic design, photography and street-art books, Onkel & Onkel also publishes its own titles, all in a library-esque atmosphere.

Voo Store

MAP P.108, POCKET MAP J7

Oranienstr. 24 ⓤ Kottbusser Tor ⓣ 030 616 511 12, ⓦ vooberlin.com. Mon–Sat 10am–8pm.

A former locksmiths turned pop-culture concept shop, Voo Store's gorgeous interior was created by Danish designer and architect Sigurd Larsen, while its highly curated stock features both big names and little-known designers.

Food market

Markthalle Neun

MAP P.108, POCKET MAP K7

Eisenbahnstr. 42/43 ⓤ Görlitzer Bahnhof ⓦ markthalleneun.com. Basic market Tues–Thurs noon–6pm; farmers' market Fri noon–6pm & Sat 10am–6pm; shops Mon–Sat noon–6pm.

This revitalized nineteenth-century market hall has become Berlin's foodie destination, thanks to a weekly farmers' market (Thurs and Fri) and events focusing on sustainable and local produce and the especially popular weekly Street Food Thursday event (5–10pm).

Restaurants

Baraka

MAP P.108, POCKET MAP K7

Lausitzer Platz 6 ⓤ Görlitzer Bahnhof ⓣ 030 61 26 330. Mon–Thurs & Sun 11am–midnight, Fri & Sat 11am–1am.

North African food fans will adore *Baraka*. The decor is authentic without slipping into kitsch (although the back room comes close) and the food – *tagines*, chicken skewers, *schwarma* – is some of the best in town, and at decent prices (mains €5–12). The mixed plate for two is immense.

Cocolo

MAP P.108, POCKET MAP K8

Paul-Lincke-Ufer 39 ⓤ Kottbusser Tor ⓣ 030 98 33 90 73. Mon–Sat noon–11pm, Sun 6–11pm.

Unarguably Berlin's best dedicated *ramen* spot, *Cocolo* started life with its Mitte branch (Gipstr. 3), expanding to this larger Kreuzberg location in 2014. Enjoy their slurp-a-licious dishes (including sweet pork belly and *kimchi ramen*) at a shared table inside, or on the canal-facing terrace. Soups start at €9.

Defne

MAP P.108, POCKET MAP J8

Planufer 92c ⓤ Kottbusser Tor/Schönleinstr. ☎ 030 81 79 71 11, ⓦ www.defne-restaurant.de. Daily: April–Sept 4pm–1am; Oct–March 5pm–1am (kitchen till midnight all year).

Defne's Turkish and Mediterranean classics include *imam bayildi* (aubergines with pine nuts, peppers and tomato sauce, €9.90) and lamb skewers (€14.50). The interior is simple and spacious; the terrace, overlooking the Landwehrkanal, is lovely in summer.

Kimchi Princess

MAP P.108, POCKET MAP K7

Skalitzer Str. 36 ⓤ Kottbusser Tor ☎ 0163 45 80 203, ⓦ kimchiprincess.com. Sun–Thurs noon–10pm, Fri & Sat noon–11pm.

Part of a trend for cool Korean eateries in Berlin, *Kimchi Princess* offers simple wooden pallets as seating, a spacious interior and cool staff. There's *bibimbap* and more on the menu, but the Korean barbecue is the thing to go for (from €16.90). The owners also run the nearby *Angry Chicken* (Oranienstr. 16), a must for spice fans.

Core Tex Records

Long March Canteen

MAP P.108, POCKET MAP K7

Wrangelstr. 20 ⓤ Görlitzer Bahnhof ☎ 0178 884 9599, ⓦ longmarchcanteen .com. Daily 6pm–midnight.

Although folk justifiably flock here for the *dim sum* (€6–10), this trendy Chinese restaurant also serves up excellent, tapas-sized portions of other dishes like *pak choi* salad and marinated chicken skewers with water chestnuts. John Malkovich is just one of the A-listers who has been spotted here.

RosaCaleta

MAP P.108, POCKET MAP K7

Muskauer Str. 9 ⓤ Görlitzer Bahnhof ☎ 030 69 53 78 59, ⓦ rosacaleta.com. Winter Tues–Sat 6pm–1am, Sun 2pm–1am; summer Tues–Fri 11 am–1am, Sat 6pm–1am, Sun 2pm–1am.

This Jamaican/European fusion restaurant has created quite a buzz in a city hopelessly devoid of Caribbean cuisine. There's plenty of jerk-style food on the menu, but also dishes like oven-roast pork fillet, mango-ginger lentil salad and tofu and vegetable stew (mains from €10). It also functions as an art space and hosts DJ parties.

EAST KREUZBERG

Kimchi Princess

Cheap eats

Maroush

MAP P.108, POCKET MAP J7
Adalbertstr. 93 Ⓤ Kottbusser Tor Ⓣ 030 69
53 61 71. Daily 11am–2am.

With a cosy dining area, Middle Eastern decor and tasty sandwiches, kebabs, falafels and fresh salads, this small Lebanese restaurant is one of the better of its type. Vegetarian options also available.

Musashi

MAP P.108, POCKET MAP J8
Kottbusser Damm 102 Ⓤ Schönleinstr.
Ⓣ 030 69 32 042. Mon–Sat noon–10.30pm,
Sun 2–10pm.

This tiny spot serves up decent sushi in a refreshingly designer-free space, decorated with posters of sumo wrestlers and populated with just a few bar tables. The Japanese chefs prepare fresh, tasty *makis* and inside-out rolls for very good prices (€6.50 for a set menu).

Ron Telesky

MAP P.108, POCKET MAP J8
Dieffenbachstr. 62 Ⓤ Schönleinstr. Ⓣ 030
61 62 11 11. Tues–Fri 12.30–10pm, Sat &
Sun 1.30–10pm.

Canadian pizza served from a canoe – how can you say no? Especially when the pizza toppings include sweet potato, mango, feta and maple syrup. Aside from the canoe (outside) the interior features national emblems like a moose head. Vegan options available.

Taka Fish House

MAP P.108, POCKET MAP J7
Adalbertstr. 97 Ⓤ Kottbusser Tor Ⓣ 0157
74 24 62 19. Mon–Thurs 9am–11pm, Fri–
Sun 9am–2am.

Tucked away on bustling Kottbusser Tor and surrounded by kebab and falafel shops, this unassuming Turkish *Imbiss* has just a handful of tables inside and out, but serves up some of the most delicious, freshly grilled fish sandwiches in the city.

Cafés and bars

Ankerklause

MAP P.108, POCKET MAP J8
Kottbusser Damm 104 Ⓤ Kottbusser Tor
Ⓣ 030 69 35 649, Ⓦ www.ankerklause.de.
Mon 4pm–4am, Tues–Sun 10am–4am.

Situated by Maybachufer, next to the Turkish market (Tues & Fri; see page 117), *Ankerklause* is a popular café during the day, with a decent range of snacks (and seats out front and a terrace overlooking the water out back). Later, there's something of the alternative scene about it when the jukebox plays rock 'n' roll classics.

Barbie Deinhoff

MAP P.108, POCKET MAP L7
Schlesische Str. 16 ⓤ Schlesisches Tor.
Tues–Sat 6pm–late.

This colourful dive bar is a lot of fun, attracting a heady mix of transvestites, gay men and curious onlookers. The decor runs from deliberately kitsch to the colourfully futuristic and there are regular DJs and happenings. A fun place to get comprehensively trashed (two-for-one happy hour Tues 7pm–midnight), though there are also often cultural events early evening.

Club der Visionaere

MAP P.108, POCKET MAP M8
Am Flutgraben 1 ⓤ Schlesisches Tor ⓣ 030 69 51 89 42, ⓦ www.clubdervisionaere. com. May–Sept: Mon–Fri 2pm–late, Sat & Sun noon–late. Admission €1–5.

Just beyond the Kreuzberg/Treptow border, this legendary summer-only techno bar enjoys a unique setting on the intersection of the Spree and Flutgraben canal. The bar and DJ booth is in an old ceramic-tiled boathouse, and punters stand (and dance) on the floating docks outside. It's minimal techno all the way and a fantastically upbeat place.

Five Elephant

MAP P.108, POCKET MAP L8
Reichenberger Str. 101 ⓤ Görlitzer Bahnhof ⓣ 030 96 08 15 27, ⓦ www .fiveelephant. com. Mon–Fri 8.30am–7pm, Sat & Sun 10am–7pm.

Opened by American and Austrian team Kris Shackman and Sophie Weigensamer in 2010, this highly regarded café not only brews (and roasts) some of the best "third wave" coffee in town, but also has a much talked about cheesecake selection. There's a second location at Alte Schönhauser Str. 14, in Mitte.

Das Hotel

MAP P.108, POCKET MAP J8
Mariannenstr. 26a ⓤ Kottbusser Tor ⓣ 030 84 11 84 33. Daily noon–open end.

Located on a residential street near the Paul-Linke-Ufer, *Das Hotel* is a combination bar, club and bistro that serves burritos and coffee. The candlelit bar is charming but get there early at weekends or you won't get a seat. The downstairs club plays music from the 1940s onwards, with a "no hits and no techno" policy.

Möbel-Olfe

MAP P.108, POCKET MAP J7
Reichenberger Str. 177 ⓤ Kottbusser Tor ⓣ 030 23 27 46 90, ⓦ moebel-olfe.de. Tues–Sun 6pm–late.

Sandwiched between a string of Turkish snack bars in a run-down building behind Kottbusser Tor, this unusual, smoky, local bar attracts gays, hipsters, ageing drunks and more. There are regular DJ nights but it's more about experiencing the diversity of the Kreuzberg crowds.

Roses

MAP P.108, POCKET MAP K7
Oranienstr. 187 ⓤ Kottbusser Tor/Görlitzer Bahnhof ⓣ 030 61 56 570. Daily 10pm–6am.

A legendary gay hangout, *Roses* provides a welcoming bosom for all manner of sexual orientations to crowd around. The kitsch decor mirrors the clientele and the fun vibe well. Sunday is the main day – and the "gayest" – but women are welcome anytime.

Schwarze Traube

MAP P.108, POCKET MAP K7
Wrangelstr. 24 ⓤ Görlitzer Bahnhof ⓣ 030

23 13 55 69. Daily 7pm till late.
Like many of Berlin's best
drinking spots, this cocktail bar
looks fairly nondescript from the
outside. Knock on the door and –
if it's not full – you'll be ushered
into a cosy, dimly lit bar with
rickety furnishings and award-
winning drinks.

Tiki Heart

MAP P.108, POCKET MAP K8
Wiener Str. 20 ⓤ Görlitzer Bahnhof ☏ 030
61 07 47 03, ⓦ tikiheart.de. Daily from
10am.

Berlin's only Hawaiian rockabilly-
themed joint is renowned for its
unapologetically kitsch interior and
innovative menu. The breakfasts,
served till 5pm, feature items
like the "Oi-Fast" – a heady mix
of scrambled eggs and chorizo.
There are veggie burgers and –
one for the serious rockers – a
Lemmy burger grilled in whisky.
Strong cocktails are served and
the *Wild at Heart* club next door
(ⓦwildatheartberlin.de) roars into
action with regular rock, punk,
metal and surf nights.

Würgeengel

MAP P.108, POCKET MAP J7
Dresdener Str. 122 ⓤ Kottbusser Tor ☏ 030
61 55 560, ⓦ wuergeengel.de. Daily
7pm–late.

One of the best cocktail bars in
Kreuzberg, "the exterminating
angel" has red walls, great tapas,
decadent decor and an extensive
cocktail and wine list. The
feel is timeless, though with a
trendy clientele.

Clubs and venues

Arena

MAP P.108, POCKET MAP M8
Eichenstr. 4 ⓤ Treptower Park ☏ 030 53
32030, ⓦ arena-berlin.de. Badeschiff
entrance: €6 (open May–Sept 8am–
midnight); other venues vary (often free).

This huge area next to the Spree
encompasses the *Arena Club*,

Glashaus, the actual Arena, the
Badeschiff and the *Hoppetosse*.
There are frequent electronic
open-air parties and live acts
at *Arena Club*, sometimes the
Hoppetosse café (on a boat) can
turn into a club, and at Arena
itself you can catch rock and
metal shows, as well as events
and festivals.

Lido

MAP P.108, POCKET MAP L7
Cuvrystr. 7 ⓤ Schlesisches Tor ☏ 030 69
56 68 40, ⓦ www.lido-berlin.de. Times and
prices vary according to event.

An old-school club in a former
theatre that's been going for
nearly ten years, *Lido* is known
for championing new music,
and is home to a younger indie
crowd, with the occasional techno
or house event. The club also
has a courtyard with canopy
that makes it suitable for winter
throw-downs.

Madame Claude

MAP P.108, POCKET MAP L7
Lübbener Str. 19 ⓤ Görlitzer Bahnhof
☏ 030 84 11 08 59, ⓦ madameclaude.de.
Daily 7pm–late.

This quirky hangout has live music
six days a week, ranging from indie-
rock and experimental to folk. Be
prepared to feel slightly unsettled
by the decor, which is upside down
and on the ceiling. Pay what you
want for entrance.

Monarch

MAP P.108, POCKET MAP J7
Skalitzer Str. 134 ⓤ Kottbusser Tor ☏ 030
61 65 60 03, ⓦ kottimonarch.de. Tues–Sat
9pm till late. Entry varies; often as low
as €3.

Unpretentious and slightly ragged
place that attracts a hip crowd who
groove to a wide range of tunes –
swing, rockabilly, folk, punk, indie
(no techno) – and enjoy views over
Kottbusser Tor from huge windows.
Entrance is via an unmarked door
and stairwell opposite the *Misir
Casisi* kebab shop.

Prince Charles

MAP P.108, POCKET MAP K7
Prinzenstr. 85f ⓤ Moritzplatz
ⓦ princecharlesberlin.com. Opening
times vary according to event; club
nights usually Thurs–Sat 11pm–open end.
Admission varies.

Hidden away in a basement near
Moritzplatz that once housed
a swimming pool, this square-
shaped, fairly upscale club has a
penchant for bass-heavy parties
that transcend techno tropes in
favour of house, jazzy beats and
hip-hop spun by a mix of local and
international DJs. Note that a new
concept for the venue is due to
launch in late summer 2019.

Ritter Butzke

MAP P.108, POCKET MAP H7
Ritter Str. 24 ⓤ Moritzplatz ⓦ club
.ritterbutzke.de. Fri & Sat from noon.
Admission €8–15.

This former factory now comprises
two main club rooms and an
outside space, generally used only
in summer. The music is usually
electronic (house, electro, techno)
and the crowd a considered but
dedicated bunch.

SO36

MAP P.108, POCKET MAP K7
Oranienstr. 190 ⓤ Görlitzer Bahnhof ⓣ 030
61 40 13 06, ⓦ www.so36.com. Opening
times and admission vary.

One of the city's most legendary
clubs, *SO36* has its roots in punk,
post-punk and alternative music –
musical heroes who've played here
include Iggy Pop, David Bowie
and Einstürzende Neubauten.
Nowadays it hosts alternative
and electronic shows, including
monthly parties like Gayhane, a
Turkish "homoriental" party, and
"Ich bin ein Berliner", where you
can catch an array of Berlin-based
artists playing everything from
garage to synth-pop.

Tresor

POCKET MAP J6
Köpenicker Str. 70 ⓤ/ⓢ Heinrich-Heine-
Str./Jannowitzbrücke. Mon, Wed, Fri & Sat
midnight–late. Admission varies.

Housed in what was the main
central-heating power station
for East Berlin, the colossal
location of the third incarnation
of this ground-breaking club is
breathtaking. Only a tiny portion
of its 28,000 square metres is
in use, but the club is sizeable
enough with three different rooms
dedicated to cutting-edge, muscular
techno played by a rotating roster
of international DJs.

Watergate

MAP P.108, POCKET MAP L7
Falckensteinstr. 49 ⓤ Schlesisches
Tor ⓣ 030 61 28 03 94. Wed, Fri & Sat
midnight–late, occasional Tues & Thurs
events. €10–20.

This slick, split-level club right
on the Spree enjoys a killer
combination of panoramic
windows, excellent sound system
and constant flow of renowned
DJs. Music is electro, house and
minimal techno. Expect to see
residents like Sven Väth and
Solomun too.

Roses

Neukölln

Neukölln, with its strings of bars, galleries, shops and cafés, is one of the city's most overtly hip districts. Once upon a time it was Rixdorf, a tiny village outside Berlin studded with windmills and boasting fantastic views from its impressive hillsides. In came the Industrial Revolution and away went the hills (used for buildings as the city expanded), and Rixdorf developed into a district of entertainment and revelry – so much so that in 1912 it was renamed Neukölln in an effort to change its riotous image. Postwar Neukölln became home to many Turkish, Aran and Kurdish communities, who still give the area its character, along with the more recent influx of expats and artists priced out of Berlin's other inner-city districts. Indeed, the resultant clash of working-class residents and middle-class creatives – reflected in intensely rising rents and the odd juxtapositions of gaudy video arcades and hipster hangouts around Weserstrasse and bustling Hermannplatz – forms the heart of Berlin's gentrification debate and lends Neukölln its somewhat edgy reputation.

Alt-Rixdorf

MAP P.117
Ⓤ KARL-MARX-STR.

The most obvious reminders of Neukölln's medieval origins lie between the main arteries of Karl-Marx-Strasse and Sonnenallee, an area known as Alt-Rixdorf. A wander around the cobbled streets – centred on historical **Richardplatz** – reveals a centuries-old blacksmith's business, attractive churches and the remains of the district's eighteenth-century Bohemian village – founded for Protestant refugees fleeing persecution – with its cute houses and attractive gardens.

Körnerpark

MAP P.117
Schierker Str. 8 Ⓢ Berlin-Neukölln ☎ 030 56 82 39 39, Ⓦ www.körnerpark.de. Park Mon–Sun 10am–6pm; café till 8pm. Free.
Refined Körnerpark might not be the biggest park in Neukölln, but

it is easily the prettiest – a stark contrast to the vast, featureless expanse of nearby Tempelhofer Park (see page 104). With its manicured hedges, elegant promenades and marble fountains, it provides an ideal setting for wedding photos and summertime events such as galas, fairs and concerts. The charming, ivy-covered **Orangerie** (Tues–Sun 10am–8pm) – unique among Berlin's parks – is a highlight, and contains the elegant covered *Café im Körnerpark*, which has a popular outdoor terrace in the warmer months.

Volkspark Hasenheide

MAP P.117, POCKET MAP J9
Entrances on Hasenheide, Columbiadamm and Karlsgartenstr. Ⓤ Hermannplatz. Open 24hr.
Originally used as a hunting ground for the Grand Elector in

the seventeenth century, then as parade grounds for the Prussian military, this green expanse in the heart of Neukölln is today the domain of local sun-worshippers and picknickers. The long rows of trees are reminders of the former shooting ranges but little else of the park's past remains; instead, the main draws are a popular petting zoo, restaurant and a (summer-only) open-air stage for music, films and theatre. A popular funfair is also held in the southern part of the park each May.

Körnerpark

Türkenmarkt

MAP P.117, POCKET MAP K8
Maybachufer Str. Ⓤ **Schönleinstr.** Ⓦ **tuerkenmarkt.de.** Tues & Fri 11am–6.30pm.

Located on the border between Neukölln and Kreuzberg (Kreuzkölln as it's widely known), the twice-weekly Turkish Market has become an institution for Berlin's significant Turkish population as well as families, hipsters and tourists. It's colourfully chaotic, complete with yelling vendors peddling the usual arrays of fruit and vegetables, fabric and shoe stalls, stands selling tasty snacks and, occasionally, live music.

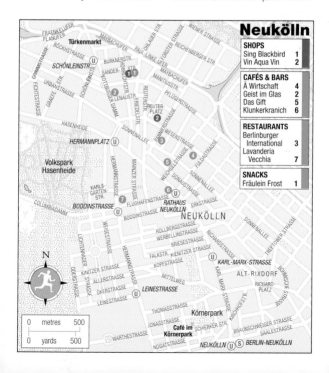

Neukölln

SHOPS	
Sing Blackbird	1
Vin Aqua Vin	2

CAFÉS & BARS	
À Wirtschaft	4
Geist im Glas	2
Das Gift	5
Klunkerkranich	6

RESTAURANTS	
Berlinburger International	3
Lavanderia Vecchia	7

SNACKS	
Fräulein Frost	1

Shops

Sing Blackbird

MAP P.117, POCKET MAP K8

Sanderstr. 11 ⓤ Schönleinstr. ⓣ 030 54 84 50 51. Mon–Sat 1.30–7.30pm.

Housed in a former phone-sex HQ, Sing Blackbird has the edge over other secondhand clothes stores thanks to a savvy selection that favours vintage garments from the 1970s, 1980s and 1990s. They also host occasional flea markets.

Vin Aqua Vin

MAP P.117, POCKET MAP K9

Weserstr. 204 ⓤ Hermannplatz ⓣ 030 94 05 28 86, ⓦ www.vinaquavin.de. Sun–Wed 4pm–midnight, Thurs & Fri 3pm–midnight, Sat 2pm–midnight.

This sophisticated wine shop and bar has introduced a new level of sophistication to this famously hipster street. In addition to a fine selection of international wines (many available by the glass), there's a roaring fireplace for the colder months, chesterfield armchairs and a dining table out back for tastings and private dinner events.

Restaurants

Berlinburger International

MAP P.117, POCKET MAP K9

Pannierstr. 5 ⓤ Hermannplatz ⓣ 016 04 82 65 05, ⓦ berlinburgerinternational com. Mon–Thurs noon–11pm, Fri & Sat noon–midnight, Sun noon–10pm.

There can never be enough burger joints in Berlin, it seems. This tiny space – just a long food bar and a smattering of outdoor picnic tables – lures punters in with fresh ingredients and generous portions: the BBI burger is enormous. Burgers from €4.90.

Klunkerkranich

Lavanderia Vecchia

MAP P.117, POCKET MAP K9

Flughafenstr. 46 ⓤ Boddinstrasse
🕿 030 627 22 152, ⓦ lavanderiavecchia
.wordpress.com. Mon–Sat noon–3pm &
7.30–11pm.

This Italian spot reached cult
status pretty quickly after
opening in 2013, chiefly for
its evening set menus, which
consist of *antipasti*, *primi*, *secondi*
and *dolci* (€65 per person). The
delicious and abundant food is
worth every penny, while the
lighter lunch deals are much
cheaper (three courses from €12).
Evening reservations essential.
Small courtyard garden at
the back.

Snacks

Fräulein Frost

MAP P.117, POCKET MAP K6

Friedelstr. 39 ⓤ Schönleinstr. 🕿 030 95
59 55 21. Mon–Fri 1pm–8pm, Sat–Sun
noon–8pm.

One of the district's best-loved ice-
cream shops, the Frosty Fräulein
serves up delicious cones and
tubs of *bioeis*, as well as sweet and
savoury waffles. In summer, the
outdoor patio provides a meeting
point for hipsters, romantic couples
and local families alike.

Cafés and bars

Ä Wirtschaft

MAP P.117, POCKET MAP L9

Weserstr. 40 ⓤ Rathaus Neukölln 🕿 030
306 48 751, ⓦ ae-neukoelln.de. Daily
5pm–late.

One of the first of many
informal bars to open up on
boho Weserstrasse, the *Ä Bar*
still holds its own as a meeting
point for young creative types,
expats and locals. Flea-market
decor, dim lighting and table
football give it a classic Berlin
dive-bar atmosphere, matched to
a soundtrack of indie and electro

and occasional acoustic gigs from
international bands.

Geist im Glas

MAP P.117, POCKET MAP K9

Lenaustr. 27 ⓤ Hermannplatz 🕿 017 655
330 450, ⓦ www.geist-im-glas.business.
site. Daily from 7pm–2am (Sat–Sun from
10am)

This trendy bar prides itself on
its large selection of infused
spirits that are skilfully mixed
into Prohibition-era-inspired
cocktails. Saturday and Sunday,
there's a "Southern American"
brunch (10am–4pm) with *huevos
rancheros*, fluffy pancakes loaded
with *dulce de leche* and lots of
caramelized bacon.

Das Gift

MAP P.117, POCKET MAP L9

Donaustr. 19 ⓤ Hermannplatz ⓦ dasgift.
de. Mon–Fri 5pm–late, Sat & Sun noon–
late.

Founded by Barry Burns, of
Scottish post-rock band Mogwai,
and his wife Rachel, this corner
pub has quickly become a local
in-spot. Its charm lies in its
simplicity: just a regular wood
interior with a long bar and an
artisan drink menu that includes
Scottish ales, German brews and
lots of whisky and cocktails. The
kitchen offers fabulous haggis,
mac 'n' cheese and an all-day
breakfast at weekends. There's
also a pub quiz, DJ sets and an
exhibition space (Das Giftraum)
that regularly hosts work by
local artists.

Klunkerkranich

MAP P.117, POCKET MAP L9

Karl-Marx-Str. 66 ⓤ Rathaus Neukölln
ⓦ klunkerkranich.org. Daily noon–2am
(see website for seasonal opening hours).

This shabby-chic rooftop hangout
is hidden on top of a distinctly
unglamorous shopping centre. The
urban bar vibe is complemented by
a sandy floor, great views over the
city and occasional concerts and
film screenings.

Charlottenburg

Part of the four boroughs that make up City West (along with Wilmersdorf, Schöneberg and Tiergarten) Charlottenburg has long been the beating heart of West Berlin and remains so today. Known for its wealthy residents and expensive shops, it's generally dismissed by the more boho east, and has much more in common with cities like London, Paris or Milan. The area's main artery, Kurfürstendamm (Ku'damm as it's colloquially known), which takes its name from the former Kurfürsten (Electors) of the Holy Roman Empire, is one of the most famous avenues in the city. It's often described as the city's Champs-Élysées, but the abundance of shops and relative dearth of impressive architecture makes it feel more like London's Oxford Street. However, many of the streets that run between Ku'damm and Kantstrasse have a charm of their own, with a wealth of independent cafés, bars, restaurants, bookstores and boutiques. The area is also home to some of the city's major sights such as Berlin's zoo and aquarium, Schloss Charlottenburg, the Kaiser Wilhelm Memorial Church and the Käthe Kollwitz Museum.

Berlin Zoo

MAP P.122, POCKET MAP B6
Hardenbergplatz 8 ⓤ/Ⓢ Zoologischer Garten ⓣ 030 25 40 10, ⓦ zoo-berlin. de. Daily: Jan, Feb, Oct-Dec 9am-4.30pm, March 9am-6pm, April-Sept 9am-6.30pm. €15.50, zoo & aquarium €21. Family tickets available.

Berlin's zoo is Germany's oldest and one of the world's most popular, attracting (along with the adjacent aquarium) more than three million visitors in 2016. It opened in 1844 with animals donated by the royal family but was decimated during World War II, leaving only 91 surviving animals. It now houses over nineteen thousand animals spanning 1300 species. The hippo house is a highlight, while famous residents include the world's second-oldest gorilla: 61-year-old Fatou.

Berlin Aquarium

MAP P.122, POCKET MAP C6
Budapester Str. 32 ⓤ/Ⓢ Zoologischer Garten ⓣ 030 25 40 10, ⓦ aquarium-berlin.de. Daily 9am-6pm. €14.50, zoo & aquarium €21. Family tickets available.

Situated next to the zoo, the city's impressive aquarium holds the title for world's most biodiverse collection. From jellyfish to crocodiles and other reptiles and tropical fish, the aquarium has over fourteen thousand creatures on three floors. Built in 1913, the aquarium has retained its old-fashioned appearance, albeit incorporating modern elements.

Museum für Fotografie

MAP P.122, POCKET MAP B6
Jebensstr. 2 ⓤ/Ⓢ Zoologischer Garten
ⓣ 030 26 64 24 242, ⓦ smb.museum/mf.

Daily 11am–7pm (until 8pm Thurs). €10.
The Museum of Photography opened in 2004 in a former casino building, and has quickly risen in popularity, drawing about 120,000 visitors a year. The city's largest museum dedicated to the art form, it covers 2000 square metres and houses a thousand images by famous *Vogue* photographer Helmut Newton, whose provocative black-and-white photographs made him famous in the world of fashion photography and beyond; his work is shown on a rotating basis in addition to exhibits of other photographers. In the large Kaisersaal, on the second floor, you'll find the Kunstbibliothek's collection, which explores all kinds of photography ranging from the nineteenth to twenty-first centuries.

C/O Berlin (Amerika Haus)

MAP P.122, POCKET MAP B6
Hardenbergstr. 22–24 ⓤ Zoologischer
Garten ⓣ 030 28 44 41 60, ⓦ co-berlin.org.
Daily 11am–8pm. €10.
Since its foundation back in 2000, C/O Berlin has hosted some of the city's best photography exhibitions,

with shows featuring international heavyweights such as Martin Parr, Annie Leibovitz, Rene Burri and Karl Lagerfeld. In 2014, C/O Berlin moved from Mitte to West Berlin's Amerika Haus, where it hosted open-air exhibitions until the venue's reopening later that year. Visitors can expect a high standard of curation and big-name retrospectives, as well as continued promotion of young and new local talent.

Kaiser-Wilhelm-Gedächtnis-Kirche

MAP P.122, POCKET MAP B7
Breitscheidplatz ⓤ Kurfürstendamm
ⓣ 030 21 85 023, ⓦ gedaechtniskirche-
berlin.de. Church: daily 9am–7pm. Hall of
Remembrance: Mon–Fri 10am–6pm, Sat
10am–5.30pm, Sun noon–5.30pm. Guided
tours: see website.
The Kaiser Wilhelm Memorial Church, built between 1891 and 1895 in neo-Romanesque style by architect Franz Schwechten, was commissioned by Kaiser Wilhelm II and served as a symbol of Prussian unity. Nearly destroyed during a World War II air raid, all that remains are the ruins of the spire and entrance hall. A

Berlin Zoo inhabitant

Charlottenburg

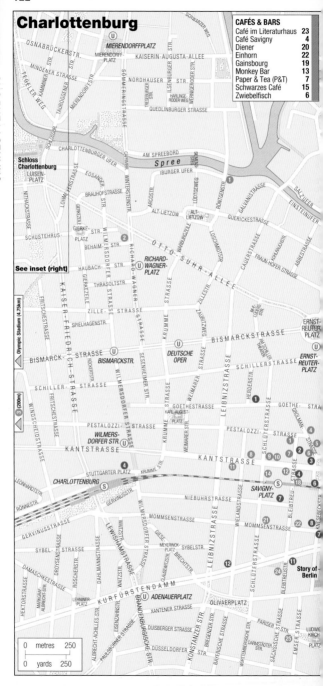

CAFÉS & BARS	
Café im Literaturhaus	23
Café Savigny	4
Diener	20
Einhorn	22
Gainsbourg	19
Monkey Bar	13
Paper & Tea (P&T)	7
Schwarzes Café	15
Zwiebelfisch	6

See inset (right)

Olympic Stadium (4.75km)

(200m)

Story of Berlin

| 0 | metres | 250 |
| 0 | yards | 250 |

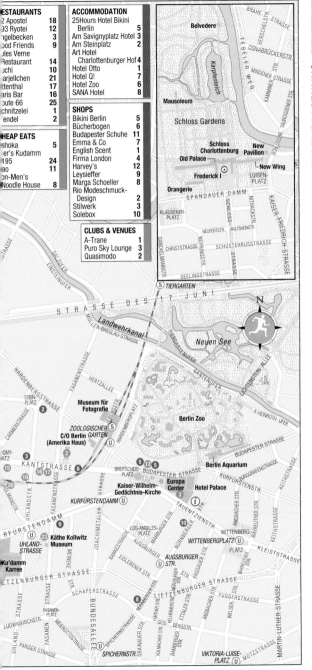

RESTAURANTS

2 Apostel	18
893 Ryotei	12
Engelbecken	3
Good Friends	9
Jules Verne	
Restaurant	14
Juchi	10
Marjellchen	21
Ottenthal	17
Paris Bar	16
Route 66	25
Schnitzelei	
Rendel	2

CHEAP EATS

Ashoka	5
Baker's Kudamm	
195	24
Mao	11
Yon-Men's	
Noodle House	8

ACCOMMODATION

25Hours Hotel Bikini	
Berlin	5
Am Savignyplatz Hotel	3
Am Steinplatz	2
Art Hotel	
Charlottenburger Hof	4
Hotel Otto	1
Hotel Q!	7
Hotel Zoo	6
SANA Hotel	8

SHOPS

Bikini Berlin	5
Bücherbogen	6
Budapester Schuhe	11
Emma & Co	7
English Scent	1
Firma London	4
Harvey's	12
Leysieffer	9
Marga Schoeller	3
Rio Modeschmuck-	
Design	2
Stilwerk	3
Solebox	10

CLUBS & VENUES

A-Trane	1
Puro Sky Lounge	3
Quasimodo	2

Schloss Charlottenburg

new structure was built in 1961, and the stunning, blue stained-glass windows fitted in concrete bricks contrast memorably with the haunting skeleton of the old. The base of the old spire and entrance hall is now a memorial hall, with exhibits documenting the old church through photos and artefacts that survived the bombing.

Käthe Kollwitz Museum

MAP P.122, POCKET MAP B7
Fasanenstr. 24 Ⓤ **Uhlandstr.** Ⓣ **030 88 25 210,** Ⓦ **www.kaethe-kollwitz.de. Daily 11am–6pm. €7.**

German artist Käthe Kollwitz's work was greatly influenced by the loss of her son in World War I and her grandson in World War II. She was a pacifist who lived in Berlin for fifty years, and was the first woman elected to the Prussian Academy of the Arts but resigned her post in 1933 in protest at Hitler's rise to power. Kollwitz's works were banned by the Nazis. Many of her pieces are powerful reminders of some of the most painful aspects of her life. Works on display here include dour self-portraits, plaintively titled sketches, woodcuts, lithographs, war protest posters and sculptures. The building itself is the oldest private home on Fasanenstrasse, built in 1871 and restored in the 1980s.

Story of Berlin

MAP P.122, POCKET MAP A7
Kurfürstendamm 207–208 Ⓤ **Uhlandstr.** Ⓣ **030 88 72 01 00,** Ⓦ **story-of-berlin. de. Daily 10am–8pm, last admission 6pm; bunker tours in English at noon, 2pm, 4pm & 6pm €12.**

The Story of Berlin aims to transport visitors to each of the eight centuries of Berlin's history through multimedia displays that include photos, films and interactive exhibits. It follows the history of the city from its founding in 1237, to the Thirty Years' War, Frederick the Great's reign, the 1920s, World War II, the Cold War and the fall of the Wall. Also included is a guided tour of an atomic bomb shelter on the site. At the time of writing, the exhibition was closed due to reconstruction work, in preparation for a new exhibition about the history of Berlin due to open in autumn 2019. See the website for current updates.

Schloss Charlottenburg

MAP P.122, POCKET MAP A4

Spandauer Damm 10–22 ⓤ Sophie-Charlotte-Platz/Richard-Wagner-Platz ⓣ 033 19 69 40, ⓦ www.spsg.de. Old Palace Tues–Sun: Jan–March 10am–4.30pm; April–Oct 10am–5.30pm; €12. New Wing daily except Tues: April–Oct 10am–5.30pm; Nov–March 10am–4.30pm; €10. Belvedere April–Oct Tues–Sun 10am–5.30pm; closed Nov–March; €4. Mausoleum April–Oct Tues–Sun 10am–5.30pm; €3. New Pavilion Tues–Sun: April–Oct 10am–5.30pm; Nov–March noon–4pm; €4. Combined ticket €17.

As you walk through Schloss Charlottenburg, you'll be in no doubt as to why its builder, Frederick I, was known as an extravagant spender who nearly bankrupted the state. The former Elector of Brandenburg, who named himself king of Prussia in 1701, had this ornate Baroque palace built as a summer home for his wife, Sophie Charlotte, in 1695. It started as a relatively modest dwelling but ballooned to its present palatial status with additions throughout the 1700s. Majestic rooms, art and plenty of porcelain characterize the interiors. In fact, the art in the palace constitutes the largest collection of eighteenth-century French paintings outside of France. There's a separate entrance fee for each of the three main buildings; The **Old Palace** features Baroque rooms, royal apartments, Chinese and Japanese porcelain and silverware chambers; the **New Wing** is more Rococo with an array of refined furniture in apartments built by Frederick the Great; and the Schinkel-built **New Pavilion** features a collection of arts and crafts. Visitors can also visit the **Mausoleum**, which contains the graves of, and memorials to, members of the Hohenzollern family, and the **Belvedere**, which displays a collection of Berlin porcelain. The reconstructed **Orangerie** is also open for concerts and the gardens are open and free. Guided tours are offered of the historic apartments and chapel.

Olympic Stadium

MAP P.122, POCKET MAP A5

Olympischer Platz 3 Ⓢ Olympiastadion ⓣ 030 30 68 81 00, ⓦ olympiastadion-berlin.de. Daily: April–Oct 9am–7pm; Nov–March 10am–4pm; Aug 9am–8pm (closed on days of concerts and games). €11. Guided tours available.

Berlin's Olympic stadium, built for the 1936 Summer Olympics (immortalized in the film *Olympia* by Leni Riefenstahl), is one of the last surviving remnants of Nazi architecture in Berlin. Occupied by the British military following the war and used by them until 1994, the stadium is now used for concerts and events and also as the official ground of Hertha BSC, Berlin's most famous football club. It was renovated for the 2006 World Cup and now has the highest all-seated capacity in Germany (74,228). The stadium remains an impressive place to visit.

Olympic Stadium

Shops

Bikini Berlin

MAP P.122, POCKET MAP B6
Budapester Str. 38–50 Ⓤ/Ⓢ Zoologischer
Garten Ⓣ 030 55 49 64 55, Ⓦ www.
bikiniberlin.de. Mon–Sat 10am–8pm.
This trendy concept mall in
a 1950s building place was,
arguably, the place that put West
Berlin back on the map. Spanning
offices and a cinema, as well as the
25hours hotel and bar (see pages
148 and 130), the lower three
floors of the Bikinihaus offer chic
retail and coffee stop options.

Bücherbogen

MAP P.122, POCKET MAP A7
Stadtbahnbogen 593 Ⓢ Savignyplatz Ⓣ 030
31 86 95 11, Ⓦ www.buecherbogen.com.
Mon–Fri 10am–8pm, Sat 10am–7pm.
You could spend hours in this
famed art book store, located
beneath Savignyplatz S-Bahn.
You'll find plenty of English-
language books in the design,
photography, art and theatre
sections, though nothing in the
literature section, sadly.

Bücherbogen

Budapester Schuhe

MAP P.122, POCKET MAP A7
Kurfürstendamm 199 Ⓤ Uhlandstr. Ⓣ 030
88 11 707. Mon–Fri 10am–7pm, Sat
10am–6pm.
A spacious and well-stocked shoe
shop whose wares run the gamut
from reasonably priced leather
classics to designer models from
Prada and Tod's.

Emma & Co

MAP P.122, POCKET MAP A7
Niebuhrstr. 2 Ⓢ Savignyplatz Ⓣ 030 88 67
67 87. Mon–Fri 11am–7pm, Sat 11am–4pm.
Lovingly decorated store with
attentive staff. They carry
alternative wooden toys, as well as
the classic brands for children, and
babywear.

English Scent

MAP P.122, POCKET MAP A6
Goethestr. 15 Ⓢ Deutsche Oper Ⓣ 030 32
44 655, Ⓦ www.english-scent.de. Tues &
Fri 10am–2pm, Sat 10am–3pm.
Located in a suitably evocative
old building, English Scent offers
a range of fragrances, skincare
products, shaving supplies, and
even toothpastes.

Firma London

MAP P.122, POCKET MAP A6
Bleibtreustr. 50 Ⓢ Savignyplatz Ⓣ 1516 88
57 268. Tues–Fri noon–7pm, Sat noon–5pm.
Run by former Stella McCartney
designer Sandra Tietje and gallerist
Florian von Holstein, this is not
for the financially faint-hearted,
but it does stock some gorgeous
vintage furniture and accessories.
There is also a large warehouse
in Lise-Meitner-Strasse 7 that's
open Saturdays from noon or
by appointment.

Harvey's

MAP P.122, POCKET MAP A7
Kurfürstendamm 56 Ⓤ Adenauerplatz
Ⓣ 030 88 33 803. Mon–Sat 11am–8pm.
A wonderland of men's designer
clothes from designers such
as Comme des Garçons and
Yohji Yamamoto.

Leysieffer

MAP P.122, POCKET MAP B7

Kurfürstendamm 218 ⓤ Uhlandstr. ☎ 030 88 57 480. Mon–Sat 9am–7pm.

This Ku'damm branch of the famed German chocolateria does a brisk trade. Aside from the usual sweet goodies, there's also a small coffee bar, useful if you're looking for a break from all the shopping.

Marga Schoeller

MAP P.122, POCKET MAP A7

Knesebeckstr. 33 ⓤ Uhlandstr. ☎ 030 88 11 112, ⓦ margaschoeller.de. Mon–Wed 9.30am–7pm, Thurs & Fri 9.30am–8pm, Sat 9.30am–6pm.

Opened in 1929 by the eponymous Frau Schoeller, this bookstore, one of the longest running in Europe, was a focal point for West Berlin's postwar literary scene. Originally located on Kurfürstendamm, the shop moved to Knesebeckstr. in 1974 and continues to sell a fantastic range of German- and English-language books on poetry, theatre and philosophy as well as fiction, history and plenty of tomes about Berlin and Germany.

Rio Modeschmuck-Design

MAP P.122, POCKET MAP A6

Bleibtreustr. 52 ⓢ Savignyplatz ☎ 030 31 33 152, ⓦ www.rio-modeschmuck-berlin. de. Mon–Wed & Fri 11am–6.30pm, Thurs 11am–7pm, Sat 11am–6pm.

Designer Barbara Kranz opened her jewellery store back in 1984 – she calls her creations "after 5pm" jewellery due to their natural evening-wear flamboyance.

Stilwerk

MAP P.122, POCKET MAP A6

Kantstr. 17 ⓢ Savignyplatz ☎ 030 31 51 50, ⓦ www.stilwerk.com. Mon–Sat 10am–7pm.

Swanky designer mall, located near Zoologischer Garten, comprising shops dedicated to home decoration, jewellery and fashion. Expect high-end stores like Bang & Olufsen, with one or two cheaper options as well. There's a café and even a babysitting service for those who want to dump the kids.

Solebox

MAP P.122, POCKET MAP C7

Nürnbergerstr. 14 ⓤ Wittenbergplatz ☎ 030 23 60 71 21. Mon–Sat 11am–8pm.

A spacious shrine to streetwear, stocking Reebok, Converse, Ellesse and Adidas sneakers plus T-shirts and hoodies.

Restaurants

12 Apostel

MAP P.122, POCKET MAP A6

Bleibtreustr. 49 ⓢ Savignyplatz ☎ 030 245 347 30, ⓦ 12-aposteli.de. Mon–Thurs 11am–midnight, Fri & Sat 11am–1am, Sun noon–midnight.

A smart, Baroque-style interior (check the kitsch religious frescoes) and generously sized thin pizzas mark this place out. They're slightly on the expensive side – around €12 – but specials on the Mon–Fri lunch menu start at €6.95. The Sunday brunch buffet (10am–3pm) is €22.50 but comes with a glass of sparkling wine and a hot drink.

893 Ryotei

MAP P.122, POCKET MAP A6

Kant Str. 135 ⓢ Savignyplatz ☎ 030 91 70 31 21, ⓦ www.893ryotei.de. Tues–Sat 6.30–11.30pm.

You arrive at a seemingly rundown building with graffitied walls, but once inside, a Japanese low-lit restaurant awaits you, with a large menu offering dishes that are inspired by Japanese, Mexican and Peruvian cuisine, such as Tiradito Hiramasa (yellowtail with Peruvian salsa €18), a ceviche 893-style or just simple sushi.

Engelbecken

MAP P.122, POCKET MAP A6

Witzlebenstr. 31 ⓤ Sophie-Charlotte-Platz ☎ 030 61 52 810, ⓦ engelbecken.de. Mon–Fri 5pm–1am, Sat 4pm–1am, Sun noon–1am.

A high-quality restaurant that serves Bavarian and Alpine cuisine – *schnitzel*, goulash – with an emphasis on organic products and home-made sauces. Vegetarian and vegan options are available, and the park-facing terrace is nice in the summer.

Good Friends

MAP P.122, POCKET MAP A6
Kantstr. 30 ⓢ Savignyplatz ☎ 030 31 32 659, ⓦ goodfriends-berlin.de. Daily noon–1am.

One of Berlin's few really authentic Cantonese restaurants, with plain decor and a full range of classics (mains €11–20). It's always busy; evening bookings recommended.

Jules Verne Restaurant

MAP P.122, POCKET MAP A6
Schlüterstr. 61 ⓢ Savignyplatz ☎ 030 31 80 94 10, ⓦ jules-verne-berlin.de. Daily 9am–1am, kitchen till 11.45pm.

The interior feels classic French but the menu is aptly global, ranging from *Flammen* (*tarte flambée*) and *schnitzel* to *couscous* and *satay*. Lunchtime deals change daily.

Kuchi

MAP P.122, POCKET MAP A6
Kantstr. 30 ⓢ Savignyplatz ☎ 030 31 50 78 15, ⓦ kuchi.de. Daily noon–midnight.

With a sister restaurant in Mitte, this place sells the same range of innovative sushi, *sashimi*, *yakitori*, as well as some Thai, Chinese and Korean recipes. Busy at peak times so it's best to reserve a table.

Marjellchen

MAP P.122, POCKET MAP A7
Mommsenstr. 9 ⓢ Savignyplatz ☎ 030 88 32 676, ⓦ marjellchen-berlin.de. Daily 5pm–midnight.

It's obvious from the window displays – books, photos and other paraphernalia – that this is a time warp kind of place. Indeed, *Marjellchen* specializes in cuisine from East Prussia, Pomerania and Silesia, all served up in a cosy, traditional atmosphere. Portions

are generous and service is friendly (mains €11.80–20.50).

Ottenthal

MAP P.122, POCKET MAP B6
Kantstr. 153 ⓢ Savignyplatz ☎ 030 31 33 162, ⓦ ottenthal.com. Daily 5pm–1am.

White-clothed tables and relatively sparse white walls lend this place an unfussy, classic feel that ties in well with the Austrian cuisine – which is simple yet some of the best in the area. Organic ingredients feature on the menu, which includes fish dishes, roast deer and a famed *Wiener schnitzel*. Good Austrian wine list too.

Paris Bar

MAP P.122, POCKET MAP B6
Kantstr. 152 ⓢ/Ⓤ Zoologischer Garten ☎ 030 31 38 052, ⓦ parisbar.net. Daily noon–2am.

There's still something tangibly bohemian about the *Paris Bar*, once one of the centres of West Berlin's art scene until the Wall fell and the East took over. Interesting artworks vie for your attention and the somewhat pricey food takes second place to the social networking action. Lunch €15–28, dinner mains €28–40.

Route 66

MAP P.122, POCKET MAP A7
Pariser Str 44. Ⓤ Hohenzollernplatz. ☎ 030 88 31 602, ⓦ route66diner.de. Sun–Thu 11am–1am, Fri & Sat 11am–3am.

A traditional '50s American diner filled with jukeboxes, red booths and bar stools and pictures of all the icons like Elvis, the cast of Grease and other flashy neon-signs. If you are in need of a real burger with a thick milkshake or some ribs, this is the place to be. The prices vary from €11 to €38 for mains.

Schnitzelei

MAP P.122, POCKET MAP A5
Röntgen Str. 7 Ⓤ Richard-Wagner-Platz ☎ 030 34 70 27 77, ⓦ www.schnitzelei. de. Mon–Fri 4pm–midnight, Sat & Sun noon–midnight

Stilwerk

The name gives it away: if you are a lover of the Austro-Germam cuisine, this is schnitzel heaven, located on the edge of the river Spree with a nice beer garden for Berlin summer evenings. A simple and well priced restaurant, which – in addition to schnitzels – serves a variety of 'German tapas' dishes like Königsberger Klopse (meat balls with caper sauce) or plums wrapped in bacon.

Wendel

MAP P.122, POCKET MAP A5
Richard-Wagner-Platz. 87 Ⓤ Richard-Wagner-Platz Ⓣ 030 34 26 784. Mon–Fri 4pm–midnight, Sat 5pm–midnight.
Being located in a 100 year-old pub gives Wendel it's unique décor – from the outside it might not look great, but once you step inside you'll be surprised. A typical German restaurant where they serve good classics like potatoes and pork knuckle.

Cheap eats

Ashoka

MAP P.122, POCKET MAP A6

Grolmanstr. 51 Ⓢ Savignyplatz Ⓣ 030 31 01 58 06, Ⓦ www.myashoka.de. Daily noon–midnight.
Ashok Sharma opened this restaurant in 1975 as he was missing the food from his home in Punjab. It offers well-priced, decent quality food in a small *Imbiss*-style place. Vegetarian options and friendly staff.

Bier's Kudamm 195

MAP P.122, POCKET MAP A7
Kurfürstendamm 195 Ⓤ Uhlandstr. Ⓣ 030 88 18 942. Mon–Thurs 11am–5am, Fri & Sat 11am–6pm, Sun noon–5pm.
One of several spots claimed as the "best in Berlin" for *Currywurst*. It also serves meat skewers and meatballs and is generally busy all night; if you feel like splashing out ask for champagne with your *Wurst*.

Dao

MAP P.122, POCKET MAP A6
Kantstr. 133 Ⓢ Savignyplatz Ⓣ 030 37 59 14 14, Ⓦ dao-restaurant.de. Daily noon–11pm.
Opened by a Berliner and his Thai wife, Dao, in the 1970s, this Thai spot serves dishes brimful

of flavour. Alongside *pad Thai* (€13.90) and fish and duck dishes (up to €20) there are specials like "Bloodnoodlesoup".

Lon-Men's Noodle House

MAP P.122, POCKET MAP A6
Kantstr. 33 Ⓢ Savignyplatz Ⓣ 030 31 51 96 78. Daily noon–10.30pm, closed on Tues.
Tiny Taiwanese noodle shop run by a friendly family who make excellent dumplings and noodle soups (small and large portions available).

Cafés and bars

Café im Literaturhaus

MAP P.122, POCKET MAP B7
Fasanenstr. 23 Ⓤ Uhlandstr. Ⓣ 030 88 72 860, Ⓦ www.literaturhaus-berlin.de. Daily 9am–midnight.
This place is every bit as classic and elegant as its name suggests. The spacious interior or beautiful summer garden are great spots for coffee and cake, lunch or dinner: the largely organic menu changes regularly and has vegetarian options.

Café im Literaturhaus

Café Savigny

MAP P.122, POCKET MAP A6
Grolmanstr. 53 Ⓢ Savignyplatz Ⓣ 0157 52 00 48 10. Daily 9am–midnight.
A small, classic spot that's been serving great breakfasts and coffee for over a decade. Lunches start at €6 (soups) with hearty Burgundy stew for €13.50. Service is good and it's also nice for an evening drink.

Diener

MAP P.122, POCKET MAP A6
Grolmanstr. 47 Ⓢ Savignyplatz Ⓣ 030 88 15 329, Ⓦ www.diener-berlin.de. Daily 6pm–3am.
This Berlin ale house is a local institution – not only because it was opened in 1954 by former German heavyweight boxer Franz Diener, but because it serves dishes like *Königsberger Klopse* (meatballs in white sauce with capers) and has an atmosphere as old school as the menu.

Einhorn

MAP P.122, POCKET MAP A7
Mommsenstr. 2 Ⓢ Savignyplatz Ⓣ 030 88 14 241, Ⓦ einhorn-catering.de. Daily Mon–Fri 10am–5pm.
A great place if you're seeking a tasty veggie lunch. There's a buffet selection including antipasti and and dishes like lentils with goat's cheese. Mostly priced by weight (€1.50/100g).

Gainsbourg

MAP P.122, POCKET MAP A6
Jeanne-Mammen-Bogen 576–577 Ⓢ Savignyplatz Ⓣ 030 313 74 64. Daily 5pm until late.
The name may pay homage to the master of risqué *chanson*, but the cocktails (€8–10) and food are more mainstream. Nevertheless, the drinks are some of the best in the neighbourhood.

Monkey Bar

MAP P.122, POCKET MAP B6
Budapesterstr. 40 Ⓤ/Ⓢ Zoologischer Garten Ⓣ 030 12 02 21 210, Ⓦ monkeybarberlin.de. Daily noon–2am.

This rooftop bar in West Berlin is found at the 25hours hotel (see page 148), making it an even more exciting place to stay. The floor-to-ceiling windows make for great sundowner vibes.

Paper & Tea (P & T)

MAP P.122, POCKET MAP A6
Bleibtreustr. 4 ⓢ Savignyplatz ☏ 030 55 57 98 071, ⓦ paperandtea.com. Mon–Sat 11am–7pm.
A Zen-style breath of fresh air in a city obsessed with coffee, this minimal and chic teahouse feels as much like a museum as a shop, with its gorgeously curated goods laid out on trays with detailed notes. Related accessories and gifts also available.

Schwarzes Cafe

MAP P.122, POCKET MAP A6
Kantstr. 148 ⓢ Savignyplatz ☏ 030 31 38 038, ⓦ schwarzescafe-berlin.de. Daily 24hr.
The slightly ragged charm of the "Black Café" makes it feel like it would be better placed in the east. The downstairs is small and intimate, but upstairs the large, airy room has a relaxed, convivial vibe. Food is served 24 hours, including breakfasts (from €4.50) – but this is a night-owl place really.

Zwiebelfisch

MAP P.122, POCKET MAP A6
Savignyplatz 7 ⓢ Savignyplatz, ☏ 030 312 73 63, ⓦ zwiebelfisch-berlin.de. Daily noon–6am.
Corner bar and 1970s throwback for would-be arty and intellectual types. Jazz, earnest debate and good cheap grub (€8–12.50), including goulash and Swabian Maultaschen, served until 1am.

Clubs and venues

A-Trane

MAP P.122, POCKET MAP A6
Bleibtreustr. 1 ⓢ Savignyplatz ☏ 030 31 32 550, ⓦ www.a-trane.de. Daily from 8pm,

Schwarzes Cafe

music from around 10pm.
Good jazz and decent cocktails in a classic jazz-style interior (small and smoky). Often hosts major international acts.

Puro Sky Lounge

MAP P.122, POCKET MAP C7
Tauentzienstr. 9–11 ⓤ Kurfürstendamm ☏ 030 26 36 78 75, ⓦ www.puroberlin.de. Thurs 10pm–6am, Sat 11pm–6am
Ensconced on the twentieth floor of the ugly Europa Center, the *Puro Sky Lounge* is filled with eye candy thanks to the beautiful people who flock here for the jaw-dropping views. What it lacks in musical edge – think 1980s classics– it makes up for with an upbeat crowd.

Quasimodo

MAP P.122, POCKET MAP B6
Kantstr. 12A ⓢ Savignyplatz ☏ 030 31 80 45 60, ⓦ www.quasimodo.de.
A classic jazz bar, *Quasimodo* (underneath the Delphi Cinema) features black-and-white photos, low ceilings and intimate tables. Aside from jazz there's funk, blues and Latin and the odd international star.

Schöneberg

Famous during the 1920s as the centre of Berlin's decadent nightlife scene and again in the 1970s when it was home to David Bowie during his dissipated sojourn in the city, Schöneberg's star waned in the 1990s as the cool kids moved east. But while East Berlin has become increasingly slick and unaffordable, this part of town has – as they say – kept it real. Nowadays the hipsters are heading back, attracted by the still-low rents and the burgeoning gallery scene in Potsdamer Strasse, and it maintains its reputation as the pinkest borough in Berlin, especially around Nollendorfplatz. It's also long-been a popular spot for writers – Christopher Isherwood had his digs in Nollendorfstrasse back in the day, and a new generation of writers including Helen DeWitt and Ida Hattemer-Higgins have called the neighbourhood home. Though it lacks any major sights, the charming Winterfeldtplatz hosts a highly popular farmers' market (Sat 8am–4pm).

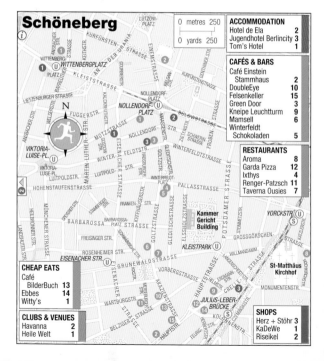

Schöneberg

0 metres 250
0 yards 250

ACCOMMODATION
Hotel de Ela	2
Jugendhotel Berlincity	3
Tom's Hotel	1

CAFÉS & BARS
Café Einstein Stammhaus	2
DoubleEye	10
Felsenkeller	15
Green Door	3
Kneipe Leuchtturm	9
Mamsell	6
Winterfeldt Schokoladen	5

RESTAURANTS
Aroma	8
Garda Pizza	12
Ixthys	4
Renger-Patzsch	11
Taverna Ousies	7

CHEAP EATS
Café BilderBuch	13
Ebbes	14
Witty's	1

CLUBS & VENUES
Havanna	2
Heile Welt	1

SHOPS
Herz + Stöhr	3
KaDeWe	1
Riseikel	2

Shops

Herz + Stöhr

MAP P.132, POCKET MAP D8
Winterfeldtstr. 52 ⓤ Nollendorfplatz
☎ 030 21 64 425. Tues–Fri noon–7pm, Sat noon–5pm.

Intelligent, elegant designs from this German fashion duo – the dresses and suits are grown-up but not dowdy, and everything can be altered to fit.

KaDeWe

MAP P.132, POCKET MAP C7
Tauentzienstr. 21–24 ⓤ Wittenbergplatz
☎ 030 21 210, ⓦ kadewe.de. Mon–Thurs 10am–8pm, Fri 10am–9pm, Sat 9.30am–8pm.

If you're tired of Berlin's austere side, check out KaDeWe (Kaufhaus Des Westerns), a temple to conspicuous consumption. The largest department store in continental Europe, it sports designer gear alongside some surprisingly affordable accessories and homewares. The legendary sixth-floor food hall will leave all but the most jaded of foodies starry-eyed.

Riseikel

MAP P.132, POCKET MAP D7
Bülowstr. 5 ⓤ Nollendorfplatz ☎ 030 54 48 37 42. Mon–Sat 2–8pm.

Formerly known as Mr Dead & Ms Free, a dusty little legend of a music shop crammed full of everything from the latest imports to rare vintage albums.

Restaurants

Aroma

MAP P.132, POCKET MAP E9
Hochkirchstr. 8 ⓢ/ⓤ Yorckstr. ☎ 030 78 25 821, ⓦ cafe-aroma.de. Mon–Fri from 5pm, Sat from noon, Sun brunch 11am–2pm, from 2pm à la carte.

Tucked into a sleepy residential street, this rustic Italian gem is the unofficial headquarters for

Berlin's slow food movement. The antipasti spread at Sunday brunch (€14.50) is legendary, while classic pastas (€9–12), pizzas (€6–9) and changing seasonal specials (€15–20) satisfy the dinner crowd. The terrace is a peaceful haven.

Garda Pizza

MAP P.132, POCKET MAP D9
Crellestr. 48 ⓢ Julius-Leber-Brücke ☎ 030 78 09 79 70. Mon–Sat 11.30am–9pm.

Locals flock to *Garda Pizza* for their trays of thin-crust Roman-style *focaccia*. Their most popular slice (€2) combines fresh aubergine, mushroom, sheep's salami and artichokes. A tray (€15) will feed a hungry group of four. Join the crowd on the pavement, or mosey down a few metres and let your children burn off the calories in the neighbouring playground.

Ixthys

MAP P.132, POCKET MAP D8
Pallasstr. 21 ⓤ Nollendorfplatz ☎ 030 81 47 47 69. Mon noon–10pm, Tues–Sat noon–9.30pm.

A tiny café run by two Korean widows (who've festooned the walls with biblical slogans), this places is all about great home-style cooking. Guests squeeze in to enjoy the home-made noodles with vegetables (€5) or seafood (€8.50) and the fiery, sizzling *bibimbap* (€7.50).

Renger-Patzsch

MAP P.132, POCKET MAP D9
Wartburgstr. 54 ⓤ Eisenacher Str. ☎ 030 78 42 059, ⓦ www.renger-patzsch.com. Mon–Sat 6–11.30pm.

An interior of dark wood and white tablecloths forms the backdrop to an expertly prepared selection of German dishes (starters €6–12; mains €16–22.50; *tartes flambées* €8–12.50). In spring, look for the dandelion salad with lardons; in winter, the braised ox cheeks with bacon-wrapped plums, turnips and mashed potatoes.

Taverna Ousies

MAP P.132, POCKET MAP D9
Grunewaldstr. 16 Ⓤ Eisenacher Str. ☎ 030
21 67 957, Ⓦ www.taverna-ousies.de. Daily
from 5pm.

This kitschy, raucous Greek
taverna is a perennial favourite.
There are no real duds, so go wild
with the meze menu (€4–7) and
be entertained by the jolly staff.
Reservations essential at weekends.

Cheap eats

Café BilderBuch

MAP P.132, POCKET MAP D9
Akazienstr. 28 Ⓢ Julius-Leber-Brücke ☎ 030
78 70 60 57, Ⓦ cafe-bilderbuch.de. Mon–Sat
9am–midnight, Sun 10am–midnight.

Lovely rambling café in the
Viennese tradition. It doesn't look
particularly special from outside,
but the comfortable back parlour
may well hold you captive for
hours. Great breakfasts (€5.40–
7.90), lovely cakes, elegant coffees
and courtyard seating, too.

Ebbes

MAP P.132, POCKET MAP D9
Crellestr. 5 Ⓢ Julius-Leber-Brücke ☎ 030
70 09 48 13. Mon–Fri 10am–7.30pm, Sat
9am–4pm.

This quirky Swabian deli is
crowded with rings of venison
salami and trays of fresh *spätzle*
(noodles). Owner Wolfgang
Steppes finds his suppliers on trips
to southern Germany. Buy a picnic
and wander north to Kleistpark, or
grab a stool outside and try one of
the daily specials (€2.50–5), such as
Maultaschen (ravioli) in broth.

Witty's

MAP P.132, POCKET MAP C7
Wittenbergplatz 5 Ⓤ Wittenbergplatz
☎ 030 21 19 496, Ⓦ www.wittys-berlin.
de. Mon–Sat 10am–midnight, Sun 11am–
midnight.

One of the city's first and finest
organic sausage stands, *Witty's* has
customers lined up along the square
for their *Currywurst* and crispy fries.

Cafés and bars

Café Einstein Stammhaus

MAP P.132, POCKET MAP D7
Kurfürstenstr. 58 Ⓤ Nollendorfplatz ☎ 030
26 39 19 10, Ⓦ www.cafeeinstein.com.
Daily 8am–midnight.

Set in a beautiful historic villa, this
classic coffeehouse and restaurant
offers fantastic breakfasts, *schnitzels*
and cakes. On sunny days
make a beeline for the spacious
garden and sip bellinis while the
shadows lengthen.

DoubleEye

MAP P.132, POCKET MAP D8
Akazienstr. 22 Ⓤ Eisenacher Str. Ⓦ www.
doubleeye.de. Mon–Fri 9.30am–6.30pm,
Sat 10am–3.30pm.

This cosy café offers some of
the most delicious coffee in the
neighbourhood – not to mention
friendly services and great pastries.
If you enjoy people watching, then
definitely get a spot outside, to soak
in the local atmosphere.

Felsenkeller

MAP P.132, POCKET MAP D9
Akazienstr. 2 Ⓢ Julius-Leber-Brücke
☎ 030 78 13 447. Mon–Sat 4pm–midnight.

The perfect destination when
you're nostalgic for old Berlin.
Founded in 1923, this bar is
famous for its eight beers on tap;
they're drawn the old-fashioned
way, so be prepared to wait.
There's hearty, simple food (dishes
from €5), such as lentil soup and
swede stew. No music, but plenty
of atmosphere.

Green Door

MAP P.132, POCKET MAP D8
Winterfeldtstr. 50 Ⓤ Nollendorfplatz ☎ 030
21 52 515, Ⓦ greendoor.de. Sun–Thurs
6pm–2am, Fri & Sat 6pm–3am

Ring the bell and enter one of
Berlin's best-loved cocktail bars.
The expert but unpretentious
staff will recommend the perfect
drink. An older crowd fills the
cosy room.

Green Door

Kneipe Leuchtturm

MAP P.132, POCKET MAP D9

Crellestr. 41 ⓤ Kleistpark ⓣ 030 78 18 519, ⓦ leuchtturm-kneipe.de. Mon–Fri 6pm–late, Sat from 6.30pm, Sun from 7.30pm.
If you think beer just isn't the same without a cigarette, head for the "Lighthouse", with its unpretentious, welcoming atmosphere favoured by former hippies and locals. The wines can be middling so go for one of the beers on tap.

Mamsell

MAP P.132, POCKET MAP D8

Goltzstr. 48 ⓤ Eisenacher Str. ⓣ 030 92 12 29 00. Mon–Fri 11am–7pm, Sat 10am–5pm, Sun 2–6pm.
Those with a penchant for pink will be delighted by this sweet café/shop. The addictive real hot chocolate is served with a dusting of freshly grated ginger.

Winterfeldt Schokoladen

MAP P.132, POCKET MAP D8

Goltzstr. 23 ⓤ Nollendorfplatz ⓣ 030 23 62 32 56. Mon–Fri 9am–8pm, Sat 9am–6pm, Sun noon–7pm.
Once an apothecary, this café-chocolate shop serves a lovely selection of pastries to cure all your ills. Scones with clotted cream and jam and warm chocolate fondant cake are popular.

Clubs and venues

Havanna

MAP P.132, POCKET MAP D9

Hauptstr. 30 Ⓢ Julius-Leber-Brücke ⓣ 030 78 48 565, ⓦ www.havanna-berlin.de. Wed from 9pm, Fri & Sat from 10pm.
With four floors and seven bars, this magnet for Latin American music fans draws a diverse clientele. Serious salsa and tango fans will find like-minded devotees to shake it on the dancefloor.

Heile Welt

MAP P.132, POCKET MAP D7

Motzstr. 5 ⓤ Nollendorfplatz ⓣ 030 21 91 75 07. Daily from 7pm.
A much-beloved destination for gay men and the women who love them. Music runs the gamut from soul and dance to house and home-brewed "Schlager". During the week, enjoy one of the friendly bar staff's famously strong cocktails and settle into a comfortable sofa. The action picks up at the weekend, when it gets too crowded for some, and just right for others.

Day-trips from Berlin

There's so much to do in Berlin that it's easy to forget there's a world outside the city. Berlin's surroundings are surprisingly sparse and beautiful – a bucolic swathe of lakes, forests and small villages. Amidst the vast landscape lie some of the city's highlights, many of them less than an hour from the centre. Easily accessible by public transport, areas such as Dahlem, Potsdam and Wannsee make for enjoyable and edifying visits (as well as memorials to the darker side of the city's past). The most popular day-trip is Potsdam, which includes Schloss Sanssouci and Babelsberg film studios as well as a town centre distinct from anything in Berlin. The Wannsee area offers lakeside beaches as well as historical villas and the magical Pfaueninsel, while Dahlem has botanical gardens and the Museum of European Cultures. History buffs will find journeys to Sachsenhausen concentration camp, Villa Wannsee and Hohenschönhausen Stasi prison both chilling and instructive.

Sachsenhausen

Str. der Nationen 22, Oranienburg Ⓢ Oranienburg (RE5 or S1 from Alexanderplatz, then follow signs for Gedenkstätte Sachsenhausen) ☏ 033 01 20 00, ⓦ stiftung-bg.de. Daily: March 15–Oct 14 8.30am–6pm; Oct 15–March 14 8.30am–4.30pm. During the winter season, the museums are closed Mon, but the Visitor Information Centre, the open-air exhibition, "Murder and Mass Murder in Sachsenhausen Concentration Camp" and the site of commemoration "Station Z", are open to the public every day. Free. Guided tours available for groups (€15–25) in a range of different languages.

Located in Oranienburg, 35km north of the city, Sachsenhausen ranks among Berlin's most emotionally wrenching wartime memorials – which is saying a lot for a city like this. Established in 1936, it was first used as a prison for political opponents. It became a training ground for SS officers, and from 1938 to 1945 the central administration for all concentration camps was located here. After the war started, prisoners from all over Europe were brought here. In 1943 a small gas chamber was added. By 1945 some 200,000 people had passed through the prison, with tens of thousands dying of starvation, disease, mistreatment or murdered systematically by the SS. In April 1945 more than 33,000 prisoners were sent on the notorious death marches, during which more than a thousand died – those who collapsed en route were routinely shot. When the camp was liberated by Russian soldiers on April 22, 1945 only three thousand prisoners remained, many of whom who died in the days afterwards. The camp became a Soviet-run prison named "Special Camp No. 7" (renamed in 1948 to "Special Camp No. 1"). Sixty thousand people were interned here over five years, including six thousand German officers transferred from Western Allied POW camps. By the time the camp closed in the spring of 1950, twelve thousand had died of malnutrition and disease. In 1961, the GDR turned the site into a memorial, removing many of the original buildings and constructing an obelisk, statue and meeting area. Today the memorial is a place of commemoration as well as a museum that includes a wealth of information on the camp, artwork by inmates, models, pictures and more. Following the discovery in 1990 of mass graves from the Soviet period, a separate museum was opened about the Soviet-era history.

Potsdam

Direct line to Wannsee, then change on S7 (20–30min; ticket for zones A,B and C); or regional trains (RE1) to Potsdam and Babelsburg. You can cover most of Potsdam on foot, though the Berlin and Potsdam WelcomeCard (see page 154), available from the tourist centre at the train station, includes transport and gives discounts on over two hundred attractions. Visit Ⓦ potsdam-tourism.com.

Located 24km southwest of Berlin, Potsdam makes for an easy and pleasant day-trip, with plenty to see and do, from the wonderful Schloss Sanssouci and its gardens to the Babelsberg film studios. There are two quaint historic quarters in the city itself that are worth seeking out. The **Russian Colony Alexandrowka** (Alexandrowka 2; Ⓣ 0331 817 02 03, Ⓦ alexandrowka.de; Tues–Sun 10am–6pm, June–Sept Fri till 9pm; €3.50), created in 1826–27 on the request of Friedrich Wilhelm III in memory of his friend Tsar Alexander I, is an artist's village with twelve picturesque wooden houses and a small Russian Orthodox chapel (1829) on Kapellenberg hill to the north. Check out the Russian tearoom in the warden's house. The **Holländisches Viertel**, or Dutch quarter (Ⓦ www.hollaendisches-viertel.net), consists of around

150 three-storey redbrick houses, and was built between 1734 and 1742 for Dutch craftsmen invited to Potsdam by Friedrich Wilhelm I. The houses are built in the classic Dutch style with shuttered windows and slanted roofs; at Mittelstrasse 8 the J**an Bouman Haus** preserves a typical house of the era (Ⓣ 0331 28 03 773; Mon–Fri 1–6pm, Sat & Sun 11am–6pm; €3), while the **Potsdam Museum** at Alter Markt 9 (Ⓣ 0331 289 68 68; Tues, Wed & Fri 10am–5pm, Thurs till 7pm, Sat & Sun 10am–6pm, €3) displays historic paintings and photos of the city.

Museum Barberini

Humboldtstr. 5–6 Ⓣ 033 12 36 01 44 99, Ⓦ museum-barberini.com. Mon & Wed–Sun 10am–7pm (closes 9pm every first Thurs of the month). €14.

In January 2017, the **Museum Barberini** opened inside Frederick the Great's former Barberini Palace on the Alter Markt. As well as exhibiting a permanent collection

Potsdam

Schloss Sanssouci

of works from the former GDR, the museum also hosts three temporary exhibitions per year, ranging in aesthetic scope from Old Masters to contemporary art.

Schloss Sanssouci and park

Park Sanssouci Ⓢ Potsdam. Around 5km from Potsdam train station; bus #695 goes from the train station, with stops at Schloss Sanssouci, the Orangerie and Neues Palais (among others). ☎ 033 19 69 42 00, Ⓦ spsg.de. Palace Tues–Sun: April–Oct 10am–6pm; Nov–March 10am–5pm, timed guided tours only (tickets at Ⓦ tickets.spsg.de). Park daily 9am–dusk. Admission to palace €12; other attractions individually priced, or €19 day ticket for all buildings. Park: free.

The highlight of any trip to Potsdam, Schloss Sanssouci was built for Frederick the Great by the magnificently titled Georg Wenzeslaus von Knobelsdorff between 1745 and 1747. It was his summer residence – the place he came for some peace and quiet and to be with his beloved dogs (*Sans Souci* means "without worries" in French); parts of the park, buildings and palaces dotted around it were added to by later Prussian kings. Having survived unscathed from the War, the palace is considered one of the most significant examples of Rococo architecture – much of the original artworks were moved to Rheinsberg during the War or were transferred as booty to the Soviet Union, though Frederick's library and 36 oil paintings were returned and can be viewed today alongside furnishings and decorations from the original rooms. The adjacent **picture gallery** exhibits works by Rubens, van Dyck, Caravaggio and other renowned artists, and the historic windmill – built in the Dutch style and rebuilt in 1993 – is worth a visit, as is the **Chinese House** (same times as Sanssouci; €4) and the **New Palace** (Neues Palais; Mon & Wed–Sun 10am–5/6pm; €8), a larger Baroque-style palace intended to display Frederick's power to the world. Best of all is the surrounding **park**, an inspiring display of terraced vineyards, flamboyant flower beds, hedges and abundant fruit trees. Note that the palaces are highly popular in summer and tours inside the main palace are limited, so arrive early or book ahead.

Filmpark Babelsberg

Grossbeerenstr. 200 Ⓢ Babelsburg, then bus #601, #619, #690 to Filmpark or RE1 to Medienstadt ☎ 033 17 21 27 50, Ⓦ filmpark-babelsberg.de. Daily: April–Sept 10am–6pm; Oct & Nov 10am–5pm (see the website for current seasonal opening hours). €22.

Some of Germany's most famous films were created at Studio Babelsberg, including masterpieces such as *Metropolis* (1927) and *The Blue Angel* (1930), starring Marlene Dietrich – in its heyday the studios were Europe's version of Hollywood. This associated theme park allows visitors to roam sets from old films, witness stuntmen in action and marvel at the special effects. It's especially good (if not better) for kids, who will enjoy the Jungle Playground and the Animal Farm.

Museum Europäischer Kulturen (MEK)

Arnimallee 25, a short signposted walk down Iltisstrasse directly opposite Ⓤ Dahlem-Dorf ☎ 030 266 42 42 42, Ⓦ smb.museum/mek. Tues–Fri 10am–5pm, Sat & Sun 11am–6pm. €8.

The **Museum Europäischer Kulturen** (Museum of European Cultures) is devoted to the life worlds of people in Europe. With around 280,000 cultural historical objects, its collection provides a unique insight into European everyday culture and popular art. The permanent exhibition "Cultural Contacts. Living in Europe" provides a cross-section of the rich collection of the MEK and deals with discussions on social movements and national boundaries in Europe.

Domäne Dahlem

Königin-Luise-Str. 49 (just west of and over the road from Ⓤ Dahlemdorf) ☎ 030 66 63 000, Ⓦ domaene-dahlem.de. Daily 8am–7pm; museum Tues–Sun 10am–5pm. €4 (free for under 18s).

A working farm and handicrafts centre, **Domäne Dahlem** attempts to show off the lifestyle and skills of the pre-industrial age. The old estate house has a few odds and ends, most intriguing of which are the thirteenth-century swastikas, but the collection of agricultural instruments in an outbuilding is more comprehensive. Elsewhere there are ponies, turkeys, pigs, sheep and cows in the grounds, and demonstrations of woodcarving, wool- and cotton-spinning and various other farm crafts. At weekends some of the old agricultural machinery is fired up and the animals are paraded. The complex also now features the **Culinarium**: a kid-friendly, interactive cultural history of food – from farm to fork – complete with locally produced goods to buy. A visit out here is best combined with a visit to the nearby **Museum Europäischer Kulturen** and/or the city's **Botanical Garden**.

Dahlem Botanic Garden and Botanical Museum

Königin-Luise-Str. 6–8 Ⓤ/Ⓢ Rathaus Steglitz, and 15min walk or bus #X83 to Königin-Luise-Str./Botanischer Garten. ☎ 030 83 85 01 00, Ⓦ bgbm.org. Daily: Jan, Nov & Dec 9am–4pm; Feb 9am–5pm; March 9am–6pm, April–Oct 9am–8pm. Gardens (inc. museum) €6.

Founded as an extension to the kitchen garden of the Berlin palace by the Elector of Brandenburg, by 1815 the royal herbarium had developed hugely thanks to extensive botanical research by C.L. Willdenow. The collection was moved to Dahlem 1897–1910 and today hosts 20,000 species of plants over 43 hectares, making it one of the largest and most diverse botanical gardens in the world. The sixteen greenhouses (Gewächshäuser) feature an array of specialist areas such as desert and rainforest. The garden resembles a planted map with "Prairie", "Himalaya" and "Alps" sections topped by aquatic and marsh plants, an aroma and touch garden and medicinal plants. The attached museum features sections of preserved fossils and plant formations on artificially constructed landscapes.

Pfaueninsel

🚇 Wannsee, then bus #208 to the passenger ferry (€4 inc. entry to the island). Castle: April–Oct Tues–Sun 10am–5.30pm (€6). Island: daily Nov–Feb 10am–4pm; Mar 9am–6pm; April–9am–7pm; May– Aug 9am–8pm; Sept, 9am–7pm; Oct 9am–6pm (€4 inc. ferry).

Formerly known as *Kanninchenwerder* ("Rabbit Island"), Peacock Island features a castle built by Prussian king Frederick William II in 1793 for him and his mistress Wilhelmine Enke. His successor Frederick William III turned the island into a model farm and from 1816 had the park redesigned by Peter Joseph Lenné. Karl Friedrich Schinkel also planned a few of the buildings, for example the former Palm House and Llama House, and also the Cavalier House in the middle of the island. The king also laid out a menagerie modelled on the Ménagerie du Jardin des Plantes in Paris, in which exotic animals and birds including peacocks were housed. In addition to several free-ranging peacocks, chickens and pheasants can be found in captivity, complemented by a rich variety of flora. The entire island is designated as a nature reserve. The Cavalier House is currently closed due to renovation work, until further notice.

House of the Wannsee Conference

🚇 Wannsee, then bus #114 (direction "Krankenhaus Heckeshorn") to Haus der Wannsee-Konferenz ☎ 030 80 50 010, 🌐 www.ghwk.de. Daily 10am–6pm. Free (guided tour €3, German only).

It's hard to imagine that this handsome villa at Wannsee lake has an iniquitous history, but it was here that the "Final Solution of the Jewish Question" was discussed by fifteen high-ranking Nazi officials, who agreed to exterminate the entire Jewish population of Europe. Since 1992 it has served as a memorial and documentation centre, with a permanent exhibit that draws on detailed historical research to profile the conference and the process of deporting Jews to the ghettoes and camps. A library on the second floor (named after Joseph Wulf, an Auschwitz survivor and campaigner for this memorial) holds thousands of books on Nazism, anti-Semitism, the Holocaust, as well as Nazi-era documents such as children's books promoting Nazism. However, the most spine-tingling experience is simply standing in the room where the plans were made for the murder of millions.

Strandbad Wannsee

Wannseebadeweg 25 🚇 Wannsee/Nikolaisee ☎ 030 22 19 00 11 🌐 berlinerbaeder.de. Daily April–Sept; check website for exact times. €5.50.

Strandbad Wannsee's impressive 1275m long (and 80m wide) sweep of sandy beach has long been a venerable summer destination for Berliners. Officially the largest lido in Europe, it's located on the eastern side of the Wannsee, just a twenty-minute train ride from the city centre. Its current "look" was formulated by architects Martin Wagner and Richard Ermisch. Today the "Mother of all Lidos" attracts up to 230,000 visitors per year and has been designated a cultural heritage site. Between 2004 and 2007, it underwent a €12.5 million refurbishment for its centenary celebrations.

Max Liebermann Villa

Colomierstr. 3 Ⓢ Wannsee then either bus #114 toward Heckeshorn to Liebermann-Villa (5min) or 20min walk ☏ 030 80 58 59 00, ⓦ www.liebermann-villa .de. April–Sept daily except Tues 10am–6pm; Oct–March daily except Tues 11am–5pm. €8.

German Impressionist Max Liebermann's "castle by the sea", built in 1909, and particularly its expansive, 7000-square-metre garden, was the subject of more than two hundred of his paintings. An exhibition documents Liebermann's life here, with prints and photographs. On the upper floor are around forty paintings, pastels and prints that revolve around his Wannsee works – pictures of the flower terrace, perennial garden, birch grove and the lawn leading down to the lake – plus portraits of family and personalities. The garden has been reconstructed today as it was originally planned by Liebermann, and brims with rare and diverse species.

Gedenkstätte Berlin-Hohenschönhausen

Genslerstr. 66 #M5 from Ⓢ Freienwalder Str. (then 10min walk) or #M6 from Hackescher Markt Genslerstr. (then 10min walk) ☏ 030 98 60 82 30, ⓦ stiftung-hsh. de. Daily 9am–6pm, English tours 10.30am, 12.30am & 2.30pm €6.

With its intact buildings, equipment and furniture, the Stasi prison at Hohenschönhausen provides a particularly authentic – and grisly – portrait of public persecution during GDR times. The Stasi used it to detain and physically and psychologically torture dissenters. The prison, which remained largely a secret until the Wall fell in 1989, was turned into a memorial in 1994, and since 2000 has been an independent foundation that researches the history of the prison and produces exhibitions, events and publications. The only way to see the memorial is via a guided tour, available in German, English and other languages; tours with former inmates are also available, though mostly in German. The tour includes a survey of the older and newer prison blocks and detailed descriptions of daily life in the prison.

Strandbad Wannsee

ACCOMMODATION

Hotel Adlon

Accommodation

Berlin's accommodation options run the gamut from cheap and cheerful hostels to corporate hotels, super-deluxe five stars and intimate boutique and "art" hotels. Prices quoted usually include taxes and service charges, though breakfast and parking are sometimes extra – it's worth double-checking when booking. While there are many rooms in the city, there are also a lot of visitors; booking ahead in the warmer, more popular months is recommended, especially during large events such as the film festival (see page 158).

Spandauer Vorstadt

CIRCUS HOSTEL MAP P.28, POCKET MAP D11. Weinbergsweg 1a ⓤ Rosenthaler Platz ☏ 030 20 00 39 39, ⓦ circus-berlin.de. One of the most popular hostels in the city, *Circus* offers pleasant, clean dorms, private rooms – even penthouse apartments – and a convivial, upbeat vibe right on buzzing Rosenthaler Platz. Bicycles for rent, free walking tours and their own microbrewery add to the appeal. Buffet breakfast €5. **Dorms from €19, doubles from €85**

CIRCUS HOTEL MAP .P28 POCKET MAP E10. Rosenthalerstr. 1 ⓤ Rosenthaler Platz ☏ 030 20 00 39 39, ⓦ circus-berlin. de. The sister establishment of the *Circus* hostel (located just over the road) is a more upmarket and more ecofriendly place. Sixty rooms include junior suites and apartments, decorated in striking colours with wooden floors and a mix of antique and modern furniture. Buffet breakfast €12. **Doubles from €95**

HEART OF GOLD MAP P.28, POCKET MAP C12. Johannisstr. 11 ⓢ Oranienburg ☏ 030 29 00 33 00, ⓦ heartofgold-hostel.de. Good-value and friendly hostel near one of the busiest strips in Mitte. Dorms and rooms are basic but clean, and staff go the extra mile to make staying here fun. Expect lots of space-themed decorative touches. Buffet breakfast €5. **Dorms from €9.50, rooms from €45**

KASTANIENHOF MAP P.28, POCKET MAP H2. Kastanienallee 65 ⓤ Senefelderplatz ☏ 030 44 30 50, ⓦ kastanienhof.berlin. This recently renovated hotel has 44 rooms in an elegant house, with decor that nods to Berlin's fascinating history, including photos, illustrations and maps. Great location for Prenzlauer Berg and Mitte. Breakfast (€9) not included. **Doubles from €87**

SOHO HOUSE MAP P.28, POCKET MAP F11. Torstr. 1 ⓤ Rosa-Luxemburg-Platz ☏ 030 40 50 440, ⓦ sohohouseberlin.com. Private

Apartment rentals

Private apartments are a popular, and often good-value choice for many travellers to Berlin. The best apartments offer value for money, are well located and usually stylish or interestingly decorated. Although Airbnb was banned from renting out complete apartments in the city in 2016 (rooms within a house are still possible), that seems to have done little to diminish offerings on the site. Also check out ⓦ brilliant-apartments.de, ⓦ ferienwohnungen-berlin.de and ⓦ oh-berlin.com, which all offer a good spread of apartments, rooms and regular special deals.

members' club in a restored Bauhaus building with forty swanky apartments, four huge lofts and forty hotel rooms that range from tiny to extra large. Decor is quirky and fun, and hints at the faded glamour of the late 1920s. There's also a lovely spa, gym, rooftop pool, restaurant, bars, screening room and private dining area. From €270

WEINMEISTER MAP P.28, POCKET MAP E11. Weinmeisterstr. 2 ⓤ Weinmeisterstr. ⓣ 030 75 56 670, ⓦ www.the-weinmeister.com. This adults-only swish hotel features 84 spacious rooms with large beds and a stylish design ethic. There's also a decent bar and lounge, a rooftop bar and a sixth-floor beauty spa. Breakfast €18. Doubles from €129

Unter den Linden and the government quarter

ADLON KEMPINSKI MAP P.48, POCKET MAP B14. Unter den Linden 77 ⓤ / ⓢ Brandenburger Tor ⓣ 030 22 610, ⓦ hotel-adlon.de. Probably the most famous hotel in the city, and definitely one of the most luxurious, the *Hotel Adlon Kempinski* matches a wealth of history (previous guests include Emperor Wilhelm II, Albert Einstein and Michael Jackson, who famously dangled his baby from one of the hotel balconies) with serious five-star swagger and an enviable location overlooking the Brandenburg Gate on Pariser Platz. Breakfast €42. Doubles from €260

ARCOTEL JOHN F MAP P.48, POCKET MAP D14. Werderscher Markt 11 ⓤ Hausvogteiplatz ⓣ 030 40 50 460, ⓦ arcotelhotels.com. Close to Gendarmenmarkt, this 190-room hotel is a slightly cheaper option than the neighbouring big guns, but has all the facilities you'll need – gym, sauna, meeting rooms, restaurant, bar. Breakfast not included. Doubles from €117

ARTE LUISE KUNSTHOTEL MAP P.48, POCKET MAP B12. Luisenstr. 19 ⓤ / ⓢ Friedrichstr. ⓣ 030 28 44 80, ⓦ luise-berlin.com. Within walking distance of the Reichstag and Unter den Linden, this art hotel has fifty charmingly appointed and

highly individual rooms, Dutch sculptures in the large lobby and an in-house restaurant serving German-Mediterranean cuisine. Breakfast €11. Doubles from €99

HOTEL DE ROME MAP P.48, POCKET MAP C14. Behrenstr. 37 ⓤ Französische Str. ⓣ 030 46 06 090, ⓦ www.roccofortecollection.com. Occupying a nineteenth-century former Dresdner Bank building, this high-class hotel mixes history with a swanky interior, luxurious rooms, an expansive spa and a fantastic restaurant (*La Banca*) and rooftop terrace. Breakfast €35. Doubles from €295

WESTIN GRAND MAP P.48, POCKET MAP C13. Friedrichstr. 158–164 ⓤ Französische Str. ⓣ 030 20 270, ⓦ westingrandberlin.com. Built during the GDR, this large hotel, well positioned on Friedrichstrasse and close to the Brandenburg Gate, has been refurbished to feature a refined *belle époque* interior and beautifully appointed rooms and suites. Breakfast €32. Doubles from €169

Alexanderplatz and the Nikolaiviertel

ART'OTEL MAP P.58, POCKET MAP F14. Wallstr. 70–73 ⓤ Märkisches Museum ⓣ 030 24 06 20, ⓦ artotelberlinmitte.com. With its impressive range of paintings by Georg Baselitz (and others), this design hotel has reasonable rates, good in-house food and drink options and friendly staff. Breakfast €17.50. Doubles from €99

CITYSTAY HOSTEL MAP P.58, POCKET MAP E12. Rosenstr. 16 ⓢ Hackescher Markt ⓣ 030 23 62 40 31, ⓦ citystay.de. Close to Hackescher Markt, the *Citystay* is a big, loft-style space in a nineteenth-century building with dorms and private rooms. No leisure facilities but the bar serves craft beer, coffee and snacks, and there's a nice courtyard (until 10pm). Breakfast buffet (partly organic) is €5.50. Dorms from €10 (bedding €2.50), doubles from €40

LUX 11 MAP P.58, POCKET MAP F12. Rosa-Luxemburg-Str. 9–13 ⓤ Rosa-Luxemburg-Platz ⓣ 030 93 62 800, ⓦ lux-eleven.com. This designer apartment-hotel oozes style and has big, comfy rooms (with kitchenettes and spacious, open bathrooms), a decent restaurant–bar (*Prince*) and a concept store with a milk bar. Breakfast buffet €18. **Doubles from €109**

NIKOLAI RESIDENCE HOTEL MAP P.58, POCKET MAP E13. Am Nussbaum 5 Ⓤ Klosterstr. Ⓣ 03 04 00 44 59 00, Ⓦ nikolai-residence.com. Cute and well-run 3-star in the heart of the Nikolaivertel. Decor is fairly modern and dotted with paintings and photos by German artists, and the 21 rooms are simple, reasonably stylish and comfortable. No breakfast. **Doubles from €90.**

PARK INN MAP P.58, POCKET MAP F12. Alexanderplatz 7 Ⓤ/Ⓢ Alexanderplatz Ⓣ 030 23 890, Ⓦ parkinn-berlin.de. This towering 37-floor GDR-era building looks better on the inside than the out. Unexciting but comfortable rooms feature cosy beds, marble bathrooms and, past the twentieth floor, panoramic views across Berlin. Gym, sauna and a rooftop terrace, too. Breakfast not included. **Doubles from €79**

Potsdamer Platz and Tiergarten

BERLIN MARRIOTT HOTEL MAP P.66, POCKET MAP A15. Inge-Beisheim-Platz 1 Ⓣ 030 22 00 00, Ⓦ berlinmarriott.de. This business hotel is a surprisingly dynamic spot for leisure travellers too. Located right on Potsdamer Platz, it boasts a slick "fashion bar" designed by local star Michael Michalsky (with DJs at weekends), an excellent restaurant (*Midtown Grill*), plus a pool and comprehensive fitness centre. Breakfast €19. **Doubles from €129**

HOTEL ALTBERLIN AT POTSDAMER PLATZ MAP P.66, POCKET MAP E7. Potsdamer Str. 67 Ⓤ/Ⓢ Potsdamer Platz Ⓣ 030 26 06 70, Ⓦ alt-am-potsdamer-platz.atberlinhotels.com. A turn-of-the-twentieth-century, Wilhelminian-era hotel with "grandma" style rooms, old-world decor and long-forgotten Berlin specialities served at its restaurant, *Rike's*. Breakfast included. **Rooms from €83**

HOTEL HANSABLICK MAP P.66, POCKET MAP B5. Flotowstr. 6 Ⓤ Tiergarten Ⓣ 030 39 04 800, Ⓦ hansablick.de. The *Hansablick*, located right on the water, has rooms with balconies and/or river views and a traditional interior that features artworks by the likes of Otmar Alt and Heinrich Zille. Rates include breakfast, wi-fi and parking. **Doubles from €79**

RITZ CARLTON MAP P.66, POCKET MAP A15. Potsdamer Platz 3 Ⓢ/Ⓤ Potsdamer Platz Ⓣ 030 33 77 77, Ⓦ ritzcarlton.com. This distinctive skyscraper hotel has 303 rooms with expensive cherry-wood closets and watercolour paintings. There are also bars, a tea lounge, a great brasserie, and fantastic five-star service. Breakfast included. **Doubles from €220**

SHERATON BERLIN GRAND HOTEL ESPLANADE MAP P.66, POCKET MAP D6. Lützowufer 15 Ⓤ Nollendorfplatz Ⓣ 030 25 47 80, Ⓦ esplanadeberlin.com. Smack between Ku'damm and Potsdamer Platz, this large, fancy hotel has two restaurants, a New York-style cocktail bar and spa. Breakfast €22. **Doubles from €99**

Prenzlauer Berg

EASTSEVEN MAP P.78, POCKET MAP F10. Schwedter Str. 7 Ⓤ Senefelderplatz Ⓣ 030 93 62 22 40, Ⓦ eastseven.de. Laid-back hostel located on the border of Mitte and Prenzlauer Berg. Rooms (singles, doubles, twins, dorms) and public areas are clean and functional, furnishings are decent quality and there's a lounge area with books and board games. No stag or hen groups. Breakfast €3. **Dorms from €14, doubles from €68.**

HOTEL TRANSIT LOFT MAP P.78, POCKET MAP K3. Immanuelkirchstr. 14a Ⓤ/Ⓢ Alexanderplatz Ⓣ 030 48 49 37 73, Ⓦ transit-loft.de. A modern hotel set in a nineteenth-century, yellow-brick factory and well located for Kollwitzplatz (see page 77). The 47 rooms (dorms included) are airy and well lit with basic furnishings and en-suite showers. The same owners run *Hotel Transit* in Kreuzberg (see page 148). Breakfast included. **Dorms from €21, doubles from €59**

LETTE'M SLEEP MAP P.78, POCKET MAP J3. Lettestr. 7 ⓢ Prenzlauer Allee ☎ 030 44 73 36 23, ⓦ backpackers.de. Located directly on Helmholtzplatz, this vaguely hip backpacker hostel has basic but clean dorms (four- to seven-bed) as well as twins and private apartments. There's a common room, kitchen (but no breakfast), free wi-fi and a beer garden in summer. **Dorms from €15, doubles from €49**

MYER'S HOTEL MAP P.78, POCKET MAP J3. Metzer Str. 26 ⓢ Senefelderplatz ☎ 030 44 01 40, ⓦ myershotel.de. Set in a nineteenth-century Neoclassical building, this tasteful hotel has 51 rooms in a range of shapes and sizes, a glass-roofed courtyard with lounge and gallery with changing exhibitions. There's also a garden with terrace. Breakfast not included. **Doubles from €87**

PFEFFERBETT MAP P.78, POCKET MAP F10. Christinenstr. 18–19 ⓤ Senefelderplatz ☎ 030 93 93 58 58, ⓦ pfefferbett.de. This welcoming hostel has clean, smart rooms and dorms, a buzzy lobby and a lovely courtyard garden that doubles as a beer garden. Bicycle hire (€12 per day), free guided tours and laundry services available. Breakfast €6.70. **Dorms from €12, doubles from €32.50**

Friedrichshain

ANDEL'S BY VIENNA HOUSE BERLIN MAP P.92, POCKET MAP M3. Landsberger Allee 106 ⓢ Landsberger Allee ☎ 030 45 30 5300, ⓦ andelsberlin.com. This sprawling design hotel has 557 small and retro-ish rooms with full amenities and spacious bathrooms. The top-floor *Skykitchen* and *Skybar* have great city views and there's a 550-square-metre spa. Breakfast included. **Doubles from €99**

JUNCKER'S HOTEL GARNI MAP P.92, POCKET MAP A16. Grünberger Str. 21 ⓤ Frankfurter Tor ☎ 030 29 33 550, ⓦ junckershotel.de. A small, family-run hotel with medium-size but good-quality rooms, friendly staff and a quiet atmosphere. Breakfast €8. **Doubles from €59**

MICHELBERGER MAP P.92, POCKET MAP M7. Warschauer Str. 39–40 ⓤ Warschauer Str. ☎ 030 29 77 85 90, ⓦ michelbergerhotel.com. Creative, welcoming and trendy, the rooms here are imaginatively and individually designed, the stylish lounge area has regular gigs and the drinks and food are good. Recent additions include a sauna, a renovated kitchen and several self-contained apartments. **Doubles from €70**

NHOW MAP P.92, POCKET MAP M7. Stralauer Allee 3 ⓢ Warschauer Str. ☎ 030 29 02 990, ⓦ nhow-berlin.com. This four-star concept hotel merges a music theme with designer hotel rooms. Recreational amenities include a health club, sauna and fitness facility and some rooms have great views over the river. Breakfast included. **Doubles from €139**

OSTEL MAP P.92, POCKET MAP L6. Wriezener Karree 5 ⓤ Ostbahnhof ☎ 030 25 76 86 60, ⓦ ostel.eu. This shrine to *Ostalgie* – nostalgia for the old Communist GDR – is kitted out with a wealth of GDR memorabilia like brown floral wallpaper, 1970s radio clocks and photographs of GDR leaders. Prices will satisfy contemporary communists too. **Doubles from €39**

PLUS BERLIN MAP P.92, POCKET MAP M7. Warschauer Platz 6 ⓤ/ⓢ Warschauer Str. ☎ 030 31 16 98 820, ⓦ plushostels. com. Upscale and vibrant backpacker hostel located inside a striking red-brick building with stylish, high-ceilinged rooms, a lively bar and restaurant, and even a pool, sauna and large garden area. Breakfast €6.50. **Dorms from €9, doubles from €120**

West Kreuzberg

GRAND HOSTEL MAP P.102, POCKET MAP F7. Tempelhofer Ufer 14 ⓤ Möckernbrück ☎ 030 200 95 450, ⓦ grandhostel-berlin .de. Set inside a listed historic building near the Landwehr Canal, this award-winning hostel ups the ante in terms of elegance and space. There's a bar and library room on site, furnishings are design-savvy and the bright, stylish rooms and dorms don't have bunks. Bed linen service €3.60, breakfast €6.50. **Dorms €12, doubles €48**

HOTEL TRANSIT MAP P.102, POCKET MAP F8. Hagelberger Str. 53 ⓤ Mehringdamm ⓣ 030 78 90 470, ⓦ hotel-transit.de. This bright, breezy hostel occupies a former factory building and has basic but decently sized rooms and an upbeat atmosphere. Breakfast included. **Doubles from €59**

JOHANN HOTEL MAP P.102, POCKET MAP H8. Johanniterstr. 8 ⓤ Prinzenstr. ⓣ 030 22 50 740, ⓦ hotel-johann-berlin.de. Close to Bergmannstrasse. and the Jewish Museum, the *Johann* is a fairly nondescript but friendly hotel, with spacious rooms and a peaceful garden. Breakfast included. **Doubles from €105**

MÖVENPICK HOTEL MAP P.102, POCKET MAP F7. Schöneberger Str. 3 ⓢ Anhalter Bahnhof ⓣ 030 23 00 60, ⓦ moevenpick-hotels.com. This former Siemens office has a unique mix of contemporary and industrial decor: Philippe Starck pieces in the rooms, wood and glass in abundance and a pleasant courtyard restaurant (*Hof zwei*) and bar. Breakfast €22. **Doubles from €99**

RIEHMERS HOFGARTEN MAP P.102, POCKET MAP F8. Yorckstr. 83 ⓤ Mehringdamm ⓣ 030 78 09 88 00, ⓦ riehmers-hofgarten.com. There's a low-key, residential atmosphere at this hotel in a historically protected building. The 22 rooms and apartments have a correspondingly nineteenth-century feel and there's a delightful living room for relaxation. **Doubles from €131**

East Kreuzberg

MOTEL ONE BERLIN-MITTE MAP P.108, POCKET MAP J7. Prinzenstr. 40 ⓤ Moritzplatz ⓣ 030 69 56 71 740, ⓦ motel-one.com. Well located for Alexanderplatz and the Oranienstrasse scene, this functional hotel has comfortable enough rooms with all necessary conveniences, a bar for snacks and drinks and free wi-fi. Breakfast €9.50. **Doubles from €77**

ROCK'N'ROLL HERBERGE MAP P.108, POCKET MAP K7. Muskauer Str. 11 ⓤ Görlitzer Bahnhof ⓣ 030 61 62 36 00, ⓦ rnrherberge.de. With six rooms designed by local artists, billiards and table football and vegan and non-vegan breakfasts and snacks, this budget hangout is especially set up for musicians and music lovers – as the graffiti of Falco and Joe Strummer testify to. Rooms for up to five people (not dorms) are available (from €34 per person). **Doubles from €52**

Charlottenburg

25HOURS HOTEL BIKINI BERLIN MAP P.122, POCKET MAP B6. Budapester Str. 40 ⓤ/ⓢ Zoologischer Garten ⓣ 030 12 02 210, ⓦ 25hours-hotels.com. The hotel that single-handedly funked up West Berlin, the *25hours* comes with a playfully cool design aesthetic, quirky bedrooms and a fabulous rooftop restaurant and bar (see page 130). The Kaiser Wilhelm Church is right across the street. **Doubles from €170**

AM SAVIGNYPLATZ HOTEL MAP P.122, POCKET MAP A6. Kantstr. 22 ⓢ Savignyplatz ⓣ 030 50 18 17 36, ⓦ am-savignyplatz-hotel.de. A beautiful old building that has been thoroughly modernized, the *Am Savignyplatz* is surprisingly stylish – its eleven rooms are spacious and modern, and one of them even has a small garden. **Doubles from €69**

AM STEINPLATZ MAP P.122, POCKET MAP B6. Steinplatz 4 ⓢ Zoologischer Garten ⓣ 030 55 44 440, ⓦ marriott.com. Sumptuous boutique set inside a heritage-listed building that was once the haunt of the more well-heeled and intellectual Weimar set. Rooms are richly appointed with a mix of vintage and modern furnishings and there's a top-notch restaurant and classy bar with craft beer and occasional DJs. Breakfast €25–35. **Doubles from €190.**

ART HOTEL CHARLOTTENBURGER HOF MAP P.122, POCKET MAP A6. Stuttgarter Platz 14 ⓢ Charlottenburg ⓣ 030 32 90 70, ⓦ charlottenburger-hof.de. Bright contemporary hotel, replete with modern art, Bauhaus design and multicoloured furniture. Perks include an on-site café-restaurant with terrace and courtyard. Rates can often be slashed by booking specials online. **Doubles from €63**

HOTEL OTTO MAP P.122, POCKET MAP A6. Knesebeckstr. 10 Ⓤ Ernst-Reuter-Platz ☎ 030 54 71 00 80, Ⓦ www.hotelotto. com. *Otto* eschews the traditional for a cheery, modern experience that's all blues, magentas and greens. The 46 rooms are chic and individually designed and the organic food at the restaurant is good too. Breakfast €18. **Doubles from €100**

HOTEL Q! MAP P.122, POCKET MAP A6. Knesebeckstr. 67 Ⓤ Uhlandstr. ☎ 030 81 00 660, Ⓦ hotel-q.com. One of west Berlin's swankiest hotels, the *Q!* has bathtubs built into bed frames, elegantly minimal rooms, chocolate massages and the *Fox Bar*, plus a lounge and garden. **Doubles from €110**

HOTEL ZOO MAP P.122, POCKET MAP B6. Kurfürstendamm 25 Ⓤ Kurfürstendamm ☎ 030 88 43 70, Ⓦ hotelzoo.de. This historic hotel reopened to great fanfare in 2014. Its 144 rooms are sumptuously appointed with tasteful fashion photographs and high-quality wooden floors and furnishings. There's a restaurant and lounge, and two sixth-floor penthouse suites if you feel like splashing. **Doubles from €150**

SANA HOTEL MAP P.122, POCKET MAP B7. Nürnberger Str. 33-34 Ⓤ Augsburger Str ☎ 030 20 05 15 10, Ⓦ berlin.sanahotels. com. A short stroll from the KaDeWe and Berlin Zoo (see page 120), this well designed hotel has 208 rooms (of which 13 are suites and 42 apartments), a restaurant and a chill-out bar/lounge, indoor pool, sauna and fitness facilities. **Doubles from €100**

Schöneberg

HOTEL DE ELA MAP P.132, POCKET MAP C8. Landshuter Str. 1 Ⓤ Viktoria-Luise-Platz ☎ 030 23 63 39 60, Ⓦ hotel-de-ela. de. A mix of twenty-first-century design in a nineteenth-century Victorian building, *De Ela* has large, comfortable rooms with a classic feel for decent prices. Family friendly too. Breakfast and wi-fi included. **Doubles from €40**

JUGENDHOTEL BERLINCITY MAP P.132, POCKET MAP E9. Crellestr. 22 Ⓤ Kleistpark ☎ 030 78 70 21 30, Ⓦ jugendhotel-berlin. de. With 170 plain but comfy beds in a renovated factory building, this is a good option for budget-conscious travellers. Pool tables, decent rooms and a convivial bar. **Dorms from €21, doubles from €65**

TOM'S HOTEL MAP P.132, POCKET MAP C7. Motzstr. 19 Ⓤ Nollendorfplatz ☎ 030 21 96 66 04, Ⓦ toms-hotel.de. This friendly gay hangout has a great bar (*Tom's*), a vibrant café and is close to the gay scene of Nollendorfplatz. Rooms are comfortable and artistically decorated and apartments feature a flat-screen TV and free wi-fi. Breakfast €6.50. **Doubles from €79**

ESSENTIALS

Beach bar on the River Spree

Arrival

By air

Flying is, predictably, the cheapest and most convenient way to get to Germany from overseas, as well as from many other European countries thanks to the proliferation of discount airlines.

Both Berlin's airports (ⓦ berlin-airport.de) are within Berlin public transport's zone ABC (Tegel is within AB, Schönefeld is within C). An ABC ticket costs €3.40 while an AB costs €2.80. From Berlin's **Schönefeld airport** (SXF) S-Bahn lines S9 and S45 run regularly (every 10–20min) to main stations like Alexanderplatz (38min), the Hauptbahnhof (44min) and Bahnhof Zoo (50min). There are also regional trains like RE7 or RB14 that head to the centre. Bus #X7 (N7 at night) runs every 20min to nearby U-Bahn Rudow. From **Tegel airport** (TXL) the frequent #TXL express bus runs to the Hauptbahnhof and Alexanderplatz, while #X9 express or local #109 and #128 buses run to Bahnhof Zoo. **Taxis** from Tegel tend to cost €20–35, depending on which part of the city you want to get to; from Schönefeld expect to pay more like €30–50.

In mid 2020, Tegel is due to close and Schönefeld extended into **Berlin Brandenburg International** airport.

By train

Germany is well connected by train with destinations throughout continental Europe. Check Deutsche Bahn's excellent website (ⓦ www.bahn.de) for international routes. From the UK, a slow but comfortable option is via Paris, with the overnight sleeper departing weekly in summer only from Paris Est (total travel time from London around 16hr); a quicker daytime route is via Brussels and Cologne (from 10hr 30min).

The huge **Hauptbahnhof** northeast of the Brandenburg Gate is well connected to the rest of the city by S- and U-Bahn. Many long-distance routes also stop at Ostbahnhof, convenient for Friedrichshain, or Bahnhof Zoo, for Charlottenburg. All are well connected by S-Bahn.

By bus

Several private bus companies, such as Flixbus (ⓦ flixbus.com) and Eurolines (ⓦ eurolines.com/en) run routes from as far afield as Barcelona and Bucharest.

Most international buses stop at the bus station (ZOB), linked to the centre by express buses #X34 and #X49, as well as regular buses #104, #139, #218, #349 and #M49; U-Bahn #2, from Kaiserdamm station; and S-Bahn from Messe-Nord/ICC.

Getting around

U- and S-Bahn

BVG (ⓦ bvg.de) operate an efficient, integrated system of U- and S-Bahn train lines, buses and trams. U- and S-Bahn trains run daily 4.30am–1am (Fri & Sat all night).

Buses and trams

The city bus network – and the tram system mainly in eastern Berlin – covers most of the gaps left by the U-Bahn; several useful **tram** routes centre on Hackescher Markt, including the M1 to Prenzlauer Berg.

A night-time network of buses and trams operates, with buses (around every 30min) often following U-Bahn line routes; free maps are available at most stations.

City tours

Original Berlin Walks ☎ 030 30 19 194, ⊕ berlinwalks.de. Offers a range of walking tours of between three and six hours, many of which cover the main sights and beyond. Prices vary according to tour.

Trabi Safaris ⊕ trabi-safari.de. Drive around the city (slowly) in a Trabant, the car of choice for the GDR (with guides and without) with live information delivered to you via radio. Day and night "safaris" available. Around €60 depending on numbers (maximum four in a car).

Slow Travel Berlin ⊕ slowtravelberlin.com. English-speaking cultural/historical walking tours (2hr), mostly run by long-term residents. €20

Alternative Berlin ☎ 0162 81 98 264, ⊕ alternativeberlin.com. Street art tours, pub crawls and other "alternative culture" trawls.

Berlin Music Tours ☎ 172 42 42 037, ⊕ musictours-berlin.com. Follow the musical trails of Bowie, Iggy Pop, Depeche Mode and U2.

Buses #100 and **#200** drive past many famous Berlin sights en route from Zoologischer Garten to Alexanderplatz, providing a cheap alternative to a sightseeing tour.

Tickets and passes

Tickets are available from machines at U-Bahn stations, on trams (machines on trams only take coins) or from bus drivers. Zone AB **single tickets** cost €2.80; zone ABC single €3.40; **short-trip tickets** (*Kurzstreckentarif*) are available for three train or six bus/tram stops for €1.80; zone AB **day-tickets** cost €7. Validate single tickets in the yellow machines on platforms before travelling.

For two, three or five days the **WelcomeCard** (see page 154) is good value.

Bike rental and tours

Cycling in Berlin is very easy, safe and very popular. Not only is the city (mostly) as flat as a pancake, there are dedicated cycle lanes throughout.

There are also numerous rental places, including: Fat Tire (daily: March–Nov 9.30am–6pm; mid-April to Sept till 8pm; call or email out of season ☎ 030 24 04 79 91, ⊕ fattirebiketours.com/berlin), beneath the TV tower at Alexanderplatz. They also offer half-day **bike tours** (4hr 30min; €28). Nearly all hostels rent bikes for around €14/day.

Taxis

Taxi fares are €3.90 flag-fall plus €2/km for the first 7km, then €1.50/km thereafter; if you hail a taxi on the street – rather than at a stand or by phone – you can ask for a short-trip price (*Kurzstreckentarif*) before the trip starts and pay €5 for a 2km ride. Taxi firms include: Taxi Funk ☎ 030 44 33 22 and Funk Taxi ☎ 030 26 10 26.

Directory A–Z

Addresses

If you are looking for an address in the former East, bear in mind house numbers run in different directions on each side of the street, as opposed to the usual odd/even system.

Children

Berlin is a surprisingly child-friendly city. There are public playgrounds all over the city (many created from transforming bombed-out areas), plenty of green areas to play in such as Tiergarten, Volkspark Friedrichshain and Viktoriapark, and, in the colder months, kindercafés (see *Kiezkind*, page 87) where parents can enjoy a frothy coffee while their kids enjoy the toys.

Cinema

Movies in English play at Babylon Kreuzberg (ⓦ yorck.de), Cinemaxx Colosseum (ⓦ cinemaxx.de), Cinestar Originals (ⓦ cinestar.de) and in the Sony Center (ⓦ sonycenter.de).

Crime and emergencies

Serious crime is relatively low in Berlin, though petty crime such as bike theft can be rife. You can get help at any police station where English is usually spoken. Reporting thefts at local police stations is straightforward, but inevitably there'll be a great deal of bureaucracy to wade through. **Emergency numbers** are: police ⓣ 110; fire and ambulance ⓣ 112.

Discount passes

The **WelcomeCard** (Berlin AB: 48hr €20, 72hr €29, 5-day €38; Berlin and Potsdam ABC: 48hr €23, 72hr €32, 5-day €42; ⓦ berlin-welcomecard. de) includes public transport and up to fifty percent off at many of the major tourist sights. Though the standard card doesn't cover the Museum Island, a version that does include these museums is available. Many of the discounts are the same as student prices.

Electricity

230 V, 50 Hz. The Continental two-round-pin plug is standard.

Embassies and consulates

Australia, Wallstr. 76–79 ⓣ 030 88 00 880; Canada, Leipziger Platz 17 ⓣ 030 20 31 20; Ireland, Jaegerstr. 51 ⓣ 030 22 07 20; New Zealand, Friedrichstr. 60 ⓣ 030 20 62 10; South Africa, Tiergartenstr.18 ⓣ 030 22 07 30; UK, Wilhelmstr. 70–71 ⓣ 030 20 45 70; US, Pariser Platz 2 (postal address Clayallee 170) ⓣ 030 83 050.

Health

Emergency room at Campus Charité Mitte (entrance Luisenstr. 65/66), ⓣ 030 450 531 000. Most doctors speak English. Pharmacies (Apotheken) can deal with minor complaints; all display local pharmacies open 24hr, including Apotheke Hauptbahnhof, at the Hauptbahnhof.

Internet

Free wi-fi at the Sony Center and at other public malls and spaces, and in most hotels and hostels. Internet cafés charge around €1.50/30min.

LGBT+ Berlin

Berlin's diverse gay scene is spread across the city, but with a focus of sorts in Schöneberg, especially around Nollendorfplatz. The magazine *Siegessäule* (ⓦ siegessaeule.de) has listings and can be picked up in many cafés and shops. Club nights by GMF (ⓦ gmf-berlin.de) at various venues, including Sundays at *House of Weekend*, are always worth checking out. The Christopher Street Day Gay Pride festival takes place every year in June (ⓦ csd-berlin.de).

Listings and websites

ExBerliner is a monthly English-language magazine focusing on arts and music listings in Berlin (ⓦ www. exberliner.com). The two main listings magazines in German are *Tip* (ⓦ tip-berlin.de) and *Zitty* (ⓦ zitty.de); all are widely available in cafés and bars. For adverts and classifications also check Craig's List Berlin (⊛ berlin.craigslist.org). Useful English-language websites include ⊛ iheartberlin.de and ⊛ slowtravelberlin.com.

Lost property

Allegedly only 25 percent of lost items in Berlin turn up again, but it's worth contacting Zentrales Fundbüro, Platz der Luftbrücke 6 (☏ 030 75 60 31 01), who will help you with the search (there are six such offices around the city). Left or lost luggage can also be reclaimed at both airports and at the Lost & Found section at the Deutsche Bahn. Look for the "Fundbüro" at Hauptbahnhof if you lost something in the subway or tram, or contact BVG-Fundbüro, Potsdamer Str. 180–182 (BVG-Callcenter ☏ 030 19 449).

Money and banks

The German currency is the euro (€). Exchange facilities are available in most banks, post offices and commercial exchange shops called **Wechselstuben**. The Reisebank has branches in most main train stations (generally open daily, often till 10/11pm) and ATMs are widespread. Basic **banking hours** are Monday to Friday 9am to noon and 1.30 to 3.30pm, Thursday till 6pm. **Credit cards** are fairly widely accepted – but certainly not universally; independent or smaller restaurants and cafés often don't take them. There can be a surcharge in hostels and smaller hotels.

    ATMs and exchange are at the airports, and major stations including: Reisebank, at the Hauptbahnhof (daily 8am–9pm), Zoo station (daily 8am–9pm), Friedrichstr. station (daily 8am–8pm) and Ostbahnhof (Mon–Fri 8am–9pm, Sat & Sun 8am–8pm).

Opening hours

Larger shops open at 8am and close around 6 to 8pm weekdays and 2 to 4pm Saturday, and often close all day Sunday; smaller shops often open at 11am/noon and keep quite erratic hours. Pharmacies, petrol stations and shops in and around train stations stay open late and at weekends. Museums and historic monuments are, with a few exceptions, closed on Monday.

Phones

Call shops are the cheapest way to phone abroad, though you can also phone abroad from all payphones except those marked "National"; phonecards are widely available. The operator is on ☏ 03.

Post offices

Post offices are open Monday to Friday 8am to 6pm and Saturday 8am to 1pm. There's a convenient branch at Dircksenstr. 2, Mitte.

Smoking

After a wave of restrictions on smoking in all bars was introduced, a lawsuit from a small bar owner resulted in the law being loosened, and Berlin bars are pretty much almost all back to being smoky or having smoking areas. Expect to get smoke in your eyes in almost all bars that don't serve food. All restaurants are smoke free, but many offer a smokers' lounge somewhere.

Sports and outdoor activities

Bundesliga football (⊛ bundesliga.de) is the major spectator sport in Germany, with world-class clubs playing in top-notch stadiums, many revamped for the 2006 World Cup such as the Olympic stadium. Important matches sell out well in advance; tickets can be purchased from the clubs' websites.

Time

Berlin is on Central European Time (CET), one hour ahead of Britain and six hours ahead of EST, with the clocks going forward in spring and back again in autumn on the same dates as the rest of the EU, although whether this will continue in the future is currently in question. Generally speaking, Berliners, like the rest of Germany, use the 24-hour clock.

Toilets

There are a few public toilets (*Öffentliche Toilette*, WC) some of which you'll find in the almost romantic-looking toilet huts in parks and close to the subway. In some, you have to put a €0.50 coin in the slot to open the door. There are mostly free toilets at petrol stations, where you have to ask the clerk for the key. Also big shopping centres have public toilets normally with a maintenance woman, who you should tip around €0.30–50. Gentlemen should head for *Herren*; ladies should head for *Damen*.

Tipping

If you're in a group, you'll be asked if you want to pay individually (*getrennt*) or all together (*zusammen*). In general, round your bill up to the next €0.50 or €1 and give the total directly to the waiter when you pay (rather than leaving it on the table afterwards).

Tourist offices

The main contact details are: ☏ 030 25 00 25 33, ⊕ visitberlin.de. Tourist offices at: Hauptbahnhof (daily 8am–9pm), Brandenburg Gate (daily 9.30am–7pm) and Alexanderplatz, inside Park Inn hotel (Mon–Sat 7am–9pm, Sun 8am–6pm).

Travellers with disabilities

Buses and trams marked with a wheelchair symbol are equipped for disabled passengers, and a footnote on the printed schedule provided at every stop indicates which trams and buses are so equipped. Look for the words *behindert* (disabled) and *ausgestattet* (outfitted). Both buses and trams also have seat-belt-like straps to prevent a wheelchair from rolling during transit.

Festivals and events

Long Night of the Museums (Lange Nacht der Museen)

January and August ⊕ lange-nacht-der-museen.de
There are two Long Nights of the Museums, when many of Berlin's museums stay open late into the night – usually until midnight or later – with special programmes and events.

Berlinale

February ⊕ berlinale.de
For two weeks each year, Berlin turns into Hollywood as the Berlinale international film festival takes over the town. Around four hundred films are shown every year as part of the Berlinale's public programme, the vast majority of which are world or European premieres.

Impro

Ten days in March ⊕ improfestival.de
Running since 2001, this event is the biggest improvisation theatre festival in Europe. Its goal is to show international developments and take part in an intercultural exchange with different ensembles.

Gallery Weekend

End April/early May ⊕ www.gallery-weekend-berlin.de
Fifty-plus galleries and small venues dedicated to design and art open for one weekend to present exclusive exhibitions and contemporary international art.

My Fest

May 1 ⊕ myfest36.de

Kreuzberg open-air festival, with music and cultural events and a lot of food stalls (especially around Kottbusser Tor). Note that May Day demonstrations in the evening in the same area have a tendency to turn ugly, though the daytime is usually very safe and fun.

Berlin Festival

May ⓦ berlinfestival.de
Acclaimed three-day dance and pop festival held at Arena Berlin. The guests tend to be world renowned – Moby, Peaches, Björk – and the event coincides with other music events, which feature additional shows in clubs across town.

Carnival of Cultures

May ⓦ karneval-berlin.de
This colourful weekend street festival has been running since 1996, with four music stages featuring acts from around the world, plus culinary delights and handmade arts and craft stands. The peak of the festivity is a street parade with around 4800 participants from eighty nations on Whitsunday.

Fête de la Musique

June ⓦ fetedelamusique.de
Over ninety concerts are put on all over town to celebrate the Fête de la Musique, a hugely ambitious event that happens across 520 cities.

Christopher Street Day (CSD)

June/July ⓦ csd-berlin.de
Held in memory of the first big gay uprising against police assaults in Greenwich Village (the Stonewall riots), Berlin's biggest celebration of gay pride has been running since 1970 and draws around half a million people.

Classic Open Air

July ⓦ classicopenair.de
Five days of classical music at the beautiful Gendarmenmarkt. Previous events have included London's Royal Philharmonic Orchestra performing the complete James Bond title themes and The Scorpions performing with the German Film Orchestra Potsdam.

International Literature Festival

September ⓦ literaturfestival.com
Berlin's biggest literary event celebrates "diversity in the age of globalization" and features an eclectic and international selection of writers over twelve days.

Berlin Art Week

Mid-September ⓦ berlinartweek.de
Started in 2012, Berlin Art Week offers an exciting and richly varied programme of outstanding exhibitions, openings and events at ten participating institutions.

Berlin Marathon

Late September ⓦ bmw-berlin-marathon.com
First held in 1974, Berlin's marathon traditionally takes place on the last weekend in September. With around forty thousand participants from around one hundred countries, it's one of the largest and most popular road races in the world.

Festival of Lights

Mid-October ⓦ festival-of-lights.de
Every autumn, Berlin's famous sights are transformed into a sea of colour and light, including the Brandenburg Gate, the Berlin TV Tower, Berliner Dom and more. The nightly light show comes with art and cultural events around the topic of light.

Berlin Jazz Festival

Early November ⓦ berlinerfestspiele.de
Running since 1964, the Berlin Jazz Festival is a world-renowned event that presents all the diverse styles of jazz. The full and varied programme is traditional and progressive in equal parts, and has tended to

focus in particular on big bands and large ensembles.

International Short Film Festival

Mid-November ⓦ interfilm.de
The five-day International Short Film Festival Berlin was founded in 1982 and is today Berlin's second largest international film festival. The event showcases numerous competitions across all genres, as well as workshops and parties.

Christmas Markets

December
Many public locations in Berlin, such as Gendarmenmarkt, Alexanderplatz and the Schloss Charlottenburg, are taken over by Christmas markets selling arts, crafts, Glühwein, Wurst, pancakes and more.

Chronology

720 The region known today as Berlin is settled by Slavic and Germanic tribes.

948 Germans take control over the area of present-day Berlin.

983 The Slavs rebel (successfully) against German rule.

Twelfth century Germans take over the land again.

1244 Berlin is first mentioned in written records.

1247 The city of Cölln is founded right next to Berlin.

1307 Cölln and Berlin become known simply as "Berlin", the larger of the two cities.

1451 Berlin becomes the royal residence of the Brandenburg electors and has to give up its status of a free Hanseatic city.

1539 The city becomes officially Lutheran.

1576 Nearly five thousand inhabitants of Berlin are wiped out by the bubonic plague.

1618 The devastating Thirty Years' War begins. Half of Berlin's population left dead.

1685 Friedrich Wilhelm offers asylum to the Huguenots. More than fifteen thousand come to Brandenburg and six thousand settle in Berlin.

1699 Inauguration of Schloss Charlottenburg, commissioned by Sophie Charlotte, wife of Friedrich I.

1701 Berlin becomes the capital of Prussia.

1740 Friedrich II – known as Frederick the Great – comes to power and rules until 1786. He turns Berlin into a centre of Enlightenment.

1745–47 Sanssouci Palace is built as the summer palace of Frederick the Great.

1788–91 The Brandenburg Gate is built by Carl Gotthard Langhans.

1806 Napoleon conquers Berlin but grants self-government to the city.

1810 Humboldt University is founded by Prussian educational reformer and linguist Wilhelm von Humboldt.

1841 The Museum Island is dedicated to "art and science" by Friedrich Wilhelm IV of Prussia.

1861 Wedding, Moabit and several other suburbs are incorporated into Berlin.

1871 Berlin becomes the capital of a unified German Empire, under Otto von Bismarck's chancellorship.

1894 The Reichstag opens.

1918 Berlin witnesses the end of World War I and the proclamation of the Weimar Republic.

1920 Berlin established as a separate administrative zone with the Greater Berlin Act. A dozen villages and estates are incorporated into the city.

1923 Tempelhof is officially designated an airport.

1933 Adolf Hitler comes to power.

1939 The beginning of World War II.

1938–45 Thousands of Jews (and other minorities) living in Berlin are sent to death camps.

1943–45 Seventy percent of Berlin is destroyed in air raids.

1945 The Allies take Berlin, and divide it into four zones.

June 1948 The Berlin airlift sees Allied planes delivering supplies to West Berlin.

1949 The Federal Republic of Germany is founded in West Berlin and German Democratic Republic in East Berlin.

June 1953 An uprising of industrial workers against the Communist regime is brutally put down.

August 1961 The building of the Berlin Wall begins.

June 1963 US President John F. Kennedy visits West Berlin, delivering his famous speech, "*Ich bin ein Berliner*".

1972 Access is guaranteed across East Germany to West Berlin with the Four Powers Agreement.

1987 During his second Berlin visit, Ronald Reagan makes a speech in front of the Brandenburg Gate, demanding Mr Gorbachev "tear down this wall!"

1989 Following mass demonstrations across East Berlin, the border crossings are finally opened on November 9.

October 3, 1990 The two parts of Berlin are unified as part of the Federal Republic of Germany.

1997 Peter Eisenman's controversial design for a Memorial to the Murdered Jews of Europe is chosen.

1999 Berlin becomes capital of a reunified Germany and the German government and parliament begin their work in Berlin.

2005 Openly gay mayor Klaus Wowereit dubs Berlin "poor but sexy", which becomes a slogan for the city.

2006 The new Hauptbahnhof is opened.

2008 Tempelhof airport is officially closed; the surrounding area is later turned into a public park.

2009 Twenty years since the fall of the Wall is celebrated with a "Festival of Freedom". Visiting dignitaries include Mikhail Gorbachev and Bill Clinton.

2014 Structural work on new Stadtschloss (City Palace) completed; scheduled to open 2019.

2014 Germany beat Argentina 1–0 in the World Cup Final.

2015–16 Berlin takes in a million refugees.

2016 12 people die during a Christmas market terror attack in Berlin.

2018 Over 200,000 people march and protest against the rise of far-right populism in Berlin

2019 On 9 November, Berlin celebrates 30 years since the fall of the Berlin Wall

German

Being the cosmopolitan city it is, it's fairly easy to get around Berlin using English. That said, it's worth learning some basics in case you find yourself needing to communicate in the native language. Needless to say, any attempt at speaking German often goes a long way.

Alphabet
Umlaut: ä, ö, ü are the letters that have the mysterious Umlaut in the German language, which can also be spelled as ae, oe or ue. The ä is pronounced like the English a, the others are comparable to speaking the German o or u with a ping-pong ball in the mouth.

The "sharp S": Whenever the s is supposed to be emphasized in German, the "sharp s", **ß**, is used, which is pronounced like the English double s. Since the spelling reform in 1996 there have been some discussions about whether to retain ß or use ss, but for now both variations are accepted.

Pronunciation
Consonants: "w" is pronounced like the English "v"; "sch" is pronounced "sh"; "z" is "ts". The German letter "ß" is basically a double "s".
Vowels: "ei" is "eye"; "ie" is "ee"; "eu" is "oy".

Basic words and phrases
Yes Ja
No Nein
Please Bitte
Thank you Danke
Good morning Guten Morgen
Good evening Guten Abend
Hello/Good day Güten Tag
Goodbye Tschüss, ciao, or auf Wiedersehen
Excuse me Entschuldigen Sie, bitte
Today Heute
Yesterday Gestern
Tomorrow Morgen
Day Tag
Week Woche
Month Monat
Year Jahr
Weekend Wochenende
Monday Montag
Tuesday Dienstag
Wednesday Mittwoch
Thursday Donnerstag
Friday Freitag
Saturday Samstag/ Sonnabend
Sunday Sonntag
I don't understand Ich verstehe nicht
How much is...? Wieviel kostet...?
Do you speak English? Sprechen Sie Englisch?
I don't speak German Ich spreche kein Deutsch
I'd like a beer Ich hätte gern ein Bier
Where is? Wo ist?
entrance/exit der Eingang/der Ausgang
Toilet das WC/die Toilette
Women Damen
Men Herren
Hotel das Hotel
HI hostel die Jugendherberge
Main train station der Hauptbahnhof
Bus der Bus
Plane das Flugzeug
Train der Zug
Cheap billig
Expensive teuer
Open offen/auf
Closed geschlossen/zu

Entrance Eingang
Exit Ausgang
Smoking/no smoking rauchen/nicht rauchen
1 Eins
2 Zwei
3 Drei
4 Vier
5 Fünf
6 Sechs
7 Sieben
8 Acht
9 Neun
10 Zehn
11 Elf
12 Zwölf
13 Dreizehn
14 Vierzehn
15 Fünfzehn
16 Sechszehn
17 Siebzehn
18 Achtzehn
19 Neunzehn
20 Zwanzig
21 Ein-und-zwanzig
22 Zwei-und-zwanzig
30 Dreissig
40 Vierzig
50 Fünfzig
60 Sechzig
70 Siebzig
80 Achtzig
90 Neunzig
100 Hundert
1000 Tausend

Food and drink

Terms and phrases

Breakfast Frühstück
Lunch Mittagessen
Coffee and cakes Kaffee und Kuchen
Dinner Abendessen
Knife Messer
Fork Gabel
Spoon Löffel
Plate Teller
Cup Tasse
Glass Glas
Menu Speisekarte
Starter Vorspeise

Main course Hauptgericht
Dessert Nachspeise
The bill Die Rechnung
Organic Bio
Vegetarian Vegetarisch

Basics

Brot bread
Brötchen bread roll
Butter butter
Ei egg
Essig vinegar
Honig honey
Joghurt yoghurt
Käse cheese
Kuchen cake
Marmelade jam
Milch milk
Öl oil
Pfeffer pepper
Reis rice
Sahne cream
Salz salt
Scharf spicy
Senf mustard
Sosse sauce
Suppe soup
Zucker sugar

Drinks

Bier beer
Eiswürfel ice cube
Flasche bottle
Kaffee coffee
Leitungswasser tap water
Mineralwasser mineral water
Saft juice
Sprudelwasser sparkling mineral water
Stroh straw
Tee tea
Teekanne teapot
Wein wine
Weissbier/Weizenbier wheat beer

Meat (Fleisch) and fish (Fisch)

Currywurst sausage served with a curry
powder and tomato ketchup
Forelle trout
Garnelen prawns
Huhn, Hähnchen chicken

Kabeljau cod
Lachs salmon
Lamm lamb
Lammkotelett lamb chop
Leber liver
Leberkäse meatloaf
Makrele mackerel
Rindfleisch beef
Schinken ham
Schweinefleisch pork
Speck bacon
Thunfisch tuna
Wiener Schnitzel breadcrumb- coated cutlet, usually veal but sometimes pork
Wurst sausage
Zander pikeperch

Vegetables (Gemüse)

Blumenkohl cauliflower
Bohnen beans
Bratkartoffeln fried potatoes
Erbsen peas
Grüne Bohnen green beans
Gurke cucumber or gherkin
Karotten, Möhren carrots
Kartoffel potatoes
Knoblauch garlic
Lauch (or Porree) leeks
Maiskolben corn on the cob
Paprika peppers
Pilze or Champignons mushrooms
Pommes frites chips or fries
Rosenkohl Brussels sprouts
Rotkohl red cabbage
Salat salad
Salzkartoffeln boiled potatoes
Sauerkraut pickled cabbage

Spargel asparagus (white asparagus is particularly popular in season)
Tomaten tomatoes
Zwiebeln onions

Fruit (Obst)

Ananas pineapple
Apfel apple
Aprikose apricot
Banane banana
Birne pear
Erdbeer strawberry
Himbeer raspberry
Kirsch cherry
Melone melon
Orange orange
Pfirsch peach
Pflaum plum
Trauben grapes
Zitrone lemon

Desserts and cakes

Eis ice cream
Käsekuchen cheesecake
Keks biscuits
Kuchen cake
Schokolade chocolate
Torte cake/tart

German specialities

Knödel/Klösse poached or boiled potato or bread dumplings
Maultaschen stuffed noodles similar to ravioli
Quark a type of strained fresh cheese
Sauerbraten pot roast, usually beef
Schweinsbraten pot-roasted pork
Spätzle egg noodles of soft texture

Publishing Information
Fifth edition 2020

Distribution
UK, Ireland and Europe
Apa Publications (UK) Ltd; sales@roughguides.com
United States and Canada
Ingram Publisher Services; ips@ingramcontent.com
Australia and New Zealand
Woodslane; info@woodslane.com.au
Southeast Asia
Apa Publications (SN) Pte; sales@roughguides.com
Worldwide
Apa Publications (UK) Ltd; sales@roughguides.com
Special Sales, Content Licensing and CoPublishing
Rough Guides can be purchased in bulk quantities at discounted prices. We can
create special editions, personalised jackets and corporate imprints tailored to
your needs. sales@roughguides.com.
roughguides.com
Printed in China by RR Donnelley Asia Printing Solutions Limited
A catalogue record for this book is available from the British Library
The publishers and authors have done their best to ensure the accuracy and
currency of all the information in **Pocket Rough Guide Berlin**, however, they can
accept no responsibility for any loss, injury, or inconvenience sustained by any
traveller as a result of information or advice contained in the guide.

Rough Guide Credits
Editor: Sarah Clark
Author: Paul Sullivan
Updater: Rob Johnsen
Cartography: Katie Bennett
Managing editor: Rachel Lawrence
Picture editor: Aude Vauconsant
Cover photo research:
Michelle Bhatia
Original design: Richard Czapnik
Senior DTP coordinator: Dan May
Head of DTP and Pre-Press:
Rebeka Davies

Reader's updates
Thanks to all the readers who have taken the time to write in with comments and
suggestions (and apologies if we've inadvertently omitted or misspelt anyone's
name):
Jonathan Bardill, Josephine Bryan, Gabriele Chi, Paul Collinson, Caroline Dale,
Pierre Flener, Jack Howell, Helen Knox, Gareth Logue, Gloria Sebulsky

Help us update

We've gone to a lot of effort to ensure that this edition of the **Pocket Rough Guide Berlin** is accurate and up-to-date. However, things change – places get "discovered", opening hours are notoriously fickle, restaurants and rooms raise prices or lower standards. If you feel we've got it wrong or left something out, we'd like to know, and if you can remember the address, the price, the hours, the phone number, so much the better.

Please send your comments with the subject line "**Pocket Rough Guide Berlin Update**" to mail@uk.roughguides.com. We'll credit all contributions and send a copy of the next edition (or any other Rough Guide if you prefer) for the very best emails.

Photo Credits

(Key: T-top; C-centre; B-bottom; L-left; R-right)

Alamy 2T, 2BL, 2CR, 6, 11T, 19C, 19B, 20B, 22C, 23T, 23C, 27, 30, 39, 52, 57, 59, 62, 68, 72, 75, 99, 103, 118, 129
AMANO Bar 36
Big Brobot 96
Burg & Schild 61
Café Einstein Stammhaus 55
Chutnify 82
Clärchens Ballhaus 22T
Diana Jarvis/Rough Guides 12/13T, 18C, 93, 124, 141
Getty Images 12/13B, 67, 69, 70
Grüne Baumpython/Aquarium Berlin 121
Helmut Meyer zur Capellen 142/143
iStock 2BR, 5, 11B, 13C, 14T, 16B, 16T, 17T, 24/25, 40, 41, 43, 56, 60, 77, 94, 117, 125, 137

Mundo Azul 81
Oliver Mahne/Oliv 63
Picfair 1
Roger d'Olivere Mapp/Rough Guides 10, 12B, 14B, 15B, 15T, 18T, 18B, 19T, 20C, 20T, 21T, 21C, 21B, 22B, 23B, 33, 34, 42, 42 47, 50, 65, 71, 73, 80, 86, 100, 101, 104, 107, 111, 112, 115, 126, 130, 131, 135
Sabine Lubenow/AWL Images 4
Shutterstock 17B, 90, 91, 138, 150/151
Suicide Sue 89
Zula 85

Cover: The Brandenburg Gate **Sabine Lubenow/AWL Images**

Index